# ESSAYS OF THE 20th CENTURY

THE NATIONAL COMMITTEE FOR  BOOKS

# ESSAYS OF THE
# 20th CENTURY

*With study suggestions*

Compiled and edited by **EDITH M. RIDEOUT**

Supervisor of Reading, Newton High School,
Newtonville, Massachusetts

**S/R BOOKS**

*Published by Farrar, Straus and Cudahy
and Scholastic Roto*
*New York*

PUBLISHER'S NOTE

Edith M. Rideout received her A.B. from Bates College (which also elected her to Phi Beta Kappa and recently awarded her a Distinguished Service citation) and her A.M. from Radcliffe. She taught in the Rockland and Augusta high schools, both in Maine, and for many years in the Newton High School, Newtonville, Massachusetts, where she is now Director of the Reading Clinic. Miss Rideout is also a teacher of Massachusetts Extension courses; staff member in the workshop at the University of Delaware; reader of the College Entrance Board Examinations; and co-editor of the Study Guide for the *Atlantic Monthly* for the past eight years. She is a member of the board of directors of the National Council of Teachers of English and a speaker and writer on many phases of the teaching of English at sectional and national meetings and for professional journals.

ACKNOWLEDGEMENTS

For permission to use material in this book, grateful acknowledgment is made to the following:

"Little People and Big Words" by Sherwood Anderson, originally published in the *Reader's Digest*. Copyright 1941 by Eleanor Anderson, reprinted by permission of Harold Ober Associates, Inc.

"The Educated Man" by Jacques Barzun, originally published in *Life,* October 16, 1950. Reprinted by permission of Jacques Barzun.

"Night on the Great Beach" from *The Outermost House* by Henry Beston. Copyright 1928, 1949 by Henry Beston. Copyright renewed © 1956 by Henry Beston. Reprinted by permission of Holt, Rinehart and Winston, Inc.

"Pleasant Agony" by John Mason Brown. Reprinted by permission of John Mason Brown.

"Can Man Live Without War?" by Vannevar Bush, originally published in the *Atlantic Monthly,* Feb. 1956. Reprinted by permission of Vannevar Bush.

"The Marginal World" from *The Edge of the Sea* by Rachel Carson. Copyright © 1955 by Rachel Carson, reprinted by permission of the publishers, Houghton Mifflin Co.

"The Mass Mind" by Joyce Cary, copyright 1952 by Harper & Brothers Publishers, Inc. First published in *Harper's,* March 1952. Reprinted by permission of the author's estate.

"Hobbies" by Winston S. Churchill, reprinted with the permission of Charles Scribner's Sons from *Amid These Storms* by Winston S. Churchill. Copyright 1932 by Charles Scribner's Sons; renewal copyright © 1960 by Winston S. Churchill.

"Dag Hammarskjold" by Andrew W. Cordier, originally published in the *Saturday Review,* October 21, 1961. Reprinted by permission of the publisher.

# CONTENTS

# WHAT ARE ESSAYS?

To the question, "What are essays?" the answer is that essays are many things. They are sources of information from the greatest minds and experts on any topic, ranging from the undersea life to the outer spaces, from the beginnings of man to the probable future of the races. They are discussions on our economic and international problems. They are propaganda intended to indoctrinate minds to the saving of mankind or to the subversive doctrines that could lead us to complete chaos. They are criticisms of the arts and of the social and political structure of our society. On the other hand, they are informal chats—even though one-sided, often furnishing the reader relaxation and chuckles concerning the foibles of the human or making one nostalgic for the long stretches of our ocean's beaches, for the scent of the forests, for the exhilaration as the writer pulls in a spotted trout or battles the wind and fog in a sailboat or swims below the sea, for the campfires, for the challenge and adventure of conquering a mountain or visiting strange lands.

What are essays? One writer attempting to define the word declares, "It is easier to say what the essay is *not* than to say what it is." By the process of elimination, then, it is *not* poetry and it is *not* fiction with the plot element. One analogy which may show its purpose is that the essay is to prose what the lyric is to poetry—to the sonnet in particular; or to quote Professor Henry Beers of Yale, "The essay is everything that any other kind of literature is not." In its brief length, usually not over four or five thousand words, the essay—or article as it is often labeled today—communicates to the reader a world of ideas which may amuse and entertain, stir indignation, or inform and broaden horizons. It may be trifling or it may be serious. There seems to be no limit to the gamut of ideas the essay presents: nature, editorial opinions, biography, reflections, philosophy, criticism, description, narration, satire, humor—all depending on the purpose of the writer who "unlocks heart or immortalizes his thoughts on the mystery of the universe." The writer chats with us, the readers, and from the many facets of his personality enriches our thinking or stirs us to delve deeper into his thought, since he can touch on only a limited treatment.

The writer reveals his own personality through his attitudes toward varied topics; his opinions, biased or broad in understanding; comments, caustic or satirical; his humor, subtle or ingenuous; his experiences in all types of situations. It is through the personality of the writer that the essay, formal or informal in style, attracts and delights the reader, but this quality is more obvious in the informal or personal essay. Even on the same subject or about the same character, opinions can be as diverse as the authors themselves: one loves the outdoor life in the country; the other, the city. The pungent odor of the pines exhilarates one; the smell of gasoline-scented highways or cities, another. This diversity of loves, of points of view, of style makes the essay of interest and importance. Since the beginnings of man with his capacity for thought and communication, this form of expression has been existent and as varied as the writers themselves and the periods of time in which they write, for they adapt to the times and to the changing trends.

Although the term *essay* was not in use for the earliest writings, yet in essence the form itself is as old as writing: in many parts of the Bible, such as the epigrammatic verses of Proverbs, the Psalms, the writings and advice of the prophets, the great passages of Ecclesiastes, St. Paul's epistles in the New Testament, and others; and in the writings in old Grecian and Roman times of Plato, Aristotle, Plutarch, Cicero—in fact in the various philosophies and ideologies. Later in the sixteenth century (1580), a French writer, Montaigne, is credited with naming the essay from *assai,* a trial or attempt: "It is of myself I write," or as some one expressed it, he was one of the first "to write as an author what he thought as a man." In English literature about the same time (1597), Sir Francis Bacon helped to establish and give recognition to this form of writing, but in a most impersonal, formal style, quite the antithesis of many later essays, such as those by Lamb, whimsical and charming; Addison and Steele, with their satires on the society of their day; Ruskin, with the aesthetic; Carlyle and Macaulay, with the historical and biographical—a galaxy of names, too numerous to mention here, has given prestige to the essay.

In America our first century was concerned chiefly with the problems of existence and not of the arts. The stern necessities of establishing homes, of the preservation of life itself from the hazards of finding sustenance and from Indians occupied the hours of the day and of the energies of the colonists. Diaries, sermons, and a few tracts, usually expository in style, compose the writings of this period and reveal in a fragmentary way the times and the philosophy of the early settlers.

After the colonists won their freedom and as the country expanded, life became more than just a struggle to exist. Days were more leisurely, and in this period appear names such as Washington Irving, whom some critics call "the first American essayist"; Benjamin Franklin, who copied the style of Addison; Thomas Paine, John Adams, Alexander Hamilton, noted for their political writings; Henry Thoreau, writing of the outdoors and his theories on problems of society; Ralph Waldo Emerson, one of the "greatest philosopher-essayists of his day"; Oliver Wendell Holmes, with his humor and wit—sometimes called the "court jester of the New England circle"; James Russell Lowell, with his scholarly critical essays—to name a few. Since these earlier periods and earlier writers, American literature, as well as the literature of all nations, has had a long list of essayists. But we are not concerned here so much with the history of names or the history of the essay as attempting to define it as a form of literature.

As the pace of the world has increased and boundaries have broadened, so has the scope of the writer varied to meet the times. No longer do we find the hours for reflection; all communications from radio, television, telephone, daily (and more frequent) newspapers, the increase in travel by train, boats, automobiles, planes—all these seem to shrink reading time, especially the more reflective. As Joseph Wood Krutch, in his "No Essays—Please," and others, have claimed the essay's decline, even disappearance, in favor of the more objective articles, the aim of which is to inform, yet careful analysis of the magazines today reveals that there are still many subjective articles with the more personal tone. The essay is not dead, but the style and the times have changed, and the essay reflects these times.

Although today the word *essay* may be used less and the words *article* and *column* more, they are not too far apart. From the pages of the newspapers, the editorials inform the reader of world events and alert, even sway, the public to take sides in local and world issues. The magazines, too, voice opinions and disseminate knowledge on all phases of life in all countries. We still have formal, more didactic writing and the informal, depending on the content and on the writer's purpose, which determine the tone and style.

While essays should be read for enjoyment or for the facts and ideas presented, the reader should also note the organization and the qualities of style with which each writer clothes his thoughts. To do this requires at least two readings: one, for the ideas; the second, for the style. Usually we speak of two types of essays, the formal and the informal. In the formal essay the style is more serious, even didactic, and the organization with a beginning, development, and conclusion is more obvious than in the informal which is more casual and conversational. Both types may make use of description and narration, although basically exposition in purpose, at least. One of the delights in reading essays is the variety of style which Lawrence Clark Powell, in *Books in My Baggage,* describes as "The inseparable fusion of personality, content, and technique into an inevitable flow of language. —Style cannot be hidden in a book. It will appear on every page, in every paragraph and sentence. Without style no book can live more than a season or two; with it, forever."

Style is as complex as the personalities of the writers and cannot be separated from them. As E. B. White writes, "Style *is* the writer and, therefore, what a man *is,* rather than what he knows, will at last determine his style," and "style takes its final shape more from attitudes of mind than from principles of composition."

Critics (defined by someone as "men who expect miracles") speak of some writing as colorless, vague, pompous, lacking in style; on the other hand, they call the style of other works colorful, vivid, realistic—to select only a few labels. A study of various styles can influence one's own writing; yet, style, as has just been said, is governed greatly by the personality of the writer, for if "style *is* the man," then he can write only what he himself observes and feels, if he is sincere. To reiterate, "The essence of a good book is the personality of the author."

The tone and the style of any writing are determined by the purpose of the author. If he wishes to ridicule some of the customs, manners, and ideas of the people, he may resort to satire; if he wishes to interpret a character, he may make use not only of exposition but also of description and some narration, to explain the person's traits and his place in the world; if, however, his sole purpose is to inform and instruct on world conditions, he may use exposition only. In the essays in this collection there is a variety of styles, both in the types and in the structure, which includes the organization, the sentence forms, the transitions, and the diction.

"Good craftsmanship in writing must be more than grammatical correctness; it must keep three cardinal principles: strength, clarity, and precision." Does the author say exactly what he means? Does he create clear impressions? Dewey says, "Thought is impossible without words," but this comment should be implemented by a statement about Churchill: "He puts the right words in the right order at the right time and in the right place." Good diction is one of the essentials of good writing. F. L. Lucas in one of the essays in this book, "What Is Style?" will discuss this subject more.

What are essays? To summarize briefly this "undefinable" form of writing, since it is impossible to include all of the almost intangible facets which constitute an essay, these general statements are accepted. The essay is a brief prose work, usually not exceeding four to five thousand words, hence limited in its scope, on any subject the writer selects. His purpose will determine his tone and style, whether informal or formal. Exposition may be implemented by the other forms of writing, narration and description. The most frequent types are the critical, reflective, character portrayals, satirical, editorial or expository, descriptive, historical. But whatever the type and the purpose, whether the nomenclature is *essay* or *article* or *column,* whether the style is personal or didactic, writers will always express opinions and emotions. These are the general characteristics of what essays are, but "essays are many things."

EDITH M. RIDEOUT

# GENERAL STUDY SUGGESTIONS FOR ALL ESSAYS

In this collection are essays and articles written in the twentieth century; hence, the earlier writers are not included, though they are important in the study of the essay as a type of writing. Since each of the essays and articles represents the opinions of one writer only and one point of view, readers should consider and discuss other facets of the topics and related issues. Some are purposely of a controversial nature to stimulate just such thinking. They vary in type and in difficulty, but no class needs to read all.

In order to avoid much repetition, these suggestions, which are applicable to all of the articles and essays, will not be repeated in the questions on specific essays unless there is an urgent or unusual need.

1. Determine first the purpose of the author: to amuse and entertain, to reminisce, to inform and instruct, to indoctrinate and persuade, to criticize, to ridicule.

2. Show how this purpose influences both the type of essay or article and the tone and style of presenting the ideas. Does the author accomplish his purpose? Justify your opinions.

3. Compare two essays similar in type and intent for style and impression made on you. Why can two, or more, essays vary even on the same subject?

4. For purposes of criticism both of content and style, list terms that show specifically your analysis of the style, such as formal, didactic, informal, chatty, ironic, satirical, caustic, philosophical, rambling, flippant, whimsical, sentimental, dull, colorless, sparkling, and others. Keep a list of critical terms to which you may refer.

5. Is the writer's diction appropriate for the content and for his purpose? List words, specific or technical, which are pertinent to the subject. Find any slanted or loaded words. Identify figura-

tive language and decide whether it is more effective than the literal.

6. Has the writer a definite plan of organization of ideas? What types of transitions are there as the thought progresses from one phase of an idea to another? Compare the beginnings of several essays: a narrative or incident; a pithy statement; a question; a focus on the purpose.

7. Analyze the sentences for length, type, and beginnings. Is there variety in these? Do they flow smoothly or are they stilted and jerky? Identify some that seem forceful.

8. Is there clarity of style? If so, from what does it come—from illustrations, from specific vocabulary, from careful organization? Test the paragraphs for unity.

9. What reflections of the writer's personality and attitudes do you discover: love of people, fondness for nature, bias, sense of humor, background, sincerity, intellectuality, powers of observation, chauvinism, and such.

10. In what ways are the times reflected? In these 20th century essays identify phrases that indicate the period.

11. Determine reasons that make you like or dislike an essay in this collection.

12. Collect sentences that deal with the verities of life.

*Vocabulary*

In each essay, list (or underline or circle if you own the book) a few words not familiar to you, but necessary for understanding. First, deduce the meanings by the context, if you can; then, and then only, consult the dictionary to verify your definition. In this way you will gain in word power.

Make a card file of these words by copying the sentence and circling the word. Below write the word in syllables and mark the pronunciation. On the other side of the card write the meaning of the word as it is used in the particular sentence. At the bottom of the card add some synonyms. File these alphabetically and review frequently. Five or six—or more—of these words from each essay will enrich your vocabulary.

# WRITING AND SOME OTHER ARTS

*All arts are one,—all branches on one tree,*
*All fingers, as it were, upon one hand.*

W. W. STORY

# PLEASANT AGONY

*John Mason Brown*

For several years now, mine has been the privilege, hence the pleasant agony, of filling a page each week, or almost every week, in the *Saturday Review of Literature*. I say pleasant agony because I know of no other words with which to describe what writing is to me.

I claim no singularity in this. There may be, there must be, writers to whom writing comes as effortlessly as breathing. There may even be (though I doubt it) writers whose happiness is complete while they are actually writing. But most of us who live by putting words together are not so fortunate. We are tortured while we write and would be tortured were we not allowed to do so. Although when we are done we feel "delivered," as Sainte-Beuve put it, this delirium of delivery is not accomplished without labor pains for which medicine has, as yet, provided no soothing drugs. If all attempts to coerce words into doing what we would have them do are at best painful pleasures, the pains and pleasures of summoning the right words to meet a weekly deadline are of a special kind.

A cook faced with getting dinner when lunch is over knows something of the routine, if not all the anguishes, of a columnist. No mortals, however, have appetites as insatiable as a column's. A column is an omnivorous beast. Its hunger is never appeased. Feed it, and almost at once it demands to be fed again.

Though he used a different image to express this same idea, even Shaw, seemingly the most easeful of writers, knew this. When he abandoned the job of drama critic on London's *Saturday Review*, he protested against the weekly deadlines which had confronted him for nearly four years. He likened himself to a man fighting a windmill. "I have hardly time," wrote he, "to stagger to my feet from the knock-down blow of one sail, when the next strikes me down."

His successor in the same job on that same fortunate magazine shared an identical dislike of deadlines. For twelve years, Max Beerbohm admitted in his valedictory article, Thursdays had been for him the least pleasant day of the week. Why Thursday? Because that was the day, the latest possible one, he set aside each week to get his writing done. On every Wednesday, therefore, he would be engulfed by "a certain sense of oppression, of misgiving, even of dread." It was only on Friday, when once the danger was passed, that the sun would shine again. Then he would move on dancing feet.

I quote my betters to console myself by the reminder that they, too, knew the pangs of weekly columnizing. Yet the consolation I seek is denied me when I discover, for example, that it took Beerbohm one, and only one, short day of pain to turn out the delectable copy which he could write. Shaw, I am certain, was also a one-day man. I wish I were. I wish even more ardently that I could claim any of the merits which glorify their reviews for what it takes me two, three, or sometimes five days of ceaseless sweating to produce as fodder for my columns.

Beerbohm ascribed his disrelish for the act of writing to "the acute literary conscience" with which he had been cursed. It was this conscience, he maintained, which kept his pen from ever running away with him. I know what he means. Unblessed with any of his gifts, I am nonetheless cursed with something of his conscience. Beerbohm insisted that "to seem to write with ease and delight is one of the duties which a writer owes to his readers." If he worked hard at his sentences, it was because Beerbohm hoped they would read easily. In other words, he was in complete agreement with Sheridan's "easy writing's vile hard reading." One statement of Beerbohm's I could truthfully apply to my own efforts for the *SRL*. It runs, "I may often have failed in my articles here, to disguise labor. But the effort to disguise it has always been loyally made."

There is a passage in *The Goncourt Journals* which has haunted me since I read it. Envy has kept it green for me, and wonder (or is it disbelief?) has kept it alive. I have in mind Gautier's boast that he never thought about what he was going to write. "I take up my pen," he explained, "and write. I am a man of letters and am presumed to know my job . . . I throw my sentences into the air and I can be sure that they will come down on their feet, like cats . . . Look here: here's my script: not a word blotted."

When I think of the one-legged kittens that land on my pages; when I remember the false starts, illegible scribblings, unfinished sentences, discarded drafts, changed constructions, and altered words which mark my beginnings, my continuings, and my endings, I blush with shame and, like the voyagers in Dante's realm, abandon all hope.

In these journalistic days the first word that pops into an author's mind is held to be the acceptable, if not the best, word. We are supposed to smile because Wordsworth, at a day's end, was wearied from his quest for the exact word. But where Wordsworth the man may win a smile, Wordsworth the writer, fatiguing himself by doing what is a writer's duty, is far from laughable. The *mot juste* is not just any word. Even if it eludes its pursuer, the search for it seems to me to remain among the obligations of authorship. Indeed, the true hope of anyone who loves the language and respects it is to stumble upon, not the correct word or phrase, but the word or phrase which is so right that it seems inevitable.

The word and the phrase are not the only hurdles—and joys—of authorship. The sentence and the paragraph, by means of which points are made, thoughts communicated, emotions transferred, pictures painted, personalities caught, rhythms established, and cadences varied, offer other challenges and should supply their own sources of delight and pride. When so much hurried writing is done for hurried reading, I find it comforting to have Shaw, a veritable geyser with words and ideas, admit in his Sixteen Self Sketches how depleting he found his labors as a weekly feuilletonist for ten years. Why? Because, says he, of "taking all the pains I was capable of to get to the bottom of every sentence I wrote."

One of the modern world's luckier occurrences was what happened at Harrow when a boy named Winston Churchill was being "menaced with Education." Three times, he tells us in *A Roving Commission,* his backwardness as a classical scholar forced him to remain in the same form and hence repeat the same elementary course in English. "Thus," writes he (and who can question him?), "I got into my bones the essential structure of the ordinary British sentence—which is a noble thing. . . . Naturally I am biased in favor of boys learning English. I would make them all learn English: and then I would let the clever ones learn Latin as an honor, and Greek as a treat. But the only thing I would whip them for would be for not knowing English. I would whip them hard for that." One trembles to think how many of us whose profession is writing would be flogged today if lapses in English, or American, were whippable offenses.

Later on in that same grand book, Churchill has his more precise say on the subtleties, intricacies, and possibilities of the writer's craft. It is his opinion, and one worth heeding, that, "just as the sentence contains one idea in all its fulness, so the paragraph should embrace a distinct episode; and as sentences should follow one another in harmonious sequence, so the paragraphs must fit on to one another like the automatic couplings of railway carriages."

I quote Churchill and these others belonging to the peerage of prose writers because, for any author with a memory, one of the disheartening and humbling aspects of writing is the recollection, as his own pen moves, of how those whom he admires have faced and solved identical problems. This recollection of what has been done, this sensing of what could and should be done, this awareness of what one hopes to do regardless of whether one can or cannot do it—these are parts of that literary conscience, mentioned by Beerbohm, which keeps a writer's pen from running away with him. I know they are factors in retarding my own pen (meaning my typewriter, pencil, or dictation) even on those happy days when a subject seems to write itself, when sentences come easily, and one paragraph gives way to another.

Style is a strange and mysterious thing. Some contemporary writers appear to get along without it and to want to do so, and most of us rightly disparage it when it shows the effort that has gone into it. Few of us, for example, can read Pater today without being irritated and put off by the labyrinthian intricacies of his sentences. His style, once held to be a model, remains a model, although as we see it it is one to be avoided rather than followed. Pater could not bring himself to say a simple thing simply. His orchestration is so elaborate that the melody of his thought is lost.

Hazlitt comes closer to present-day tastes. More than being the enemy of the gaudy and "Occult" schools of writing, Hazlitt was not only a champion but at his best a matchless practitioner of "The Familiar Style." Although he had the art to make a long sentence seem short, he knew the value of short sentences. "I hate anything," wrote he, "that occupies more space than it is worth. I hate to see a load of band-boxes go along the street, and I hate to see a parcel of big words without any meaning in them."

The perpetual challenge of writing, the challenge presented by each new sentence is to say exactly what one wants to say exactly as one wants to say it. This is where the anguish of composition mixes with the delights. This is where, too, style, as I see it, comes into the picture. Style is merely the means, chosen or instinctive (doubtless both), by which a writer has his precise and personal say.

Certainly, style is not affectation. Conscious though it may be, when self-conscious it is an obstruction. Its purpose, to my way of thinking, is to give the reader pleasure by sparing him the work which the writer is duty-bound to have done for him. Writers, notwithstanding their hopes or ambitions, may or may not be artists. But there is no excuse for their not being artisans. Although in the final and spiritual sense the style is the man, it is more than that. It is the writing man *in print*. It is, so to speak, his written voice and, if it is truly his voice, even in print it should be his and his alone. The closer it comes to the illusion of speech, perhaps the better. Yet the closeness of the written word to the spoken can, and in fact should, never be more than an illusion. For the point of the written word is planning, as surely as the charm of the spoken word can be its lack of planning.

Without shame I confess that, regardless of how unsatisfactory the results may be, I have labored when writing my weekly pieces to lighten the labor of those who may read them. That I have failed again and again I know to my own chagrin, but I can honestly say I have tried. I not only rewrite; I often rewrite and rewrite again. I do this though I am well aware that the result is sentences and paragraphs which do not bear rereading. I rewrite partly in longhand, partly by dictation, occasionally sitting down, sometimes walking, but most often snaking my way across the floor on my stomach. My desk, a migratory one, is the small piece of beaverboard I push before me. On it are sheets of typewriter paper darkened with hieroglyphics which must be deciphered immediately to be read at all.

Endeavoring to square my writing with my writing conscience, and having to live with the difference between what I would like to have done and am able to do, is one of the reasons why writing is to me an agony, however pleasant.

### Study suggestions

1.   Explain the seeming paradox in his title.
2.   Compare his attitudes toward deadlines, writing, and choice of words with your own.
3.   Analyze Churchill's opinion on the writer's craft. Read *A Roving Commission* to explore how well he follows his remarks.
4.   What does he mean by a "literary conscience"?
5.   Note his comments on style and compare with the ideas expressed in the two essays which follow.
6.   Also note his emphasis on rewriting.
7.   What evidences of humor do you find in this?
8.   Write an essay on your experiences with writing.

# THE WRITER'S CRAFT

*André Maurois*

The starting-point of a writer's life is the sense of a vocation. The child or the adolescent feels impelled to give expression in the written word to the emotions or the ideas which people and things have aroused in him. At a very early age Marcel Proust was conscious of a desire to lay hands on an imprisoned beauty which, so he believed, was hidden under the appearance of certain objects. He had a confused notion that it was incumbent upon him to free some captive truth from confinement. At that time in his life he was as yet incapable of reaching down to truths which he felt to be lurking under the bushes, the orchards, and the sunlight of La Beauce. In *Louis Lambert,* Balzac gives us a portrait of himself as a youth chock-full of works clamoring to be born. Victor Hugo, Byron, Musset, Valéry all wrote poems when they were young. It occasionally happens that the vocation of letters is a late-flowering growth (as in the case of Rousseau), but when that is so, numerous attempts in secret have preceded the ultimate fulfillment.

How comes it that this vocation is present in some people and not in others? One may say in answer to that question, though without laying it down as a rule, that the need to express oneself in writing springs from a maladjustment to life, or from an inner conflict which the adolescent (or the grown man) cannot resolve in action. Those to whom action comes as easily as breathing rarely feel the need to break loose from the real, to rise above and describe it. That is why so many of the finest writers have been the victims of ill health (Poe, Proust, Flaubert, Chekhov), men whose lives have known frustration from an early age or found their natural development impeded by some obstacle. Dickens, Balzac, Hugo, Kipling, and Stendhal all had an unhappy childhood which was too soon dislocated by family conflicts. With others the conflict was social or religious (Voltaire, Anatole France, and Tolstoy), while in some an oversensitive nature has been driven back on itself as the result of some invincible timidity (Mérimée). I do not mean that it is enough to be maladjusted to become a great writer, but writing is, for some, a method of resolving a conflict, provided they have the necessary talent.

It may be objected that many writers have been happy in their lives and endowed with a healthy temperamental balance. That, no doubt, is true, but I do not know a single instance in which that balance has not had to be achieved by a struggle from which a considerable body of work has resulted.

The only writers I have known who were perfectly contented with themselves and with the world in which they lived, were, I am sorry to say, bad writers. This is not to say that in order to write well a man must be a pessimist, but only that "optimism in an artist is something that has to be won by hard fighting" (Alain).

First, then, the vocation and the early attempts at authorship. Next, the problem of publication. Why is it so necessary for a writer to have a public? If his purpose is to express himself, ought it not to be enough for him that he should succeed in doing so? Is a cloud of witnesses really essential? The answer to this question is almost always in the affirmative. I say "almost" always because there have been writers of memoirs, Saint-Simon, for instance, and Pepys, who cared nothing for public applause. They wrote for themselves or for a posterity which they could never know. But such cases are rare. Nearly every writer wants to have readers, even though they should amount to only a small number of the elect. That is but natural. He has written with the deliberate purpose of revealing the truth about himself and about the world as he sees it. The revelation can have no point unless it reaches those for whom it is intended. To find readers who shall understand him, who may perhaps love, or at least admire him, is reassuring to an author, and if his own conflict resembles that of many of his fellow men, it may, through his efforts, become less obsessive and troublesome to them, in which case he will have the additional pleasure of having been helpful.

The aim of a writer worthy of his chosen profession is never merely to achieve Power and Glory. It does sometimes happen that these rewards come the way of those who deserve them, but many great men have been cheated of them in their lifetime. Mallarmé was the idol of a few discriminating admirers: to the wider public he was unknown. Stendhal said, with considerable perspicacity: "I shall have readers in 1860"; he has still more in 1960, but he had few before his death. Tolstoy, on the other hand, Balzac and Dickens, enjoyed an enormous popularity. Success proves nothing either for or against a writer. It is desirable, because it gives him an assured independence, on condition that it does not come to him through scandal, the employment of such artificial means as excessive publicity, or vulgarity. The public interest in certain literary prizes does ill service, in the last analysis, to those who receive them. A sudden and exaggerated notoriety leaves them precisely where they were before. They may, indeed, show themselves worthy of their fame, and capable of responding to the hopes reposed in them. If, on the other hand, they drop back into obscurity, then failure is the more painful by reason of the generous promises of success so unexpectedly extended to them.

Power, Glory, and Money are only secondary objects for the writer. No man can be a great writer without having a great philosophy, though it may often remain unexpressed. A great writer has a high respect for *values*. His essential function is to raise life to the dignity of thought, and this he does by giving it a shape. If he refuses to perform this function, he can be a clever juggler and play tricks with words such as his fellow writers may admire, but his books will be of little interest to anybody else. If, on the contrary, he fulfills it, he will be happy in his writing. Borne aloft by the world as reflected in himself, and producing a sounding echo of his times, he helps to shape it by showing to men an image of themselves which is at once true and disciplined.

"There is as much craft in the making of a book as there is in the making of a clock," said La Bruyère. About this one might argue up and down for a long time. Undoubtedly, the making of a book involves the learning of a craft, and one that is mastered by the exercise of writing. Few succeed at the first attempt. Those whose earliest published efforts seem to show real skill are not, as a rule, strictly speaking, beginners. They will be found to have worked long and arduously in the privacy of their study, either writing themselves or absorbing the secrets of the masters. But though authorship is a craft it differs from that of the clockmaker in that the latter assembles pieces ready to his hand in a strictly determined order, whereas the writer, in the very process of putting pen to paper, has to invent not only the constructional plan of his book but the materials which go into it. Of what a nature, therefore, should his training be?

A book is made up of words. The first concern of the writer-to-be is to acquire a vocabulary and to master the rules of grammar. He must have so infallible a knowledge of his native tongue and its syntactical usages that he will never run the risk of employing a word to convey a meaning other than that normally attached to it, or of constructing an unintelligible or defective sentence. I am quite prepared to have it pointed out to me that very great writers have sometimes given a new meaning to an old word, or played tricks with syntax. That is so, but such liberties, though they may win approval when they stand out against the background of a perfect norm, will seem ridiculous when taken by a beginner, for in his case they will merely give the impression of ignorance.

The first essential, therefore, on which the young writer must concentrate is the acquisition of an accurate vocabulary. Should it be more than usually extensive? No general rule can, I think, be laid down. The beginner's choice depends upon the nature of his subject. Technical phrases, admirably suited to the treating of technical matters, will seem pretentious when applied to narrative. The clear and simple words of common usage are always better than those of erudition. The jargon of the philosophers not seldom conceals an absence of thought.

The best training for the young writer is to be found in a reading of the masters. A close study of them will show him how a masterpiece is made. Familiarity with the methods of the great will provide him with great examples. At first he will read for pleasure, like any young enthusiast with a taste for books. Then, having become familiar with this or that work, he will return to it again and again with the purpose of "taking it to pieces" and seeing just how its effects are obtained.

But is there not danger in following a master too slavishly? What we ask of a young writer is not that he should be a second Balzac, a new Dickens, but himself. The danger is, I think, imaginary. In the first place, should the young writer suddenly and miraculously produce the very novel, dealing with our contemporary society, which Balzac himself would have written had he been alive today, that would be a great and happy event. In fact, if he is truly gifted nothing of the sort is likely to happen. He will have learned from his masters certain tricks of the trade, but he will use them differently. Even if he deliberately sets out to imitate them, a moment will come when, his own genius having taken charge, he will forget all about the imitation, take a good look at his subject, and handle it in his own way. Nobody expects us to write as though no one had ever written before we came upon the scene. In literature everyone is somebody's spiritual child. What matters is that the beginner, by studying other men's styles, should ultimately develop a style of his own.

But what, precisely, is style? It is the hallmark of an individual, which shows clearly in his use of language and in his view of life. Every man has a temperament which is personal to himself. But most men are incapable of impressing their temperaments on what they write. For most, the act of writing is something outside their usual competence. Consequently, they lack that flexibility which would allow them to give free rein to their instincts and their passions. As soon as they get a pen between their fingers, they find that nothing comes but a flood of commonplace clichés. They are used to reading bad prose, and cannot break free from it. Saint-Simon, who was a master of language and wholly indifferent to popular applause since he was writing only for himself, could give full play to his furies and his memories. The supremely right adjective came to him simultaneously with the thought he wished to express, or, rather, a cascade of adjectives which gradually encircled it. Passionately intent on what he was feeling and wanted to record, he did not much worry about the form in which it should be presented. He took the first word that occurred to him, no matter how trivial, with the result that he hit on those astonishing "finds," those powerful images which both surprise and flay. So torrential is the movement of his prose that the incidents flood the page. Circumstances come into his mind even while he is in the act of writing, but the very disorder in which they jostle gives life to his words. The touchy duke shows through the writing. That is what style means.

Alain laid it down that in anything worth calling style two conditions must be fulfilled: grace and ease in the movement of the prose, and, in the work itself, its visible trace. Grace and ease can be acquired as a result of that double training to which I have already referred: reading and working. A certain degree of modesty must also be linked with them. He who takes too much obvious trouble to write well falls below the highest level. Flaubert in his letters, where he is being himself without effort, is better than the Flaubert of the novels, in which every sentence has been so frequently worked over that the style loses all natural movement and becomes rugged or clumsy. Let me, once again, quote Alain: "Style, like good manners, should never be self-conscious, but must express a free improvisation in a way that laborious application can never achieve." The resistance of the material will do the rest, as can be seen in hand-wrought iron-work or sculptured stone. That is why, as we realize in classical tragedy, style is the outcome of constraint.

It is useless to advise a writer who is seeking to express himself to be a Kipling, a Chateubriand, a Flaubert, or, indeed, anyone but himself. But it is not easy to be oneself. Many writers have died without ever finding their true selves, or, at least, without succeeding in imparting their selves to their style. This is sometimes due to lack of culture and of skill in the handling of words, though sometimes, on the contrary, to an excess of culture. They have admired so many styles that they have failed to form one of their own. What advice, then, should be given to the beginner? That he should remain a rough diamond? No, for the rough diamond has no luster. The source of light is doubtless in it, but it remains invisible. My own advice would be to seek out those masters who best suit the young learner, those for whom he feels a natural sympathy and, having found them, to be assiduous in his study of their work.

*Nulla dies sine linea.* The aspiring author, whether genius or not, should never let a day pass without writing at least a few lines. The habit of writing is a good one, always on condition that one sets down on paper what one *really* wants to say, and does not fall a victim to the allurements of the easy cliché. Journalism can easily become a danger if it is not conducted with passionate sincerity. There is an art of saying nothing which is the very reverse of style. Journalism undertaken in the manner of Paul-Louis Courier or Diderot is, on the contrary, a wonderful training-school of good and succinct writing. Goethe's advice—start with short pieces—is, I think, excellent. The very fact of carrying through a piece of work *to the end* is of great encouragement to the beginner. To embark upon a "saga-novel" at twenty would be doubly foolish. At that age few men have the necessary technical skill or a sufficient first-hand experience of life on which to draw. Writing should never be allowed to become a substitute for living. Style cannot breathe in a void. It should not be forgotten that Dickens was at one time a reporter, Balzac a lawyer's clerk, and Chekhov a country doctor. Art is different from life but cannot exist without it.

"The business of getting going," says Alain, "should be reduced to a minimum," by which he meant that one should never spend months and years in planning how to start on a book. I have known writers, or, rather, men who wanted to be writers, whose whole life has been wasted in deciding to take the first step. "I still lack certain important elements," they say, "before I can begin my novel," or "I am burning to get on with this biography but there are still several essential documents on which I haven't, so far, been able to lay my hand." So, time goes by, and nothing is done. Once the choice of a subject has been made, one must jump into a book as one jumps into water. If one goes on testing the temperature with one's toe one will never learn how to swim.

The first thing that a certain Scots professor used to say to his students when they handed in their essays was: "Did it never occur to you to tear up the first page?" Without reading it, he could guess that it was bad, because beginnings are the most difficult things to manage successfully. "It is there," said Chekhov, "that we do most of our lying." Before we are properly warmed up, we run the risk of being flat and pedantic. Speaking personally, I am never quite sure how I am going to begin, but, once afloat, instinct takes over the controls. That is why so many of the great masters make an abrupt opening. They fling the reader straight into a dialogue between characters about whom he knows nothing. It is for him to strike out and find his own way. The Scots professor was right. It is an admirable rule to "cut" the first page, which is almost certain to be groping, slow and didactic, as well as wholly unnecessary for the intelligent reader.

As to the art of concluding, that depends on the nature of the subject. If the whole purpose of a book has been to argue a thesis, it should end, as Beethoven ended, with a passage of affirmation in which the musical material was resolved. In biography and history it is well to gather all the motifs in the final pages, after the manner, say, of Wagner. In the case of a novel, or any imaginative work, especially if the tone is poetic, my own preference is for ending with a touch of symbolism which shall leave the reader brooding. A fine novel, a well-written story, "proves" nothing. Certain characters have played their parts, life goes on, and the final passage may be allowed to remain with one foot in the air, as is the case with some of Chopin's conclusions. But there is no absolute rule in such matters, and there are epic novelists who like to end on a powerful crescendo, as Ravel does in *Boléro,* or Dvořák in the *New World Symphony.* Composition has features which are common to all the arts, and the author can learn as much about his business in the concert hall as in the library.

## Study suggestions

1.    This essay deals first with the writer and, secondly, with the writer's craft. Summarize his ideas on each.

2.    Study the paragraphs for the topic sentences and note by what methods he develops these paragraphs.

3.    Discuss his feeling that "writing springs from a maladjusted life or from an inner conflict." Are there any recent American writers who have been maladjusted? If so, how have their difficulties affected their writing? Why is it necessary to have a public?

4.    Comment on the following epigrammatic sentences—the

meanings and their effect on the clarity and the vigor of the paragraph:

    a.  "No man can be a great writer without having a great philosophy, though it may often remain unexpressed."

    b.  "The first concern of the writer-to-be is to acquire a vocabulary and to master the rules of grammar."

    c.  "The best training for the young writer is to be found in a reading of the masters."

    d.  "But what, precisely, is style? It is the hallmark of an individual which shows clearly in his use of language and in his view of life."

    e.  "The aspiring author, whether genius or not, should never let a day pass without writing at least a few lines."

    f.  "Style cannot breathe in a void."

    g.  "Did it never occur to you to tear up the first page?"

    h.  "Composition has features which are common to all the arts. . . ."

# WHAT IS STYLE?

*F. L. Lucas*

When it was suggested to Walt Whitman that one of his works should be bound in vellum, he was outraged—"Pshaw!" he snorted, "—hangings, curtains, finger bowls, chinaware, Matthew Arnold!" And he might have been equally irritated by talk of style; for he boasted of "my barbaric yawp"—he would *not* be literary; his readers should touch not a book but a man. Yet Whitman took the pains to rewrite *Leaves of Grass* four times, and his style is unmistakable. Samuel Butler maintained that writers who bothered about their style became unreadable but he bothered about his own. "Style" has got a bad name by growing associated with precious and superior persons who, like Oscar Wilde, spend a morning putting in a comma, and the afternoon (so he said) taking it out again. But such abuse of "style" is misuse of English. For the word means merely "a way of expressing oneself, in language, manner, or appearance"; or, secondly, "a *good* way of so expressing oneself"—as when one says, "Her behavior never lacked style."

Now there is no crime in expressing oneself (though to try to *im*press oneself on others easily grows revolting or ridiculous). Indeed one cannot help expressing oneself, unless one passes one's life in a cupboard. Even the most rigid Communist, or Organization-man, is compelled by Nature to have a unique voice, unique fingerprints, unique handwriting. Even the signatures of the letters on your breakfast table may reveal more than their writers guess. There are blustering signatures that swish across the page like cornstalks bowed before a tempest. There are cryptic signatures, like a scrabble of lightning across a cloud, suggesting that behind is a lofty divinity whom all must know, or an aloof divinity whom none is worthy to know (though, as this might be highly inconvenient, a docile typist sometimes interprets the mystery in a bracket underneath). There are impetuous squiggles implying that the author is a sort of strenuous Sputnik streaking round the globe every eighty minutes. There are florid signatures, all curlicues and danglements and flamboyance, like the youthful Disraeli (though these seem rather out of fashion). There are humble, humdrum signatures. And there are also, sometimes, signatures that are courteously clear, yet mindful of a certain simple grace and artistic economy—in short, of style.

Since, then, not one of us can put pen to paper, or even open his mouth, without giving something of himself away to shrewd observers, it seems mere common sense to give the matter a little thought. Yet it does not seem very common. Ladies may take infinite pains about having style in their clothes, but many of us remain curiously indifferent about having it in our words. How many women would dream of polishing not only their nails but also their tongues? They may play freely on that perilous little organ, but they cannot often be bothered to tune it. And how many men think of improving their talk as well as their golf handicap?

No doubt strong silent men, speaking only in gruff monosyllables, may despise "mere words." No doubt the world does suffer from an endemic plague of verbal dysentery. But that, precisely, is bad style. And consider the amazing power of mere words. Adolf Hitler was a bad artist, bad statesman, bad general, and bad man. But largely because he could tune his rant, with psychological nicety, to the exact wave length of his audiences and make millions quarrelsome-drunk all at the same time by his command of windy nonsense, skilled statesmen, soldiers, scientists were blown away like chaff, and he came near to rule the world. If Sir Winston Churchill had been a mere speechifier, we might well have lost the war; yet his speeches did quite a lot to win it.

No man was less of a literary aesthete than Benjamin Franklin; yet this tallow-chandler's son, who changed world history, regarded as "a principal means of my advancement" that pungent style which he acquired partly by working in youth over old *Spectators;* but mainly by being Benjamin Franklin. The squinting demagogue, John Wilkes, as ugly as his many sins, had yet a tongue so winning that he asked only half an hour's start (to counteract his face) against any rival for a woman's favor. "Vote for you!" growled a surly elector in his constituency. "I'd sooner vote for the devil!" "But in case your friend should not stand . . . ?" Cleopatra, that ensnarer of world conquerors, owed less to the shape of her nose than to the charm of her tongue. Shakespeare himself has often poor plots and thin ideas; even his mastery of character has been questioned; what does remain unchallenged is his verbal magic. Men are often taken, like rabbits, by the ears. And though the tongue has no bones, it can sometimes break millions of them.

"But," the reader may grumble, "I am neither Hitler, Cleopatra, nor Shakespeare. What is all this to me?" Yet we all talk—often too much; we all have to write letters—often too many. We live not by bread alone but also by words. And not always with remarkable efficiency. Strikes, lawsuits, divorces, all sorts of public nuisance and private misery, often come just from the gaggling incompetence with which we express ourselves. Americans and British get at cross-purposes because they use the same words with different meanings. Men have been hanged on a comma in a statute. And in the valley of Balaclava a mere verbal ambiguity, about *which* guns were to be captured, sent the whole Light Brigade to futile annihilation.

Words can be more powerful, and more treacherous, than we sometimes suspect; communication more difficult than we may think. We are all serving life sentences of solitary confinement within our own bodies; like prisoners, we have, as it were, to tap in awkward code to our fellow men in their neighboring cells. Further, when A and B converse, there take part in their dialogue not two characters, as they suppose, but six. For there is A's real self —call it $A_1$; there is also A's picture of himself—$A_2$; there is also B's picture of A—$A_3$. And there are three corresponding personalities of B. With six characters involved even in a simple *tête-à-tête,* no wonder we fall into muddles and misunderstandings.

Perhaps, then, there are five main reasons for trying to gain some mastery of language:

We have no other way of understanding, informing, misinforming, or persuading one another.

Even alone, we think mainly in words; if our language is muddy, so will our thinking be.

By our handling of words we are often revealed and judged. "Has he written anything?" said Napoleon of a candidate for an appointment. "Let me see his *style.*"

Without a feeling for language one remains half-blind and deaf to literature.

Our mother tongue is bettered or worsened by the way each generation uses it. Languages evolve like species. They can degenerate; just as oysters and barnacles have lost their heads. Compare ancient Greek with modern. A heavy responsibility, though often forgotten.

Why and how did I become interested in style? The main answer, I suppose, is that I was born that way. Then I was, till ten, an only child running loose in a house packed with books, and in a world (thank goodness) still undistracted by radio and television. So at three I groaned to my mother, "Oh, I *wish* I could read," and at four I read. Now travel among books is the best travel of all, and the easiest, and the cheapest. (Not that I belittle ordinary travel—which I regard as one of the three main pleasures in life.) One learns to write by reading good books, as one learns to talk by hearing good talkers. And if I have learned anything of writing, it is largely from writers like Montaigne, Dorothy Osborne, Horace Walpole, Johnson, Goldsmith, Montesquieu, Voltaire, Flaubert and Anatole France. Again, I was reared on Greek and Latin, and one can learn much from translating Homer or the Greek Anthology, Horace or Tacitus, if one is thrilled by the originals and tries, however vainly, to recapture some of that thrill in English.

But at Rugby I could *not* write English essays. I believe it stupid to torment boys to write on topics that they know and care nothing about. I used to rush to the school library and cram the subject, like a python swallowing rabbits; then, still replete as a postprandial python, I would tie myself in clumsy knots to embrace those accursed themes. Bacon was wise in saying that reading makes a full man; talking, a ready one; writing, an exact one. But writing from an empty head is futile anguish.

At Cambridge, my head having grown a little fuller, I suddenly found I *could* write—not with enjoyment (it is always tearing oneself in pieces)—but fairly fluently. Then came the War of 1914-18; and though soldiers have other things than pens to handle, they learn painfully to be clear and brief. Then the late Sir Desmond MacCarthy invited me to review for the *New Statesman;* it was a useful apprenticeship, and he was delightful to work for. But I think it was well after a few years to stop; reviewers remain essential, but there are too many books one *cannot* praise, and only the pugnacious enjoy amassing enemies. By then I was an ink-addict —not because writing is much pleasure, but because not to write is pain; just as some smokers do not so much enjoy tobacco as suffer without it. The positive happiness of writing comes, I think, from work when done—decently, one hopes, and not without use —and from the letters of readers which help to reassure, or delude, one that so it is.

But one of my most vivid lessons came, I think, from service in a war department during the Second War. Then, if the matter one sent out was too wordy, the communication channels might choke; yet if it was not absolutely clear, the results might be serious. So I emerged, after six years of it, with more passion than ever for clarity and brevity, more loathing than ever for the obscure and the verbose.

For forty years at Cambridge I have tried to teach young men to write well, and have come to think it impossible. To write really well is a gift inborn; those who have it teach themselves; one can only try to help and hasten the process. After all, the uneducated sometimes express themselves far better than their "betters." In language, as in life, it is possible to be perfectly correct—and yet perfectly tedious, or odious. The illiterate last letter of the doomed Vanzetti was more moving than most professional orators; 18th Century ladies, who should have been spanked for their spelling, could yet write far better letters than most professors of English; and the talk of Synge's Irish peasants seems to me vastly more vivid than the later style of Henry James. Yet Synge averred that his characters owed far less of their eloquence to what he invented for them than to what he had overheard in the cottages of Wicklow and Kerry:

*"Christy.* 'It's little you'll think if my love's a poacher's, or an earl's itself, when you'll feel my two hands stretched around you, and I squeezing kisses on your puckered lips, till I'd feel a kind of pity for the Lord God is all ages sitting lonesome in His golden chair.'

*"Pegeen.* 'That'll be right fun, Christy Mahon, and any girl would walk her heart out before she'd meet a young man was your like for eloquence, or talk at all.' "

Well she might! It's not like that they talk in universities—more's the pity.

But though one cannot teach people to write well, one can sometimes teach them to write rather better. One can give a certain number of hints, which often seem boringly obvious—only experience shows they are not.

One can say: Beware of pronouns—they are devils. Look at even Addison, describing the type of pedant who chatters of style without having any: "Upon enquiry I found my learned friend had dined that day with Mr. Swan, the famous punster; and desiring *him* to give me some account of Mr. Swan's conversation, *he* told me that *he* generally talked in the Paronomasia, that *he* sometimes gave in to the Plocé, but that in *his* humble opinion *he* shone most in the Antanaclasis." What a sluttish muddle of *he* and *him* and *his!* It all needs rewording. Far better repeat a noun, or a name, than puzzle the reader, even for a moment, with ambiguous pronouns. Thou shalt not puzzle thy reader.

Or one can say: Avoid jingles. The B.B.C. news bulletins seem compiled by earless persons, capable of crying round the globe: "The enemy is re*port*ed to have seized this im*port*ant *port,* and reinforcements are hurrying up in sup*port.*" Any fool, once told, can hear such things to be insupportable.

Or one can say: Be sparing with relative clauses. Don't string them together like sausages, or jam them inside one another like Chinese boxes or the receptacles of Buddha's tooth. Or one can say: Don't flaunt jargon, like Addison's Mr. Swan, or the type of modern critic who gurgles more technical terms in a page than Johnson used in all his *Lives* or Sainte-Beuve in thirty volumes. But dozens of such snippety precepts, though they may sometimes save people from writing badly, will help them little toward writing well. Are there no general rules of a more positive kind, and of more positive use?

Perhaps. There *are* certain basic principles which seem to me observed by many authors I admire, which I think have served me and which may serve others. I am not talking of geniuses, who are a law to themselves (and do not always write a very good style, either); nor of poetry, which has different laws from prose; nor of poetic prose, like Sir Thomas Browne's or De Quincey's, which is often more akin to poetry; but of the plain prose of ordinary books and documents, letters and talk.

The writer should respect truth and himself; therefore honesty. He should respect his readers; therefore courtesy. These are two of the cornerstones of style. Confucius saw it, twenty-five centuries ago: "The Master said, The gentleman is courteous, but not pliable: common men are pliable, but not courteous."

First, honesty. In literature, as in life, one of the fundamentals is to find, and be, one's true self. One's true self may indeed be unpleasant (though one can try to better it); but a false self, sooner or later, becomes disgusting—just as a nice plain woman, painted to the eyebrows, can become horrid. In writing, in the long run, pretense does not work. As the police put it, anything you say may be used as evidence against you. If handwriting reveals character, writing reveals it still more. You cannot fool *all* your judges *all* the time.

Most style is not honest enough. Easy to say, but hard to practice. A writer may take to long words, as young men to beards—to impress. But long words, like long beards, are often the badge of charlatans. Or a writer may cultivate the obscure, to seem profound. But even carefully muddied puddles are soon fathomed. Or he may cultivate eccentricity, to seem original. But really original people do not have to think about being original—they can no more help it than they can help breathing. They do not need to dye their hair green. The fame of Meredith, Wilde or Bernard Shaw might now shine brighter, had they struggled less to be brilliant; whereas Johnson remains great, not merely because his gifts were formidable but also because, with all his prejudice and passion, he fought no less passionately to "clear his mind of cant."

Secondly, courtesy—respect for the reader. From this follow several other basic principles of style. Clarity is one. For it is boorish to make your reader rack his brains to understand. One should aim at being impossible to misunderstand—though men's capacity for misunderstanding approaches infinity. Hence Molière and Po Chu-i tried their work on their cooks; and Swift his on his menservants—"which, if they did not comprehend, he would alter and amend, until they understood it perfectly." Our bureaucrats and pundits, unfortunately, are less considerate.

Brevity is another basic principle. For it is boorish, also, to waste your reader's time. People who would not dream of stealing a penny of one's money turn not a hair at stealing hours of one's life. But that does not make them less exasperating. Therefore there is no excuse for the sort of writer who takes as long as a marching army corps to pass a given point. Besides, brevity is often more effective; the half can say more than the whole, and to imply things may strike far deeper than to state them at length. And because one is particularly apt to waste words on preambles before coming to the substance, there was sense in the Scots professor who always asked his pupils—"Did ye remember to tear up that fir-r-st page?"

Clarity comes before even brevity. But it is a fallacy that wordiness is necessarily clearer. Metternich when he thought something he had written was obscure would simply go through it crossing out everything irrelevant. What remained, he found, often became clear. Wellington, asked to recommend three names for the post of Commander-in-Chief, India, took a piece of paper and wrote three times—"Napier." Pages could not have been clearer—or as forcible. On the other hand the lectures, and the sentences, of Coleridge became at times bewildering because his mind was often "wiggle-waggle"; just as he could not even walk straight on a path.

But clarity and brevity, though a good beginning, are only a beginning. By themselves, they may remain bare and bleak. When Calvin Coolidge, asked by his wife what the preacher had preached on, replied "Sin," and, asked what the preacher had said, replied, "He was against it," he was brief enough. But one hardly envies Mrs. Coolidge.

An attractive style requires, of course, all kinds of further gifts —such as variety, good humor, good sense, vitality, imagination. Variety means avoiding monotony of rhythm, of language, of mood. One needs to vary one's sentence length (this present article has too many short sentences; but so vast a subject grows here as cramped as a djin in a bottle); to amplify one's vocabulary; to diversify one's tone. There are books that petrify one throughout, with the rigidly pompous solemnity of an owl perched on a leaf-less tree. But ceaseless facetiousness can be as bad; or perpetual irony. Even the smile of Voltaire can seem at times a fixed grin, a disagreeable wrinkle. Constant peevishness is far worse, as often in Swift; even on the stage too much irritable dialogue may irritate an audience, without its knowing why.

Still more are vitality, energy, imagination gifts that must be inborn before they can be cultivated. But under the head of imag-ination two common devices may be mentioned that have been the making of many a style—metaphor and simile. Why such magic power should reside in simply saying, or implying, that A is like B remains a little mysterious. But even our unconscious seems to love symbols; again, language often tends to lose itself in clouds of vaporous abstraction, and simile or metaphor can bring it back to concrete solidity; and, again, such imagery can gild the gray flats of prose with sudden sun-glints of poetry.

If a foreigner may for a moment be impertinent, I admire the native gift of Americans for imagery as much as I wince at their fondness for slang. (Slang seems to me a kind of linguistic fungus; as poisonous, and as short-lived, as toadstools.) When Matthew Arnold lectured in the United States, he was likened by one newspaper to "an elderly macaw pecking at a trellis of grapes"; he observed, very justly, "How lively journalistic fancy is among the Americans!" General Grant, again, unable to hear him, remarked: "Well, wife, we've paid to see the British lion, but as we can't hear him roar, we'd better go home." By simile and metaphor, these two quotations bring before us the slightly pompous, fastidious, inaudible Arnold as no direct description could have done.

Or consider how language comes alive in the Chinese saying that lending to the feckless is "like pelting a stray dog with dumplings," or in the Arab proverb: "They came to shoe the pasha's horse, and the beetle stretched forth his leg"; in the Greek phrase for a perilous cape—"stepmother of ships"; or the Hebrew adage that "as the climbing up a sandy way is to the feet of the aged, so is a wife full of words to a quiet man"; in Shakespeare's phrase for a little England lost in the world's vastness—"in a great Poole, a Swan's-nest"; or Fuller's libel of tall men—"Ofttimes such who are built four stories high are observed to have little in their cockloft"; in Chateaubriand's "I go yawning my life"; or in Jules Renard's portrait of a cat, "well buttoned in her fur." Or, to take a modern instance, there is Churchill on dealings with Russia: "Trying to maintain good relations with a Communist is like wooing a crocodile. You do not know whether to tickle it under the chin or beat it over the head. When it opens its mouth, you cannot tell whether it is trying to smile or preparing to eat you up." What a miracle human speech can be, and how dull is most that one hears! Would one hold one's hearers, it is far less help, I suspect, to read manuals on style than to cultivate one's own imagination and imagery.

I will end with two remarks by two wise old women of the civilized 18th Century.

The first is from the blind Mme. du Deffand (the friend of Horace Walpole) to that Mlle. de Lespinasse with whom, alas, she was to quarrel so unwisely: "You must make up your mind, my queen, to live with me in the greatest truth and sincerity. You will be charming so long as you let yourself be natural, and remain without pretension and without artifice." The second is from Mme. de Charrière, the Zéide whom Boswell had once loved at Utrecht in vain, to a Swiss girl friend: "Lucinde, my clever Lucinde, while you wait for the Romeos to arrive, you have nothing better to do than become perfect. Have ideas that are clear, and expressions that are simple." (*"Ayez des idées nettes et des expressions simples."*) More than half the bad writing in the world, I believe, comes from neglecting those two very simple pieces of advice.

In many ways, no doubt, our world grows more and more complex; sputniks cannot be simple; yet how many of our complexities remain futile, how many of our artificialities false. Simplicity too can be subtle—as the straight lines of a Greek temple, like the Parthenon at Athens, are delicately curved, in order to look straighter still.

## Study suggestions

1.    Compare the author's definition of style with that in the preceding essay. Too, compare the two articles for content and style.

2.    In his opinion how can handwriting reveal one's self?

3.    Analyze the value of the statements below:
     a.    "Consider the amazing power of mere words."
     b.    "And though the tongue has no bones, it can sometimes break millions of them."
     c.    "We live not by bread alone, but also by words."
     d.    "Men have been hanged on a comma in a statute."
     e.    "One learns to write by reading good books, as one learns to talk by hearing good talkers."

4.    Study the five reasons he gives for gaining some mastery of language.

5.    Give your opinion on pupils' writing on topics about which they have no knowledge.

6.    What suggestions does Lucas give in usage, in philosophy, and in style? What is his attitude toward American slang?

7. How much is involved in the statement: "Have ideas that are clear, and expressions that are simple"?

8. In his own writing does he follow the advice he gives? Justify your opinion.

# THE ART AND MEANING OF FICTION

*Orville Prescott*

Several years ago I was asked to feel sorry for a young writer because he had to earn his living in a business office. Wasn't it a shame that he had to work from nine to five and so had no time to produce his masterpieces? Wasn't his lot as a sensitive intellectual in this age of clamorous crises nearly unbearable? With some dudgeon I expressed no sympathy whatever and indignantly denied that the mere desire to be a writer is a qualification for an endowed ivory tower in which to be one. I cited Hawthorne, whose duties in the customhouse and as a consul in the diplomatic service did not prevent him from writing books which have been well thought of; Trollope, who worked all his life as a civil servant in the British Post Office; Lamb, who did not feel abused because he spent his days perched on a high stool among the other clerks of the East India Company; and Cervantes, Bunyan and Marco Polo, who found imprisonment no barrier to authorship.

And as for the theory that intellectuals occupy an especially pitiable position today—that's ridiculous when we remember the many millions of persons whose lot is truly terrible, the victims of the totalitarian tyrannies. Did Sophocles, who fought the Persians, or Socrates, who fought the Spartans and saw the defeat of Athens in the Peloponnesian War, know a world unplagued by war and dangerous ideologies? Or did Shakespeare, or Milton, or Goethe? The answer is that the true writer writes, whether he can live off his writings or not, whether the din of battle assails his ears and the shock of doubt and fear troubles his mind or not.

The modern world in which we are condemned to live through no choice of our own is a cold and drafty place. It offers no safe haven for the timorous. Most of the portentous questions with which it challenges us have no answers; or, at least, we have not found them yet. But the world has never been much different. Few men have ever found living in it easy. But to live in it with courage is a high adventure and to write about living in it with skill and understanding is a fine achievement.

There are no rules to guide a novelist in what he should write and very few that can tell him how to write it. He must write what he wants to write, about what he knows best and about what he feels most strongly. He must write as well as he can and record the truth as it is given him to see the truth. And if he wishes to attract any considerable number of readers to his book he must do three things.

The first is to persuade. A novelist, whether he is writing the most trivial of ephemeral entertainments or the most solemn and ambitious study of man's soul and his place in the universe, must make his characters seem believable. Readers will meet him halfway. They are willing to believe in the King of Elfland if the novelist makes him both kingly and an elf.

The second thing the novelist must do is make his characters not only believable, but interesting people whose company seems worth keeping for several hours or several days. The easiest way to do this on a superficial level is to make some of his characters sympathetic and some not, and to involve them in conflict, the old heroes-and-villains formula. Then the reader can feel concern for the welfare of some of them because he has identified himself with them. And if the blacks and whites of heroism and villainy are washed out and replaced by the subtle shading of more complicated characters a more intelligent and critical reader will be attracted.

And the third thing the novelist must do is to remember that a work of fiction is a story which must be about something, whether flight and pursuit or an emotional or moral crisis deep within the subconscious mind. Narrative interest depends on a sufficiently dramatic central situation or conflict to make what happens next seem important. The reader must be made to care. His own emotions must be involved.

But if a novelist is a genius, and sometimes even if he is only greatly gifted, he can refuse to do any of these three things and still delight his readers by the originality of his approach and the impact of his personality. This is the hard way and not many writers can take it, only a few in each generation, a Laurence Sterne in the eighteenth century, a Meredith or a Melville in the nineteenth, a Joyce or a Faulkner in the twentieth.

There are three varieties of successful novels (there is no point worrying about the thousand and one sloppy, gooey, foolish and miserable ways in which a novel can be a dismal failure) and the most successful usually are all three at once. The three are: an entertainment, a fictional work of art, an interpretation of life.

Some readers and critics are inclined to look down their noses at fictional entertainment with a ridiculously pompous air of self-righteousness. Several years ago a talented American woman novelist and critic expressed in my hearing her conviction that in times of world crisis, general calamity and mass suffering there is no place for novels which seek merely to entertain.

A novel, she proclaimed, should at least grapple honestly with the great truths and emotional problems of human life and experience if it did not concern itself with urgent issues of war and peace. When I asked her if she never read just for amusement, just for relaxation or just to take her mind off her worries and compose herself for a good night's sleep, she said grimly, "No. Never. When I read I want something I can get my teeth into." And I had a mental picture of her worrying a $3.50 novel as a terrier a rat.

It is easy to understand how she felt. Any good reader feels the same way much of the time. But such a perfectionist standard of criticism upheld with such fervent moral earnestness is as blindly fanatical, as arrogant and as opposed to other people's pleasures as the fulminations of a seventeenth-century Puritan divine. If writers, readers and publishers paid any attention to it a great portion of the books which give the human race the most pleasure would be drowned at birth like kittens.

Surely there is a need and there will always be a welcome for adventure and spy stories, detective stories and even science fiction, a need for novels which retain the increasingly old-fashioned virtue of narrative pace, novels which are stories! Farcical novels, high and low comedies, fantasies and romances all have their place in a balanced literary diet. How much duller the world would be if Conan Doyle had never written about Sherlock Holmes, if P. G. Wodehouse had never invented Bertie Wooster, if Angela Thirkell had never taken over Barchester, if C. S. Forester had not chronicled the adventures of Horatio Hornblower! One of the differences between a free world and a totalitarian world is that in the free one the individual's tastes can be catered to and the amenities of life, such as light fiction and butter, can have a place, as well as solemn art and guns. Fiction which makes no claim to be anything except entertainment may not require much critical discussion; but it is one of the props of a civilized life.

The second thing a novel can be is a work of art. If it is to be one its author must have mastered the technical craft of writing fiction. This is not so easy as it looks, as many a hopeful writer has found out who thought that he had all the necessary tools when he owned a typewriter and some paper. A sound craftsman in fiction must be skillful in the use of words. He must know how to arrange them in the most effective patterns, be aware of their rhythms and connotations, humbly venerate that noble achievement: a good English sentence.

He must know how to create characters through dialogue, thought and action (not in unsupported statements). He must have the creative imagination to think his way into somebody else until, for the time being, while he is hunched over his manuscript, he is that somebody else, a mixture of himself and of what he knows and imagines about others. He must be a good observer and be able to remember colorful and factual details, rhythms of speech characteristic of different kinds of people, typical gestures and special habits. And he won't be able to do this unless he is always interested in people and always noticing them. He must know how to develop his story in dramatic terms so that his characters are revealed in their relationships to one another.

And, perhaps most important of all, he must look at the inchoate mass of human experience, so bare of tidy demarcations and neat denouements, and impose a form upon it, a pattern which will give it unity and clarify its meaning as he sees it. This form is obtained by skill in the art of selection, what to put in and what to leave out. What Edith Wharton thought should be chosen she expressed in her famous maxim for novelists: "The art of rendering life in fiction can never, in the last analysis, be anything, or need to be anything, but the disengaging of crucial moments from the welter of experience."

The more finished a craftsman the novelist is, the more concerned he is with this matter of selection, of including only the significant, of not burying his story beneath a mountain of documentation and useless cataloguing. After all, a novel is not primarily a sociological document. It is a story about people living in society. The best and most effective way of telling it, of disengaging Mrs. Wharton's "crucial moments," is by compression, suggestion and implication. The danger is that the novelist may become too fascinated by such refinements of technique and succumb to the false charms of ambiguity and obscurity. But this danger is only a means of telling his story, of conveying ideas and emotions. It must not be an end in itself.

The third thing a novel can be, an interpretation of life based on the author's experience, ideas, private vision and conditioned reflexes, has been referred to regularly throughout this book. It is the summation of a writer's literary personality, the essence of it as it is transferred into print. It is his way of looking at the world, his convictions about God, destiny, love, marriage, society, virtue, sin and the problem of finding a reliable baby-sitter at short notice. It is this vision, this total personality, which impresses readers more than anything else, which they remember long after particular fictional characters have faded from their minds, which is the most conspicuous difference among writers.

It is this vision which excites or amuses thoughtful and critical readers, which makes one writer seem infinitely more rewarding than another perhaps equally skillful, which makes the writer himself more important than his individual books. Most literary criticism is devoted to it; most casual literary conversation is about it. After all, there is little to say about light fictional entertainment beyond saying that is is entertaining. And there is little which readers uninterested or untrained in literary technique can say about a novel's artistic craftsmanship. But everyone who likes to read, who reacts strongly to books, recognizes the stimulating difference between Thomas Hardy's outlook on life and Jane Austen's, between John O'Hara's and Rumer Godden's.

Everything a novelist sets down in his book contributes to his reader's impression of his outlook and personality: his choice of words and subject matter, his attitude toward his characters (which can never be concealed no matter how arduously the novelist may strive for objectivity), his manipulation of events. Everything fits together like pieces in a puzzle until the novelist who has written a number of books has also written a self-portrait. His readers know how he thinks, what he believes and what he cares about. Often they know these things more intimately than they know them about their friends.

In this way fiction is a never-failing source of intellectual stimulation. From novelists, sometimes wise, sensitive and tolerant, sometimes bitter, prejudiced and angry, we learn how other people feel about life and character, how they felt in the past and how they feel today in circles and even in countries not our own. No one who reads the best fiction sympathetically and attentively can remain so parochially minded, so narrow in outlook, so uninformed about points of view diametrically opposed to his own, as he would be if he read only the sporting pages. Fiction is the great educator for millions of people from childhood to old age.

Just as we may profit in a general way from the personal vision of authors, so we may also learn specifically from novels. They teach us about human nature as revealed in the minds and lives of fictional characters. All of us lead restricted lives, see the same face across the breakfast table, encounter the same group of people at our work and see the same circle of friends in our leisure. We have no way of knowing what it is like to be a South Sea trader, an Arkansas share-cropper, a New York City advertising account executive or a Welsh coal miner except through fiction, or, although the opportunity comes rarely, through a good play. By learning about such people in books we become better informed about the varieties of human experience and, unless we have minds of wood and hearts of stone, we should become wiser, more sympathetic, more tolerant through this vicarious participation in the lives of others.

The mystery of human personality and character may never be solved to the satisfaction of both priests and psychoanalysts. Information alone cannot do it. With increased information about environment, heredity, psychology and the sex habits of five thousand American males we lessen the circumference of the mystery by only a minute fraction, remove only some of the fuzziness from around its edges. One of the basic and most difficult things for anyone to understand is that someone else does not think the same way, does not even inhabit the same world.

Knowing better through experience, we expect others to be logical when we are not logical ourselves. Conscious of our own sins of commission and omission, we irrationally insist that our children and friends have no sins of their own. We may learn the folly of such conduct; but we never learn not to be a little disappointed by the bewildering confusion of a world in which every individual is, to a certain extent, a traveler from another country, a country where the natives worship strange gods and paint themselves blue.

But, even if we persist in being human and fallible, we can learn a more understanding kind of humanness through fiction. The importance of novels as interpretations of life has never been properly recognized. They demonstrate it best when the novelists succeed in creating memorable characters who are significant for their individual, personal efforts to meet eternal human problems.

I do not believe that the novelist can succeed in this respect unless he himself believes in the individual worth and dignity of men, in men's capacity of choice and their moral obligation to choose as well as they can, in the something within them that makes them worth writing about, that makes them worth saving from atomic extinction and from totalitarian terror.

## Study suggestions

1. What are the author's attitudes toward the writer in "an ivory tower"? In fact, what is the value of a writer's living among people while he is writing?

2. In the third paragraph what does the author reveal of his thinking?

3. Study the three criteria for attracting readers and also three varieties of successful novels. Illustrate these from your own reading of novels.

4. Explain the meaning behind calling fiction "one of the props of the civilized world"; and also, "the great educator for millions of people from childhood to old age."

5. Analyze the specific items he gives for the craft of writing.

6. Write an essay yourself on novels (or a novel) as interpretations of life—or on the quotations in question 4. Be definite and illustrate from novels you have read.

# BUILD YOUR OWN LIBRARY

*Gilbert Highet*

You should build your own library, as though you were building something which would last all your life, and perhaps longer. Not the bookshelves and such external things; the books themselves, chosen, and read, and placed, with understanding and affection. Everyone except illiterates and quasi-illiterates has a little library of his or her own, even if it is only a few novels picked up haphazardly or a shabby collection of paperbacks. Everyone starts with *some* books: a Bible, a do-it-yourself manual, a mystery story. The standard of education throughout the United States is more or less paced by the sales of books in various regions: the stupider any area is, the fewer good schools it has, the fewer books its inhabitants buy and borrow from libraries. Books are not all of civilization, but they are one of the essential carriers of civilization.

Since we are nearly all building our own libraries, here are a few hints which might be useful, hints from an old lover of books who acquired his first volume forty-eight years ago, bought his first volume forty-five years ago, and bound his first volume with his own hands forty years ago. (I still have it too, though the glue is beginning to dry up and the sewing to come apart.)

Naturally, we start with the few indispensable books for consultation, not for reading—the books of reference without which we can scarcely have an intelligent discussion or read an intelligent book: the dictionary, the encyclopedia, and all the other settlers of arguments. Every week, sometimes every day, people take the trouble to telephone me or write me at Columbia University in order to ask me some perfectly simple question which they themselves could have solved within five minutes if they had had two or three simple, cheap, and widely distributed reference books at their hand. Ridiculous.

Beyond those, we all have our individual look-it-up shelves, depending on our personal interests and hobbies. Everyone ought to have a first-aid book; most people need cookery books; anyone who spends any time in the country needs a garden book and a bird book and a tree book; there are books on the maintenance of automobiles, on income tax, on child care. (Just make sure that you buy reasonable books, and not the works of crackpots: I still remember a period of great unhappiness when my wife and I were misdirected by a book about raising small babies, and when we all three suffered a great deal. It is a grave responsibility to write a book.)

Now for real reading. We begin with the central books, which are part of almost every educated person's mind, which are thought about and referred to (consciously or unconsciously) every day: the Bible and Shakespeare. From these we go on to the more or less permanent works of fiction which have been created during the last century or so: Tolstoy's *War and Peace* and *Anna Karenina;* Dostoevsky's *Crime and Punishment* and (probably) *The Brothers Karamazov;* Melville's *Moby Dick;* a few of the best of Mark Twain and Charles Dickens; the perverted pageant of Proust; some of Thomas Mann; Faulkner's central works; add to these the novels which have most powerfully impressed you and seem unforgettable.

Now you have part of the core of a library. You need poetry also, and good nonfiction. In buying poetry to keep, follow your own taste. If your taste is still developing, then buy several good anthologies of poetry, ancient and modern, original and translated; keep them; read them off and on for a year or two, and then your taste will form itself. You will know whether you prefer Robinson Jeffers or Robert Frost, Browning or cummings. Personally, I buy every anthology of poetry which looks intelligent and varied and rich; even if I find only a dozen good poems in it which I did not possess, they are my reward. As for permanent nonfiction, that depends entirely on your habit of mind. If you are inclined to philosophy or to religion, to science or to economics or to history, there are many good books which promise to last.

But then you should have a couple of shelves devoted purely to fun: ease, relaxation, pleasure—something to pick up in odd moments when you cannot face the logic of life or the effort of thought; something to read while in bed with a mild virus infection; something for a peaceful evening when you cannot stand any more guffawing audiences and shouted commercials. (YES! SHOUTED COMMERCIALS!) Something easy. Similar books should be put in every guest room. Not *Whither Are We Drifting?* books, nor books about *Our Role in Tristan da Cunha,* but books which produce the same effect as a chicken sandwich and a glass of champagne: the works of James Thurber; some fantasy fiction; some intelligent whodunits; light books of travel; some well-written ghost stories (like those of M. R. James, *Ghost Stories of an Antiquary*)—books which you need not read, but go on reading for pure diversion.

Now this is becoming a personal library. As you read books and buy them, you will find that your own tastes come out more

and more strongly. There are special hobbies which interest
you. There are problems still unsolved on which good books are
written. Neglected aspects of human activity deserve more attention. You have been to some strange and charming place, and
wish to explore its past and its present. For all these reasons you
will buy books. A man who was captivated by a lecture on astronomy which he heard at school may well recall it twenty years
later, and begin to read more about modern astronomy; or else
he may pass on to the new topic of space travel, or to the important
and still misunderstood subject of weather and climate. The young
fellow who deciphered one of the ancient Greek scripts called
Minoan was not a professional scholar at all: he was an architect
by profession, but he recalled that he had heard, when he was
still a schoolboy, a lecture on the problem of these scripts by
Sir Arthur Evans, who had dug up many of the clay tablets on
which they are written; the problem fermented in his mind for
years; he devoted his mind to it as soon as he had some leisure; he
collected books and articles about it; and, with the brilliance of an
amateur (which sometimes brings tears to the eyes of the profes-
sionals), he solved it. Another man, who recognizes reluctantly
that his temperament will never allow him to be a good chess
player, will still collect books on the history of the game, biographies of its masters, analyses of its problems. Another, again,
may buy books on mathematics, its puzzles and its personalities;
on extrasensory perception; on business cycles; on psychoanalysis;
on the ballet; on local and family history; even (I am glad to say)
on nonsense.

Your library will now go on growing, almost by itself. But it
needs a little care. It is not an external thing, like a doormat; it
is more personal than a car. Like your furniture and pictures and
ornaments, it is a reflection of your feelings and your mind. No
more than you would have a cracked piece of linoleum under your
dining-room table, should you have a collection of dirty, dog-eared,
crippled books on your shelves. No more than you would have
your phonograph blaring out a random selection mixing Tebaldi
with Spike Jones and old Carusos with new Presleys, should you
have shelves in which Mickey Spillane leans against Edith Sitwell.
Books need a little arranging, and a little maintenance.

To make sure that they will remain with you it is a good idea to have your own bookplate inside the front cover. There are many pleasant bookplates which can be adapted for individual use on sale in stationers' shops. Or you can persuade an artist friend to design one specially for you; or if you are a photographer you can make your own. Back in 1929, when I had just a few books which I treasured, a friend of mine who was an artist and a calligrapher designed a bookplate for me. Those were the days of sharp, angular, modernist designs, and this bookplate was highly unfashionable, being calm and balanced and reposeful and harmonious—a head and a landscape out of the pictorial tradition of the early Italian Renaissance. But I liked it; I saved up some money and had a plate made of it; I have used it ever since. James Wardrop, who drew it for me, is dead now, but his friendship and his sensitive taste remain alive for me whenever I open one of my books.

As well as putting your own bookplate into your books (by the way, you know that you should never lend a book? Never, unless you have at least two copies. You always lend books that you like; the other fellow likes them too; and you never see them again), you might also jot down the date you bought them: just a few figures, the month and the year, will be enough later to remind you of a stage in your life which had been half forgotten.

There is also an almost indispensable addition to your library, which is not a book, but a collection of book material. This is a box file, or a large decorative envelope, or anything more or less permanent and not too disagreeable to look at, into which you can put newspaper clippings, and magazine articles, and interviews, programs of concerts and catalogues of art exhibitions, and so forth. It is surprising how many things like this turn out to be worth keeping. There is no need to make a system of it; but if some particular piece seems interesting when you read it, drop it into the file. In five years or so you will be surprised to find how much that is curious and stimulating has survived, which might otherwise have perished. Of course there will be a lot of rubbish too, and you can throw that into the wastebasket; but there will be some interviews with authors which have never been reprinted in book form, and which supplement what you yourself have been thinking about them; there will be some reviews of new plays or first novels which confirm, or perhaps contradict, later impressions; there will be some impressive or amusing public utterances, when some prominent writer breaks into speech. You will often reread an article from your own file, when you would not think of handling the back numbers of the magazine in which it first appeared.

One further hint, which is sometimes forgotten. Public libraries are fine things, and we all ought to use them; but they do not replace a personal library. When you see a book which really attracts you, *buy* it. Take it out of the library first if you like, and read it to see whether you are sure. But if you are sure, then buy it. In part, this is a kindness to the author, who has to live and pay his taxes and his mortgage; one of the surest ways to wound any writer, however insignificant, is to write telling him that you *loved* his book even though you had to wait *six months* before your name came up on the waiting list at the lending library. In part, it is insurance. Books are apt to go out of print, when their authors die; they disappear even before that, and cannot be discovered except with inordinate effort.

Remember also that there are many guides to help you in building a good personal library. To begin with, there are some very competent, level-headed, and candid book critics in the United States. If you pick two or three of them and read their reviews regularly, you will recognize their strengths and their weaknesses, and learn within limits to trust their taste. Again, at the end of every calendar year, the best magazines and newspapers usually list the hundred books produced during that year which have most chance of surviving with distinction; from these lists you could easily assemble two or three highly interesting shelves. Then there are a number of exceedingly useful books about books, which classify and describe hundreds, even thousands, of important works in all fields. The best is probably Hester Hoffman's *Bookman's Manual* (Bowker, New York, 8th edition, 1958); there is a fine paperback called simply *Good Reading* (New American Library), which would keep most people going for a lifetime; and I often recommend a book list made up for Trinity College, Hartford, Connecticut, by Professor Harry Todd Costello, called *Books for a College Student's Reading* (Trinity College, Hartford, 1951). When in doubt, always ask a librarian. Trained librarians always have lists ready at hand; some even distribute their own; they are always willing to help, for they love books.

I have been talking about forming a personal library as though it were a pleasure and a way to pleasure; and indeed so it is. But it is also something of a duty. It is the mind that makes us truly human. If the mind is never fed on anything more than television stunt programs and old movies and short reports in the newspapers and casual conversations, it will never operate at more than half its capacity; it will start to atrophy like an arm with a withered muscle. A house without books usually means a mind without either knowledge, or thought, or enjoyment of its own powers.

## Study suggestions

1.  Compare Highet's statement that "books are one of the essential carriers of civilization" with Orville Prescott's comments on novels in his essay, "The Art and Meaning of Fiction." Discuss these opinions.

2.  What works does Highet call the *core* of a library? What others would you feel come under this category?

3.  After these titles, note his emphasis on the personal. What books would you choose for your own interest?

4.  Would a file be more helpful if you organized your clipings?

5.  Discuss his concluding paragraph.

6.  Theme suggestions:
    My Personal Library
    Lending Books
    My Favorites Among Books
    Browsing in Book Stores

# THE THREE SONS IN HAMLET

*Jean Paris*

It is difficult, André Gide once said, "to imagine a text more super-subtle and crafty, more full of ambiguities, snares, and pitfalls" than *Hamlet*. This is certainly no exaggeration. For some three centuries countless poets, critics, scholars, philosophers, and psychologists have sought to explore every nook and cranny of *Hamlet's* endless labyrinth of meaning, but the only points on which any of them seem to be able to agree are that it is a masterpiece of pessimism whose central figure is a procrastinating prince. Yet even these are points which are still vigorously debated to this day.

Now it is evident that the interpretation of a play will vary according to the point of view from which you approach it. Most interpretations of *Hamlet* have been centered on Hamlet himself, with lesser degrees of attention being lavished on Claudius, Gertrude, Ophelia, Laertes, and the other characters in descending order. These interpretations have been, we might say, "Hamlet-centric." More than a hundred years ago Goethe in his *Wilhelm Meister* was already inveighing against this tendency and denouncing "the error of judging a play in terms of a single role, and of not considering this role itself in relationship with the whole." For no dramatist are these warning words more appropriate than for Shakespeare. Almost all his plots are of an extraordinary intricacy and complexity, and it is characteristic of his plays that his protagonists are as much governed by the dramatic structure of the events in the midst of which they move as these are determined by the temperament and actions of the protagonists them-selves. In virtually every one of his plays the characters are sub-ject to natural and supernatural forces which are imposed from the outside—like the fairies in *A Midsummer Night's Dream,* the witches in *Macbeth,* Ariel in *The Tempest,* and the Ghost in *Hamlet.*

Let us take this last as a starting point. The role of the Ghost in *Hamlet,* as everyone knows, is to announce to young Hamlet that his father was murdered by his brother, Claudius. This, in the accepted view of the play, is the real beginning of the tragedy. But in the very opening scene, and before the Ghost has spoken, we are given an inkling of the fact that the tragic cycle goes back further than that. When the two sentinels, Marcellus and Bernardo, wish to know why the kingdom is in such a frenzy of military prep-aration, Horatio explains to them that some time before, the late king, Hamlet, had taken on Fortinbras, king of Norway, in single combat, had slain him and annexed a large portion of his lands. To regain them young Fortinbras, his son, "of unimproved mettle hot and full," was now busy gathering together a force of "lawless resolutes,"

> and this, I take it,
> Is the main motive of our preparations,
> The source of this our watch, and the chief head
> Of this post-haste and romage in the land.

Strange as it may seem, I know of no major Shakespeare critic or scholar who has given to this speech of Horatio's the attention it would seem to deserve. This is all the more extraordinary in that it occurs at the very beginning and was apparently intended to point up the genesis, the "original sin," in the fateful cycle of events that make up the tragedy of *Hamlet.* If we want proof of this, we can find it in the gravedigger's scene in the last act. When asked by Hamlet how long he has been digging graves, the grave-maker replies:

> I came to't that day that our last king Hamlet overcame Fortinbras . . . the very day that young Hamlet was born —he that is mad, and sent into England.

There is no reason to suppose that Shakespeare gave the grave-digger these pregnant lines to establish an odd coincidence. It seems clear enough that in this scene, one of the most meaningful in the entire play, the gravedigger speaks not just for himself, but for inexorable destiny. Prior to this he asks of his fellow grave-digger: "What is he that builds stronger than either the mason, the shipwright, or the carpenter?" and he answers his own question: "A grave-maker. The houses he makes last till doomsday." The crucial importance of this scene seems to lie in the fact that it is a symbolic anticipation of the final laying to rest of the tragic cycle of unrest first unleashed by Hamlet's father,

> the King
> That was and is the question of these wars,

as Bernardo says in the first scene.

Far from being the first victim of an act of violence, King Hamlet is himself the first slayer of another's father and the conqueror of another's lands. This helps to throw some light on the Ghost's cryptic reference to his previous "foul crimes done in my days of nature." The slaying of their king and the annexation of their lands could only have appeared to the Norwegians as a crime, no matter how valorous an act it may have seemed to the Danes, and for Fortinbras' son such an act called inexorably for vengeance. Even Horatio seems to imply as much, for in recalling these events and "our valiant Hamlet" (the late king) he adds: "(For so this side of our known world esteem'd him)" as much as admitting that others on earth, no less than in heaven, might feel differently about him.

The action in *Hamlet,* therefore, really begins with the slaying of Fortinbras' father rather than with the murder of Hamlet's father. It is this which gives *Hamlet* its quality of ineluctable trag-edy. In the complex scheme of events that have occurred prior to the raising of the curtain, there are wrongs to be righted that cannot simply be atoned for by the killing of Claudius. Such an act would avenge Hamlet's father, but it would not avenge the elder

Fortinbras. Young Hamlet himself must die in order to redeem the initial injustice committed by his father in making an orphan and a landless prince of Fortinbras the younger.

The slaying of a man in single combat cannot, of course, be equated in terms of villainy with the poisoning of a sleeping brother. There is quite a gulf separating King Fortinbras' death on the battlefield from Claudius' fratricide. But we should not forget that the Elizabethans had a sense of morality, justice, and destiny that was considerably different from ours. The death of a kinsman, and above all of a father, on the battlefield as elsewhere was an act of violence calling for revenge, no matter how fairly or honorably it might have been inflicted. In *Henry VI,* for example, justice constantly passes from the House of York to the House of Lancaster and vice versa, each successive vengeance for a previous slaying rendering the dialectic of destiny more and more implacable. In *Romeo and Juliet* a duel is considered as much of an evil as murder, and when Tybalt kills Mercutio, Romeo immediately feels it his duty to avenge his kinsman by killing Tybalt. In this conception of things destiny is implacable, and a valorous act can engender a tragic cycle of war and vengeance no less than a crime. In killing King Fortinbras, King Hamlet may have acquitted himself honorably and for the welfare of Denmark, but his action nonetheless unleashed the fateful drama from which the younger Fortinbras was destined to emerge triumphant.

Properly considered, then, *Hamlet* is the final phase in a three-act tragedy begun by the slaying of Fortinbras, continued by the murder of Hamlet's father, and further complicated by the killing of Polonius. This last event is, as Victor Hugo was the first to see, one of the crucial moments in the play. "All of Shakespeare's plays, with only two exceptions—*Macbeth* and *Romeo and Juliet*—" he remarked in his book *William Shakespeare,* "that is, thirty-four plays out of thirty-six, present a strange peculiarity . . . this is the double nature of the action in each drama, in which the larger is reflected in the small. Beside the storm in the Atlantic there is the storm in the waterglass. Thus Hamlet makes along-side of him another Hamlet; he kills Polonius, Laertes' father, and here is Laertes in the same situation that he is in vis-à-vis

Claudius. There are two fathers to avenge, and there might well have been two ghosts."

There is, indeed, a troubling similitude between Hamlet and Laertes. If we look closely at their relationship, we note that it passes through three distinct phases. In the first, the two are bound together by a certain rivalry regarding Ophelia, a rivalry which seems to have been a source of some concern to Hamlet, since he twice accuses Ophelia of betraying him and of obeying another's will. Similarly Laertes is bent from the start on ending the romance between the prince and his sister.

This first phase is followed by a second, a strange period of storm and eclipse, in which Laertes absents himself from Elsinore to go abroad, while Hamlet "alienates himself," as it were, by assuming the actions and words of a madman. It is in this twilight period that Hamlet, suspected by Laertes and distrusted by the rest of the court, realizes the full depth of his isolation and distress and ends by accidentally avenging himself on one of its artisans— Polonius. This period of rupture and separation is then followed by a third phase of identification, which begins with an extremely significant act—when the two leap into the same grave during Ophelia's burial. It continues with such strange phrases as this one of Hamlet's: "by the image of my cause I see the portraiture of his"; and it culminates in a duel, a mutual forgiveness, and a twin transfiguration.

Thus, beneath the evident disparities distinguishing these two heroes, there lurks a profound kinship; the same duty weighs upon them, the same love haunts them, the same end awaits them. The one great difference between them lies in their attitude toward the murder of their respective fathers. Whereas Hamlet ponders his revenge at length, Laertes rushes recklessly at his and makes himself the blind instrument of Claudius' wiles. The two are, indeed, complementary opposites, like two detached halves of an integrated personality. Symbolically speaking, Hamlet is the incarnation of conscience more or less bereft of action, while Laertes is the embodiment of action more or less bereft of thought. And behind and midway between them looms Fortinbras, in whom the halves are reunited and in whom these contradictions are triumphantly summed up.

Viewed in this light, the observation of Hugo, astute though it is, is obviously incomplete. In saying that there are "two fathers to avenge," he forgot Fortinbras' father. The truth is that there are not two, but three fathers to be avenged. There are also lands and a throne to be won. If Fortinbras ends by winning them, it is because he shares what is essential in the roles and virtues of his "brothers." Like Hamlet, he is the son of a slain monarch and subjected to the authority of an uncle; like Laertes, he is a man of action in word and deed. Above all, he is the predestined victor because only by regaining his father's lost lands can he re-establish the original order of things and restore concord and unity to a world of division and chaos.

Thus the three sons are linked together in this play by a common duty—the vengeance of their fathers—and they may be said to represent three different aspects of one type: the Son.

In the original *Hamlet* saga, as recorded by Saxo Grammaticus, there is no such person as Laertes, nor Fortinbras either. Ophelia is Hamlet's foster sister, and Hamlet himself perishes at the end in a battle with another uncle. Laertes, therefore, is an original invention of Shakespeare's and obviously created to be a foil, a violent contrast to the brooding, pensive prince.

This scission of a once single and harmonious person, family, or estate into two distinct and warring halves is a significant feature of many Shakespeare plays. Its most perfect geometric exemplification, perhaps, is in *The Comedy of Errors,* where the merchant Egeon and his wife Emilia are separated by a shipwreck, the father regaining Syracuse with one of his twin sons and another adopted one, while the mother with her other twin and the twin of the adopted son makes her way to Ephesus, which is at war with Syracuse. Only after many vicissitudes and adventures are the two disjointed halves of the family once again happily reunited, and its pristine harmony restored. The same pattern of divorce can be found in *A Midsummer Night's Dream,* where the conflict between Oberon and Titania plunges the mortals into multiple errings and aberrations that are only dissipated when the strife of the gods is ended.

Shakespeare's predilection for this pattern of unity, scission, and reunion was not accidental. This symbolism had become fashionable at the time Shakespeare was writing his greatest tragedies through the philosophy of the Rosicrucians, which had just been introduced into England. The leading English exponent of this form of occultism was Robert Fludd. According to Fludd, in the beginning of things there reigned a state of unity called the *Ain Soph:* a state characterized by nothingness, the unknowable, the absolute. All creation springs from the original void by a series of divisions engendering being. God himself proceeds from it, and following his self-relevation he divides everything into two basic principles: *voluntas,* the active, luminous, masculine principle, and *noluntas,* the passive, dark, feminine principle. From the mating of these two opposites are born primordial matter, chaos, and by successive differentiations, the three alchemical substances (sulphur, mercury, and salt), the four elements, and finally all the varied creatures and things that make up our teeming world. As the end products of this cosmic genesis, Nature, Beasts, and Men constitute the lowest creations in a hierarchy that loses itself in the eternal. Whence the necessity of a liberating metamorphosis through death which, by dissolving matter, frees the divine fire inhabiting it. Like Jesus, we must die in the flesh so as to live again in the spirit. Creation, fall, and redemption are the three great acts in the drama of the universe, repeated in nature by the cycle of the seasons and in human society by the accession of each new king.

This symbolism is, of course, one that has appeared in various forms in a number of religions and myths, as, for example, in the medieval myth of the Knights of the Holy Grail—Percival, Gawain, and Galahad. In the case of *Hamlet* it is applied not just to young Hamlet, who is at war with himself and with Laertes, but to society as a whole. Beginning with a profound corruption in the existing nature of men and things—"there is something rotten in the state of Denmark"—Shakespeare leads us through spiritual strife, dissension, and war toward an ultimate purification and recapture of the pristine state of innocence. Hamlet's world is the rotten world destined to return to dust, while Fortinbras' is the "shape of things to come," perfect once more in its order, unity, and purity. This double movement of fall and redemption is accentuated throughout the play by a violent antagonism of images, as, for example, in these words of Hamlet's:

> I have of late—but wherefore I know not—lost all my mirth, forgone all custom of exercises; and indeed, it goes so heavily with my disposition that this goodly frame, the earth, seems to me a sterile promontory; this most excellent canopy, the air, look you, this brave o'erhanging firmament, this majestical roof fretted with golden fire—why, it appeareth no other thing to me than a foul and pestilent congregation of vapours. What a piece of work is a man! how noble in reason! how infinite in faculties! in form and moving how express and admirable! in action how like an angel! in apprehension how like a god! the beauty of the world, the paragon of animals! And yet to me what is this quintessence of dust?

A British scholar, D. S. Savage, has shown how Hamlet's speeches contain many allusions to alchemical processes, and how his reflections take the form of an "inverted transmutation," whereby a kingdom is transformed into a prison, glory into mire, monarch into beggar. Yet to this we should add that such a degradation is here the precondition for a greater good. The science of alchemy taught that matter, like spirit, must first be vilified before attaining its final purity. All must rot and rust in order to be changed to gold. In accordance with the logic inherent in tragedy, pain and horror must reach their ultimate exasperation so that from the very excess there may issue an ultimate salvation. Thus we find in Fortinbras' apotheosis that catharsis which Aristotle held to be the supreme function of the theater. Past the night of terror man finds himself restored to his first powers, to the prerogatives of his semidivinity. Issuing from hell he finds once more the harmony, the sense, the universal plenitude of justice. In *Hamlet* all is summed up, redeemed, regenerated in Fortinbras, so that to reduce him to an insignificant figure, or still more to leave him out entirely, as Laurence Olivier did in his film version of the play, is to upset and to destroy the deep symbolic meaning of this great tragedy.

It may well be asked why, if Fortinbras plays such a crucial role in *Hamlet,* he was only given a few unimportant lines by Shakespeare and was allowed to appear but twice upon the stage.

But here again we catch a glimpse of Shakespeare's instinctive genius. Like the Ghost, who conjures up the past, Fortinbras, who embodies the future, is for the most part invisible, yet he haunts the play from beginning to end. Like the future he is ever on the horizon of the present, dimly but inexorably felt, until the moment comes when, like a *deus ex machina,* he must put a final seal to the tragedy. That this is so even Hamlet seems vaguely to sense, for as he dies he requests that Fortinbras be made his legitimate successor:

> But I do prophesy th' election lights
> On Fortinbras. He has my dying voice.

To which Fortinbras a few lines later replies:

> For me, with sorrow I embrace my fortune.
> I have some rights of memory in this kingdom,
> Which now to claim my vantage doth invite me.

Thus the tragic cycle is finally buried in an apotheosis of reconciliation.

This dialectic of fall and redemption can be found in all of Shakespeare's historical dramas. Here the moral of history is the eternal degradation of mankind. In triumphing over a corrupt king, a prince regenerates the kingdom. The welfare of the kingdom itself seems bound to this periodic sacrifice, to this cycle of ritual death and resurrection. The Father must die, so that the Son may live and reign.

Such is the symbolic cycle of things that we find also in *Hamlet.* Unlike most of Shakespeare's historical dramas, the prince who triumphs here is not the legitimate pretender, but a foreign prince, Fortinbras, alien to the House of Denmark. But his accession to the throne, if anything, accentuates the ultimate redemption of the kingdom's rotten condition. For so corrupted has the dynasty become by the end of the play that we find Laertes suddenly become the hero of a popular revolt and envisaging the overthrow of Claudius and the seizure of the throne.

Thus the three sons, the ambitious Fortinbras, the impetuous

Laertes, and the luckless Hamlet, who has been cheated out of his kingship, are linked by a common aspiration for the throne. Each in his own way is confronted with a struggle to free himself from the bondage of the past by assuming the control of the morrow. The three are linked, not only by the duty of avenging their slain fathers, but by their need to find their own liberation from it. Hamlet, Laertes, and Fortinbras may thus be regarded as three affirmations of the Son against the Father, of the future against the past.

To grasp the fundamental import of this symbolism we must remember that Shakespeare wrote *Hamlet* around 1603, at the very end of the Renaissance. By that date the medieval conception of the universe, society, and man had crumbled beneath the hammer blows of at least three great demolishers. The old geocentric order had been shattered by Copernicus, the moral order undermined by Montaigne, the political order destroyed by Machiavelli. This triple convulsion in the accepted scheme of things explains in large measure the violence and uncertainty that finds its dramatic expression in the Elizabethan theater. From Thomas Kyd to Webster, from Marlowe to John Ford, the tumult of this upheaval fills the air with clamors of desperate doubt and dread. This is an age in which the old order is dying. Nothing is absolutely certain, absolutely sacred, absolutely immutable, absolutely eternal any more. All is in flux, doomed to perdition, but also to rebirth.

As perhaps it is given to only one work in any century to express, *Hamlet* is the epic portrayal of this renaissance apocalypse. But its crowning glory and significance lie precisely in the fact that the doubt and anxiety it so splendidly depicts eventually find their term. Amidst the longing for an order that has vanished and given way to confusion, this play emerges as a supreme effort to recover man's power of affirmation. For if in the image of the slain Father is to be seen the symbolism of the old, moribund medieval order, in the figure of the triumphant Son can be found the presage of the new. Supreme expression of a cosmic, spiritual, and social transition, *Hamlet* is the dramatization of this metamorphosis of civilization, from the death of one to the birth of another.

Far from being a somber masterpiece of nihilism, as it has sometimes been accused of being, it marks in Shakespeare's works, and for the Elizabethan theater as a whole, the decisive turning point where despair, pushed to its paroxysm, turns back upon it-self. The dying Hàmlet is born again in Fortinbras, thus prefigur-ing the mystique of *The Tempest*—the mystery of reconciliation and the final triumph of human reason and virtue.

## Study suggestions

To understand this article, one must be familiar with Shakespeare's play. This point of view gives much material for discussion. That Fortinbras was mentioned early in the play, that he appeared and then reappeared at the conclusion to receive the dying voice for election to the throne substantiates the feeling of many that he had more significance than former critics have given him.

1. In what way does the linking together of the three sons "in a common duty" give a unified pattern?

2. Explain that because of the death of the elder Fortinbras young Hamlet must die.

3. Show how the Elizabethan standards of "morality, justice, and destiny," quite different from ours, probably influenced Shake-speare.

4. Why did Victor Hugo call the slaying of Polonius one of the "crucial moments in the play"?

5. Contrast the attack of the three sons on their problems. Explain: "They may be said to represent three different aspects of one type: the Son."

6. Compare Hamlet and Laertes.

7. How does the writer use other Shakespeare plays, symbol-ism, and the science of alchemy to analyze certain patterns and trends in developing his dramas? Explain Aristotle's idea that catharsis is the "supreme function of the theater."

8. Discuss the logic of this analysis.

# THE PLACE OF MUSIC IN GENERAL HISTORY

*Romain Rolland*

Music is only now beginning to take the place due to it in general history. It seems a strange thing that concepts of the evolution of man's soul should have been formed while one of the strongest expressions of that soul has been ignored. But we know what difficulty the other arts have had in obtaining recognition in general history, even when they were more favored and easier of approach by the French mind. Is it so long ago that this did not apply to the history of literature and science and philosophy and, indeed, the whole of human thought? Yet the political life of a nation is only a superficial part of its being; in order to learn its inner life—the source of its actions—we must penetrate to its very soul by way of its literature, its philosophy, and its art, where the ideas, the passions, and the dreams of its people are reflected.

We know that history may find resources in literature; we know the kind of help, for example, that Corneille's poetry and Descartes' philosophy may bring to the understanding of the Treaty of Westphalia; or, again, what a dead letter the Revolution of '89 might be if we were not acquainted with the thought of the Encyclopedists and eighteenth-century salons.

Nor do we forget the valuable information that the plastic arts give us about different epochs, for in them we behold an age's very countenance—its type, its gestures, its dress, its fashions, indeed its whole daily life. What a storehouse for history! One thing hangs to another: political revolutions have their counterpart in artistic revolutions; the life of a nation is an organism in which all is bound together—economic phenomena and artistic phenomena alike. In the resemblances and differences of Gothic monuments a Viollet-le-Duc could trace the great highways of commerce in the twelfth century. The study of some detail of architecture—a belfry, for instance—would show the progress of royalty in France, the thought of the Ile-de-France imposing a peculiar construction upon provincial schools from the time of Philip Augustus onward. But the great service that art renders history is to bring it close to the soul of an epoch and so let it touch the springs of emotion. On the surface, literature and philosophy may seem to give us more definitive information by reducing the characteristics of an age to precise formulas. On the other hand, this artificial simplification may leave us with inelastic and impoverished ideas. Art is modeled on life, and it has an almost greater value than literature because its domain is infinitely more extended. We have six centuries of art in France, and yet we are often content to judge the French spirit by four centuries of literature. Further, our medieval art, for example, can show us the life of the provinces, about which our classical literature has hardly anything to say. Few countries are composed of elements more disparate than ours. Our races, traditions, and social life are varied and show evidence of the influence of Italians, Spanish, Germans, Swiss, English, Flemish, and inhabitants of other countries. A strong political unity has dissolved these antagonistic elements and established an average and an equilibrium in the civilizations that clashed about us. But if such a unity is apparent in our literature, the multiple nuances of our personality have become very blurred. Art gives us a much richer image of French genius. It is not like a grisaille but like a cathedral window where all the colors of earth and sky blend. It is not a simple picture but like those rose windows which are the product of the purely French art of the Ile-de-France and Champagne. And I say to myself: Here is a people whose characteristics are said to be reason and not imagination, common sense and not fancy, drawing and not coloring; yet this is the people who created those mystical east-windows!

And so it is that acquaintance with the art enlarges and gives life to the image one has formed of a people from their literature alone.

Now by turning to music we may extend this idea still further.

Music perplexes those who have no feeling for it; it seems to them an incomprehensible art, beyond reasoning and having no connection with reality. What help can history possibly draw from that which is outside ordinary matter and therefore outside history?

Well, first of all it is not true that music has so abstract a character, for it has an undoubted relationship with literature, with the theater, and with the life of an epoch. Thus no one can fail to see that a history of opera will throw light on the ways and manners of society. Indeed, every form of music is allied with some form of society and makes it easier to understand; also, in many cases, the history of music is closely connected with that of other arts.

It constantly happens that the arts influence one another, that they intermingle, or that, as a result of their natural evolution, they overflow their boundaries and invade the domains of neighboring arts. Now it is music that would become painting, now painting that would be music. "Good painting is music, a melody," said Michelangelo, at a time when music was extricating itself, so to speak, from the very decadence of other arts. The doors between the arts are not closely shut as many theorists would pretend, and one art is constantly opening upon another. Arts may extend and find their consummation in other arts; when the mind has exhausted one form, it seeks and finds a more complete expression in another. Thus is a knowledge of the history of music often necessary to the history of the plastic arts.

But the essence of the great interest of art lies in the way it reveals the true feeling of the soul, the secrets of its inner life, and the world of passion that has long accumulated and fermented there before surging up to the surface. Very often, thanks to its depth and spontaneity, music is the first indication of tendencies which later translate themselves into words, and afterward into deeds. The *Eroica* Symphony anticipated by more than ten years the awakening of the German nation. The *Meistersinger* and *Siegfried* proclaimed ten years beforehand the imperial triumph of Germany. There are even cases where music is the only witness of a whole inner life which never reaches the surface.

What does the political history of Italy and Germany in the seventeenth century teach us? A series of court intrigues, of military defeats, of princely weddings, of feastings, of miseries, and of one ruin after another. How is one, then, to account for the miraculous resurrection of these two nations in the eighteenth and nineteenth centuries? The work of their musicians gives us an insight. It shows in Germany the treasures of faith and activity which were silently accumulating; it shows simple and heroic characters like Heinrich Schütz who, during the Thirty Years' War, in the midst of the worst disasters that ever devastated a country, quietly went his way, singing his own robust and resolute faith. About him were Johann Christoph Bach and Michael Bach (ancestors of the great Bach), who seemed to carry with them the quiet presentiment of the genius who followed them. Besides these were Pachelbel, Kuhnau, Buxtehude, Zachau, and Erlebach— great souls who were shut up all their lives in the narrow sphere of a little provincial town, known only to a few men, without wordly ambition, without hope of leaving anything to posterity, singing for themselves alone and for their God; and who, among all their sorrows of home life and public life, slowly and persistently gathered reserves of strength and moral well-being, building stone by stone the great future of Germany. In Italy there was, at the same time, a perfect ebullition of music which streamed all over Europe. It flooded France, Austria, and England, showing that Italian genius in the seventeenth century was still supreme; and in the splendid exuberance of musical production a succession of thoughtful geniuses like Monteverdi at Mantua, Carissimi at Rome, and Provenzale at Naples gave evidence of the loftiness of soul and purity of heart which was preserved among the frivolities and dissoluteness of Italian courts.

Here is a still more striking example. It is scarcely likely that there has ever been seen a more terrible age than that of the end of the old world—the time of the decomposition of the Roman Empire and the great Invasions. The flame of art, however, con-

tinued to burn under that heap of smoking rubbish. A passion
for music served to reconcile the Gallic Romans with their barbarian conqueror, for the detestable Caesars of Rome's waning
empire and the Visigoths of Toulouse had an equal relish for concerts; and both the Roman houses and the half-savage camps re-
sounded with the noise of instruments. Clovis had musicians
brought from Constantinople. And the remarkable fact was not
that art was still loved but that the age created a new kind of art.
From this upheaval of humanity sprang an art as perfect and as
pure as that of the most finished products of happier times. According to Gevaert, the Gregorian chant made its first appearance
in the fourth century in the *Alleluia* song—"the cry of the victory
of Christianity after two and a half centuries of persecution." The
musical masterpieces of the early church seem to have been produced in the sixth century, between 540 and 600; that is to say,
between the invasions of the Goths and the invasions of the Lom-
bards, "at a time which we imagine was represented by an uninterrupted series of wars, massacres, pillages, plagues, famines,
and cataclysms of such a kind that St. Gregory saw in them evidence of the decreptitude of the world and premonitory signs of the
Last Judgment." In these chants, however, everything breathes
of peace and hope in the future. Out of barbarity sprang a gentle
art, in which we find pastoral simplicity, clear and sober outlines
like those of Greek bas-reliefs, free poetry filled with love of nature, and a touching sweetness of disposition—"a speaking witness
of the soul of those who lived amid such terrible disturbance." Nor
was this an art of cloisters and convents, shut away in confinement.
It was a popular art which prevailed through the whole of the
ancient Roman world. From Rome it went to England, Germany,
and to France; and no art was more representative of its time.
Under the reign of the Carolingians it had its golden age, for the
princes were enamored of it. Charlemagne and Louis the Pious
spent whole days in singing or listening to' chants and were absorbed by their charm. Charles the Bald, in spite of the troubles of
his empire, kept up a correspondence about music and composed
music in collaboration with the monks of the monastery of Saint-
Gall, the musical center of the world in the ninth century. Few occurrences have been more striking than this harvest of art, this

smiling efflorescence of music which was gathered, in spite of everything, amid the convulsions of society.

Thus music shows us the continuity of life in apparent death, the flowering of an eternal spirit amidst the ruin of the world. How then should one write the history of these times if one neglected some of their essential characteristics? How should one understand them if one ignored their true inner force? And who knows but that such an omission might falsify not only the aspect on one period of history but the whole of history itself? Who knows if the words "Renaissance" and "Decadence" do not arise, as in the preceding example, from our limited view of a single aspect of things? An art may decline, but does Art itself ever die? Does it not rather have its metamorphoses and its adaptations to environment? It is quite evident, at any rate, that in a ruined kingdom, wrecked by war or revolution, creative force could express itself in architecture only with difficulty; for architecture needs money and new structures, besides prosperity and confidence in the future. One might even say that the plastic arts in general have need of luxury and leisure, of refined society, and of a certain equilibrium in civilization, in order to develop themselves fully. But when material conditions are harder, when life is bitter, starved, and harassed with care, when the opportunity of outside development is withheld, then the spirit is forced back upon itself, and its eternal need of happiness drives it to other outlets; its expression of beauty is changed and takes a less external character, and it seeks refuge in more intimate arts, such as poetry and music. It never dies—that I believe with all my heart. There is no death or new birth of the spirit there, for its light has never been extinguished; it has died down only to blaze anew somewhere else. And so it goes from one art to another, as from one people to another. If you study only one art you will naturally be led to think that there are interruptions in its life, a cessation of its heartbeats. On the other hand, if you look at art as a whole, you will feel the stream of its eternal life.

That is why I believe that for the foundation of all general history we need a sort of comparative history of all forms of art; the omission of a single form risks the blurring of the whole picture.

History should have the living unity of the spirit of humanity for its object and should maintain the cohesion of all its thought.

### Study suggestions

1.    Study the author's attitude towards the place of the arts in the understanding of history and the interrelation of the arts.

2.    How can music "throw light on the ways and manners of society" in learning the inner life of a nation?

3.    How can the arts influence each other?

4.    Explain the author's belief in the need of a comparative history of all forms of art.

5.    Theme suggestions: Folksongs, Spirituals, Jazz, Music of the War Periods, Sea Chanties, Classical versus Popular Music. These broad topics call for research which will show the origins and the development.

# ART IN EVERYDAY LIFE

*Helen Gardner*

We are all potential artists—almost all of us. There are but few who seem entirely wanting in capacity for understanding or creating; many have considerable ability; a few become great artists. It is a matter of degree. Art and the way of art exist for most of us —not only exist but permeate all life, today as well as yesterday. Today life is most complex and its activities and contacts, however much they differ in number and breadth with the individual, are varied and pressing. With this immediate present we are concerned primarily.

A current opinion, far too common, holds that art is a luxury, a monopoly of wealth, a matter of museums, something to be indulged in only in one's leisure, and quite inessential to and divorced from one's daily activities. How far from the truth! It *is* true that to understand a great painting one must look at it long and contemplatively; that to understand a sonata one must hear it, undistractedly, many times. Few poems reveal all their beauty and meaning in one reading. Real understanding requires concentration of eye or ear, feelings, and intelligence. Granted, however, that great art is relatively rare and requires contemplation and leisure for its true appreciation, still art and a way of art permeate the world in which we live.

But what, you ask, has a *Skyscraper* or a *Navajo Blanket* or Leonardo's *The Last Supper* to do with my everyday life, my humdrum seven days a week? To be sure, our study of some of the arts has been restricted to the work of great masters, often of foreign lands, and far-away ages. But in them all, as we begin "to see what we know how to look for," we begin to discern certain qualities and characteristics so constantly recurrent that we conclude that they are the result of some fundamental, universal principles. What words have we used constantly in our discussion, whether it be of buildings or statues or paintings, of books or textiles or pottery? *Unity, variety, harmony, rhythm, balance, contrast, proportion, emphasis.* What words do we use in discussing music, the dance, literature? Are they not the same? Are there not, then, some guides to point out the way to art in everyday life?

Let us be specific. The way we look at things may or may not be an art. Consider the view framed by your own window—a yard, a street, a lake bordered by woods, a group of roofs. Can you apply to it the words we have just mentioned? Is it lacking in contrasting lines and masses, or colors? Would you shift the position of some objects, imaginatively, or by shifting your own position can you obtain a better balance? Everything in the view has a form. When we look at these forms as artists, we re-form them. Is this not what we have seen the artist doing in all his works that we have studied? We have found him nowhere imitating what he sees, but everywhere taking forms that he sees as his raw material and out of them creating new forms that are more beautiful, more real and significant than the original, sometimes the new form is close to the original; sometimes far removed. To see everything as form or a group of forms and with imaginative insight to re-form these forms into something which has harmony, unity with variety, balance, rhythm—this is to see the world as an artist. Thus everything we see, from the small objects about our rooms to skyscrapers and mountains, we see, if we are artists, as forms and unities of forms which give us a far greater sense of their reality and significance than any exact copy of their appearance can give. To see significant aspects of commonplace things is to transform what is mediocre, if not ugly, into something that is lovely and worth our while.

> She has a sensitivity that was very wide, eager and free. . . . It lighted on small things and showed that perhaps they were not small after all. It brought buried things to light and made one wonder what need there had been to bury them.

Do not the same principles hold in what we hear? In our music? As I sit writing on my porch someone on the road below is whistling a melody. He repeats it again and again. The monotony becomes irritating. Ah! He changes the key. This change brings in a pleasing variety. The whistler is the potential artist creating through the medium of tones a form for his melody. I listen for him to create a still more complex form, perhaps by the addition of another melody. In imagination I hear him interweave and contrast these two melodies (each a form) and unite them into a harmonious form which is the entire song. Just as the weaver of the *Navajo Blanket* selected two motifs, the step and the zigzag, which he varied and united into the harmonious form which is the work of art. Thus the whistler and I are two potential artists working together: one an artist in understanding because the ear can hear forms; the other an artist in creating because he can use forms. The eye too, to a limited extent, reinforces the ear in the comprehension of a musical form if one looks at the score. The pattern which a simple folk melody makes on the printed page contrasts in appearance as well as in sound with that of a theme which consists of a group of melodies in much the same way in which the simple boldness of the *Navajo Blanket* contrasts with the complex richness of the royal *Persian Carpet*.

To see and to hear as an artist is a necessary foundation stone for doing things in an art way—creative activity. For this too most of us have some capacity, if it is not left latent. Let us consider a few of our daily activities. Can we be creative artists in their pursuance? We might select four, almost at random: writing letters, furnishing our rooms, selecting our clothes, and using our leisure.

Can letter writing be an art? Are not some letters more pleasing than others? Why? Probably for at least two reasons. First, because the letter presents to the eye a pleasing form. The writing is legible and is thoughtfully spaced with ample margins; and page follows page in a logical, harmonious way. The effect of the form is an enhancement of the content. A pleasing form alone arouses in the recipient an emotional response. But how much greater the response if, in the second place, the content too has a pleasing form! To write a letter, in fact any kind of literature, one starts with an idea, which he expresses through the medium of words. Words are to the writer what stone is to the builder or sculptor, tone to the musician, pigment to the painter, or clay to the potter. By means of words he creates a form for the conveyance of his idea. The better the form, the more forceful the expression, provided the idea is worth expressing. He may elaborate the idea, add other ideas for emphasis or contrast, just as the musician contrasts his melodies (musical ideas) or Leonardo, the figure of Christ (an idea of agitation).

In any kind of literature as well as in the letter, the visual form of the printed words bears a direct relation to the form of the content, just as does the visual score to the audible form of the music. The grouping of words into paragraphs and the separation of paragraphs by space devices is a simple illustration of how the eye assists the mind to grasp a break in the thought. Many poems by Carl Sandburg will afford a more complex illustration in which the grouping of the printed words on the page creates as definite a pattern of light and dark as do the light and dark colors in the

Sienese *Madonna*. In both cases the purpose and result are the same: a form presented to the eye reinforces the idea presented to the mind. Thus we see that the fundamental principles of music and painting (we might carry the comparison further) are the fundamental principles of letter-writing also—in fact of any kind of writing, from the simple memorandum to a complete story or drama.

To turn to our second activity, do we find these principles at work in the furnishing of our rooms? Everyone lives in an abode. Does he enjoy it or dislike it? Does he have a feeling of "rightness" about it? Or is he indifferent to it? To which of the two types does your room belong? Is it overloaded with furnishings that are largely useless, and irritating in their demand of time for their care? Or is it reposeful and harmonious, a place in which one really likes to live?

Interior architecture is a complex art with many branches, involving the purpose of the room; its space design by the placement and proportion of walls, ceilings, and openings—the permanent elements; and the furnishings and people—the changeable elements. Its ultimate character is dependent upon not one but all of these elements; working in accord, if harmony results; at cross purposes, if discord results.

For many of us our room is already built. It may be furnished or partly so. If it is ugly to start with, is our objective hopeless? By no means. The room may well be small and disproportionately low; a door and windows break three sides and leave the fourth a long monotonous wall surface. Let us consult, imaginatively, our sense of balance. If the room is too small, a quiet, inconspicuous, lightly broken wall treatment of retreating color will add a feeling of spaciousness; while an advancing color and wallpaper of strongly contrasted light and dark would make the room appear even smaller. If it is too low, an emphasis upon verticality (as in the hangings and other furnishings) and a suppression of horizontality (as in the avoidance of horizontal moldings and borders) will increase the appearance of height. The *Parthenon* is long and low, but the insistent verticals of the fluted columns create a balance and a feeling of "rightness." *Chartres* is very vertical, hardly held in restraint by horizontals. Here too is "rightness." Both are "right." Behind the design lie the purpose and the people with their ideas and feelings. Balance for the Greek was different from balance for the Gothic. One must not be dogmatic. Each must determine for himself what constitutes balance in his own room. But balance there must be; without it everything collapses.

What then of the monotonous wall space? It may be needed to balance the broken walls of the other sides. If, on the other hand, the wall still remains monotonous and overbalances with its unbroken space, the furnishings (perhaps a picture or hanging) can be used to break the large area and establish a balance.

In the furnishings, the first question is that of function: what is there in the room that has no use in function or design? What can be eliminated without sacrificing efficient use and pleasing appearance? Having reduced the furnishings to the necessary minimum with a modicum for that which delights by indulging the personal tastes of the owner (for too much impersonality is as bad as none), one may then consider each piece, first as a form and then as related to the other forms and to the form of the room as a unit. A good chair, for instance, *looks* its use. The supporting parts are proportioned to the weight; the back and arms are related to the seat so as to insure comfort. The materials fittingly harmonize and contrast. The upholstery, in pattern, color, and texture, depends upon the material of the frame: massive wood, woven reed, light metal. The construction of a good chair is dependent upon the same guiding principles as the *University Chapel*. In both it is a matter of materials, the way in which they are used, and the purpose for which they are used, subject to the creative sensitivity of the artist who can proportion and balance, contrast and unify. In the *Chapel* the thick stone walls, the great windows, the relative open and solid stone areas of the tower, the relative proportions of all parts—every detail presents itself to our eyes as a contributing element to the unified and harmonious whole; and the visual impression of strength and aspiration dignifies every event which takes place in the building. It is true that the *Chapel* gains in majesty and power through its size. A fine chair, small in comparison, is as architectural in principle and may appeal to some as strongly as the *Chapel*.

To return to our room, though the chair may be fine of itself, does it belong in the room? Have you not seen a chair look ugly in one place and "just fit" in another? Study that chair, not in itself but in its relation to its surroundings, and you will probably find the explanation. Its form or some details of its form—its materials, their color or texture, its shape, size, or proportions—clash too dissonantly or harmonize too mildly with the table, for example, or with the room as a whole. Our objective, the harmony of the whole, is a stern master. Yet by it every piece of furnishing in a good room—furniture, hangings, wall decoration, rugs, pictures, ornaments, lighting fixtures—is measured. Each is a form of a definite material—wood, stucco, tile, metal, textiles, glass—subject to its own guiding principles of material, function, and design, and each is also a contributing element to the whole.

If we can make of our rooms works of art, can we not do the same with ourselves in our personal appearance? Just as we began with what was given us, in making a work of art out of our room, so in the matter of ourselves we begin with what nature has given us. It may or may not be beautiful. We reformed the ugly room into an attractive one by infusing into it, by means of the furnishings, qualities of balance, proportion, unity, and harmony in accordance with our own personal interpretations of those qualities. In the same way the physical self is re-formed by clothing into something attractive or unattractive in proportion as the garments are selected to secure these qualities. Have you watched people on the street with this observation in mind? How often does a tall gaunt person wear garments that accent verticality! And the stout person, those which emphasize horizontality! A pale type—pale complexion, light eyes and hair—often selects a pale uncontrasted color when it should have a color that in hue and intensity brings in the needed contrasting strength. Some types need brown; some, blue. Not the prevailing style but suitability to myself. My physical self and my personality (ideas to be expressed) are the basic forms to be reformed and hence set forth in their essential qualities, not obliterated. Each article of clothing is partly a form in itself and largely a contributing element to the whole. How attractive is a hat in a shop window! How ugly on me!

One more activity may be mentioned for discussion—the way in which we use our leisure. Here too can we see the way of art?

It depends upon whether we see life itself as an art—a balanced, unified, harmonious whole. If we do, then we know that variety is essential for this harmony.

After all, there is not only variety, but also unity. The diversity of the Many is balanced by the stability of the One. That is why life must always be a dance, for that is what dance is: perpetual slightly varied movements which are yet always held true to the shape of the whole.

The great wall of the *Egyptian Temple* is more unified when broken by carving and color. The rapid zigzag motif of the *Navajo Blanket* brings in so refreshing a contrast to the more austere step pattern that the unity of the entire design is greater. In Leonardo's *Last Supper* the reposeful room and the poiseful central figure would be uninteresting were they not set over against and united with the restless, moving masses of the disciples. Is there a work of art which does not illustrate this principle of variety in unity? If life, then, is a work of art, may we not see in leisure a vitalizing variety to the main business of life? May we not look upon leisure as a form and ask whether the character of the form is such that it exists partly for itself and partly for the intensification which its contrasts bring to the larger whole? The pattern of life may be like that of the *Navajo Blanket:* simple and forceful; or like that of the royal *Persian Carpet:* complex and rich. It is a difference not of value but of kind. One thing, however, is certain: neither the *Navajo Blanket,* nor the *Persian Carpet,* nor any kind of life is a work of art without wisely placed, balanced variety. As for life, the activities of our leisure time form one of the chief sources of this variety.

There is a tendency, in these days of specialization, to pigeon-hole our activities—work, play, religion, civics, art—and when engaged in one, to banish all others to their tight compartments. An illustration of the possibility of breaking down these partitions is the late Prof. A. A. Michelson, one of the world's great physicists, who when asked why he persisted in his attempt to measure the velocity of light even more precisely when the present measurement was an acknowledged absolute, said that it "amused" him. A profound scholar, relentless in his demands for accuracy, found "amusement" in his work. Fittingly he has been called the "scientist-artist."

If we conclude that it *is* possible to look at everything with the artist's vision and to pursue all activities in accordance with art principles, let us restate what is involved. Life is the raw material of the artist, as it is of everyone's living. The artist, in the first place, as he looks out upon the world, sees things, people, and incidents as forms and grasps their significance, both outward and inward, and the significant aspects of commonplace things, in proportion as he has within himself the capacity to perceive and feel such significance. In the second place, he creates an appropriate form in appropriate material for a convincing expression of this significance. In the third place, he is a craftsman grounded in the technique of his craft. Some of these activities he pursues consciously, some subconsciously. No one of them is *a priori,* nor are they to be isolated. Each acts on and is inextricably fused with the others. They do not account entirely for the artist. Other forces are at work—social, economic, religious, geographic. But these three are distinguishable and essential wherever we find great art. There is, it is true, a difference in degree between profound, imaginative, universal art and the art of our daily activities—but not in kind. We are all potential artists.

### Study suggestions

1. Explain fully the significance of the first and also of the concluding sentences.

2. How does the author's concept of art vary from that of the average person? How does art permeate the world?

3. Note her list of words common to all of the arts and her application of them.

4. How do her four illustrations from our daily activities prove her thesis? Analyze her details of proof.

5. Apply her "ingredients of universal principles" to the structure of this essay. Note, for instance, her transitions that give her discussion *unity.* What other elements are there in her organization?

6. Explain: "Life must always be a dance"; "Life is the raw material of the artist, as it is of everyone's living."

7. Louis Bromfield has said that Grandma Moses' paintings "show her feeling for the eternal importance of little things." Compare this with the author's sentence: "To see significant aspects of commonplace things is to transform what is mediocre, if not ugly, into something that is lovely and worth our while."

8. Theme suggestions:
   A Room I Love
   Purpose in Costumes (men and women)
   Comparison of Two Buildings
   The Art of Letter Writing
   Use of Leisure Time
   Planning a Garden

# ASPECTS OF BEAUTY

*Santha Rama Rau*

There is a very famous story in Japan about a man who was renowned throughout the country for the magnificent chrysanthemums he cultivated in his garden. Soon his fame reached even to the imperial palace, and the emperor announced that he wished to see these remarkable chrysanthemums. Greatly honored, the man went out into his garden before the emperor arrived and cut down all except one of his treasured flowers, leaving only the most beautiful of all to delight the eyes of the emperor. It was the highest compliment he could offer.

To foreigners this story needs, perhaps, a little explanation. But to the Japanese the point is immediately clear—the appreciation of something beautiful is so important a human activity that there is nothing surprising (only admirable) in the action of a man who can destroy hundreds of wonderful plants so that the emperor may enjoy the one flawless flower undistracted by lesser blooms, so that he can offer perfection the concentration it deserves. A friend of mine once explained the matter to me fairly succinctly. "Almost anyone," he said, "has at least some appreciation of art, but the Japanese have gone a little further. They have made an art of appreciation. Other people don't always realize that this is a genuinely creative function."

In more vigorously externalized societies one is apt to feel that one must express oneself, be "creative," be active and contributing in some way. There is a subtle but constant pressure on one to meet the demands of an aggressive society in outward expressions even if the medium is only conversation. Many people mean by this that you must have something to *show* for your effort—to be creative you must write or paint or even be a good cook. You must express yourself in conversation, in music or perhaps in dancing. The aspect of living that is so often forgotten—or at best relegated to an inferior position—is the sense of appreciation. What of the people who read the books, see the pictures, hear the music or even eat the cooking? What about their "creative" offering, their sensitive and developed art of appreciation? It is just as hard to come by, and to the Japanese, at least, just about as valuable.

Whether this sense of appreciation is a cause or an effect in Japanese society I suppose only anthropologists can decide, but certainly to the traveler or the foreigner in Japan it lends a surprising and new perspective to a life that has often been interpreted as too rigidly mannered for spontaneity. It adds, besides, a richness and an unsuspected depth to a society in which women (on the surface at least) appear to lead dull and restricted lives.

An American friend of mine, a girl who had lived in Japan for the two years that her husband was stationed there, told me the story of one of her most unexpectedly pleasant experiences in Tokyo. In Japan, with servants to do her housework, an amah to help with the children, she suddenly and disconcertingly found herself with a good deal of time on her hands. She had rather despairingly decided that she was "uncreative" and had no particular inclination to take up amateur painting or attend classes in flower arrangement. At a fairly pedestrian party one day she expressed something of the sort to a Japanese woman there, the wife of one of her husband's business associates.

"I see," the Japanese woman replied seriously, "but what do you *like* to do?"

"Well, in America," my friend said, feeling rather frivolous, "I keep house for my husband, and the children take up a lot of time, and I like pretty clothes and good perfumes——"

"Perfumes?" the Japanese woman interrupted with interest. "Perfumes are very difficult to appreciate."

And eventually my American friend found herself attending the meetings of an "incense-smelling society," where a number of Japanese women spent the afternoon enjoying the fragrances of scented wood smoke—cedar, lime, verbena, camphor, pine, plum and many more—learning their special characteristics, appreciating the subtle changes of quality in a piece of wood a hundred years old as contrasted with a new fragment cut the day before. It was an activity that the members of the society considered important enough to employ an expert to instruct them, and my American friend discovered not only a new and fascinating pastime but began to understand a whole new approach to the pleasure and appreciation of daily living, to the smells, sounds, textures or sights that previously had not seemed worth her notice. It all contributed to a fresh and sharper awareness of the world about her.

The Japanese live in heavily overpopulated islands, and possibly it is the years of crowded life that have developed in them a keener sense of privacy; an interior and allusive quality in their arts; a particular feeling for the detail, the small but important experience; the value of the quiet, personal satisfaction rather than the exuberantly outward approach to life. Besides this, Japan is a poor country, and possibly out of this fact has grown the deeply individual enjoyment of the universally available pleasure, the aspects of life that are in most parts of the world taken for granted.

In the springtime, for instance, the nationally accepted pleasure is "cherry blossom-viewing." Groups of people or romantically inclined couples or individuals make a point of going out to the country by bus, by train or even on foot to catch the special moment of splendor in the spring when the trees flower. This may be a shared amusement, a private pleasure or a background for an emotional moment. Some people are so moved that they write a poem about the moment; others, equally appreciative, savor an inarticulate refreshment of the mind.

Equally, in autumn, the same intensity is directed to the viewing of the incredible scarlets and golds of the maples and beeches on the slopes of Mount Arashi outside Kyoto, or the flaming hillsides of Nikko. You might, in Japan, be invited to a moon-viewing party—this is a time for elegance, graciousness and repose. You watch the moon rise and you watch it in silence. Apart from the initial formalities of greeting and hospitality, no conversation is expected of you. It is assumed that your mind is fully occupied by watching the changing light the moon throws on gardens, countryside or rooftops. People recognize that your entire attention is needed to absorb the shifting shadows, the play of clouds across the moon, the growing luminosity of the night sky. Some houses, in fact, have a special "moon-viewing window," a treasured architectural feature, silently expressing the value of the experience of profound appreciation of beauty.

The first snow has elicited countless poems and paintings in Japan and remains a celebrated occasion calling for the exercise of talents that, in the West, are too often considered passive rather than active. A woman I once met in Kyoto, old-fashioned, beautifully mannered, conventionally retiring, made me realize the importance of this annual experience in her life. She had a small pavilion in her garden built to offer her the best view of the snow. With her it was a special ritual. She would sit, in silence, with her friends in her snow-viewing pavilion. Normally she never drank anything even mildly alcoholic, but on this occasion she would sip a tiny cup of the special sake that the Japanese brew exclusively for snow-viewing (it is beaten up with a raw egg and is supposed to enhance your appreciation of the changed look of the land under snow) "After this," she said, "it is possible to continue with the memory in your head for the rest of the year."

These refinements of appreciation extend far beyond the accidental beauties of nature into the smallest details of one's daily life in Japan. You find yourself exercising a talent—rusty and often ignored in other societies—to find an unexpected satisfaction and charm in the trivial or familiar details of day-to-day life. If, for instance, you are invited to dinner in Japan, you will see at the bottom of your bowl of consommé a slice of vegetable—say carrot—cut into some beautiful or fantastic shape. A hostess is as much complimented by the guests who say, "How beautiful!" and don't taste the soup as by those who say, "How delicious!" and eat it all. If you are offered a cup of orchid tea, you are expected to get as much enjoyment from watching the delicate, changing patterns of the tiny dried orchid floating in your cup as from the faint, slightly salty fragrance of the tea itself.

If you stop at the stall of a *sushi*-vender on any city street to buy a couple of the snacks that they sell—small, delicious, vinegary rice cakes with different kinds of savories embedded in them —you will judge his expertness as much by the grace and design of the bamboo leaf that he clips into a feathery decoration for your plate as by the taste of the *sushi* itself. If you make the most plodding purchase in a shop—a package of pins and buttons, say— you will watch enthralled while the shop attendant exerts an astonishing skill in wrapping and tying the package in a manner that makes it almost a work of art. In some cases—as, for example, when you write a formal letter—you can be judged as much for the elegance with which you fold the paper as by the contents of the letter itself; your calligraphy will be as much appreciated as the actual message. All trifles, but to the Japanese all potentially moments of beauty.

At certain seasons of the year your neighbors will probably invite you in for an "airing of household treasures." On such occasions whatever the family owns that it considers particularly beautiful will be displayed for a while to neighbors and guests. You will drink tea and admire (with or without conversation according to your wish) perhaps some ancient Noh masks that have come into the possession of the family, or a couple of unusually lovely kimonos, possibly some picture scrolls or pieces of brocade. Afterward it will all be packed away for the rest of the year—the interior of a Japanese house is so spare and carefully measured in its elegance that there is no place for a permanent display. A fine table, a picture, a vase of flowers, a couple of bright silk cushions

—this is the extent of decoration that is possible in a Japanese room, and the point is still the same: you can't appreciate something unless you are prepared to exercise your faculties, to allow your eye or your mind or your ear an undistracted concentration.

Probably the best known of Japanese occasions (though in many ways the most confusing to foreigners) is the tea ceremony, for this ritual of drinking a bowl of rather bitter green tea and the eating of a dry, not very appetizing wafer has implications far beyond its apparent aspects of a tea party. The tea-making utensils are special. The methods of preparing the tea are carefully prescribed. Each movement must be graceful, controlled, economical, perfect. You lavish as much attention on the beauty of the bowl in which the tea is served as on the taste of the tea itself. You consider with care the harmony of your surroundings, the water bubbling on the charcoal brazier, the texture of pottery, silk, wood. You can make of the occasion anything from a deep, contemplative spiritual experience to a merely formal, peaceful moment in a crowded day. It all represents a peculiarly Japanese infusion of meaning and importance into something as banal as the drinking of a cup of tea.

All this is not simply the expression of an overfussy formalism but something much more satisfactory. It is the recognition of the value of genuine appreciation, a feeling for the interior effects of a kind of constant awareness, a sensitivity to even the most insignificant aspects of the most ordinary activity or occurrence—the look of soapsuds in a wash tub or the sudden yellow of the first spring willow shoots, the arrangement of food on a plate or the brief snatch of music you hear from an upstairs window when you pass by on a quiet street. This approach is so well accepted in Japan that even in the most highly developed of Japanese arts a degree of participation is expected from the spectator, a degree that assumes a willingness and an ability to share in the completion of the artistic experience. To put it with quite un-Japanese bluntness, it takes two to make, say, a Japanese poem or a Japanese dance.

In the famous and much-loved Haiku poems of Japan—those brief, suggestive and yet carefully composed verses—the poet offers you, in a way, the raw material of an experience. Your own faculties for appreciation, sharing, enlarging are assumed to be up to the challenge of completing the experience in your mind, of embellishing or imbuing it with special meaning. For instance, the great poet Bashō wrote:

> A sick wild duck
> Falling in the evening cold—
> These traveler's lodgings!

And from this the reader is supposed to elaborate not only the picture of the wild duck, stricken while it is in flight, fluttering down to come to rest at the first haven that it finds, but simultaneously he makes the identification of the duck with the traveler arriving somewhere in the cold evening, compelled to take shelter in whatever lodgings he can find. And from there one can continue with his own associations of the winter countryside and the sadness of traveling away from home.

In Japanese dances, too, the best of the exponents will give you only the most fragmentary of gestures, a few fleeting indications of the mood or meaning of the dance. The rest is up to you— the interpretation, the completion of the idea, the individual reference. The slight raising of the dancer's kimono sleeve may indicate sadness and tears—it will be the lightest of movements to suggest, perhaps, all the sorrow in the world. A quick glance over a fan may condense in a second all the seductive flirtatiousness of a seasoned courtesan or may indicate only a moment of farewell. In any case, you are given some hints, a sense of mood, the capturing of an elusive beauty, and with these materials you translate the dance into your own singular experience. The place of the observer (or of the reader of poetry) is, in these ways, considerably enlarged. You are not a passive spectator but an active participant, for the element of appreciation is the highly developed essential that will complete the art in its fullest sense.

Apply the same principle in your life, the Japanese believe, and it becomes not a passive progression from day to day but an active, stimulating and "creative" way of living.

## Study suggestions

1.    Contrast the incident in the opening paragraphs with what would probably be the case in America.

2.    Note the turn of phrase from "appreciation of art" to an "art of appreciation"—and her explanation.

3.    Through what illustrations and details does the author make us realize the appreciation of the Japanese for the small details of daily living?

4.    How does she reveal their "constant awareness" or "sensitivity to the most trivial or ordinary activity?" What does she mean by a creative way of living?

5.    Contrast their enjoyment of beauty with that of the average American.

6.    Theme suggestions: Write descriptions of a page or two on one or more of the following:

Dawn at the Lake
Snow-covered Trees
From the Airplane
The Birds in My Feeding Station
Drifting in a Canoe
Above the Clouds

# ABOUT PEOPLE

*The history of the world is but the biography of great men.*

THOMAS CARLYLE

# BIOGRAPHY, TRUE AND FALSE

*Iris Origo*

I do not remember who it was who once remarked that every great man has his disciples, but it is always Judas who is the biographer.

Whether or not this is entirely true, there are certainly more ways than one in which a biographer can betray his subject—and not all of them spring from bad intentions. "Whatever you do, do not prettify me!" said Walt Whitman to his friend Horace Traubel, the author of *With Walt Whitman in Camden.* "Include all the hells and damns." But other great men have considered that any biography can hardly fail to be a betrayal, for the very sound reason that no one really knows anything about anyone else. "The world will never know my life," said Carlyle, "if it should write and read a hundred biographies of me. The main facts of it are known, and are likely to be known, to myself alone, of all created men." And these words stand on the first page of the long life written by his closest friend, James Froude.

We would all agree as to which is the most satisfactory biography—most satisfactory owing to the unmistakable, unrelenting veracity of the biographer. Boswell has told us very clearly what he was aiming at: he thought that a life should be "like a flawless print struck off from the engraved plate which is bitten into our memory." Biography, in his view, should not be a selection or a monument or a thesis, but the *duplication* of an image in the mind. Unfortunately, as Geoffrey Scott remarked in his penetrating preface to Boswell's *Notes and Journals,* "This is an aim beyond human reach." But Scott also shrewdly added: "The knowledge that his arrow pointed to that impossible mark, was Boswell's source of confidence. Other biographies might forestall his book; that they could rival it, he never, in his most sombre moments, conceived. Those others did not even know that biography is impossible."

Impossible or not, the biography written by a man's daily companion belongs to a genre that has a perennial charm: it gratifies our wish to believe. When a biographer records—with a sharp ear and a selective eye—what a great man actually said to him, he awakens a degree of conviction that no other form of narrative or analysis can achieve. "I wonder why we hate the past so," says Howells ruminatively to Mark Twain, and when Mark Twain replies, "It's so damned humiliating!" we know, without a doubt, that that is precisely what the great man did say. To open such a book is like entering a room—a room, I think, in an old-fashioned English country house—greeted by a mixture of wood smoke, old books, wet dogs, and fresh roses. One enters, and one is at home.

This is, perhaps, why Dr. Johnson himself asserted: "Nobody can write the life of a man, but those who have eaten and drunk and lived in social intercourse with him." Failing personal acquaintance, he maintained that a biographer must at least be able to talk with his subject's friends, though he also admitted that their reports were often highly unsatisfactory. In his own youth, he related, he determined to write a life of Dryden, and applied to two men who knew him, Sweeney and Cibber. "Sweeney's information," he said, "was no more than this, that at Will's coffeehouse Dryden had a particular chair for himself, which was set by the fire in winter and was called his winter chair; and that it was carried out for him to the balcony in summer, and was then called his summer chair."

What, then, is the wretched biographer who is not a contemporary to do, the writer who has no plate bitten into his memory, who must juggle, two or three centuries later, bare facts and documents, and who has, at best, an occasional portrait to look at? The further back we go, the more evident our presumption becomes. From the seventeenth century onwards we have at least some private papers to help us: someone writes a love letter, someone scolds an erring daughter, someone else sets down in a diary his fear of death; but earlier, what is there? A mass of public documents, but a terrible dearth of private ones. How can we dare, from such fragmentary and formal knowledge, to reconstruct a man?

Two methods are open to the biographer: he can try, in the

manner of the three-volume Victorian biography and of the exhaustive modern biographies which are again becoming popular, to set down everything he can find out; or he can attempt the selective portrait, the "work of art." The first method, unavoidably, must be that of the official biographer, who writes at the request of the family or of the state, or sometimes, nowadays, is financed by some great foundation. He works with one great advantage—a vast supply of material—and sometimes with a corresponding disadvantage, that part of it must be suppressed. For him the only solution seems to be the one recommended by William Allen White to a young historian: "Kill the widow!" Sometimes, too, it is the subject himself who has taken a great deal of trouble to cover his own tracks. In an essay on George Sand, Henry James suggested that the artist who fears to become the subject of a biography should take an unlimited degree of trouble to destroy all his private papers, leaving only his considered creation behind him. "Then," he wrote, "the cunning inquiry will exceed in subtlety and ferocity anything we today conceive, and the pale forewarned victim, with every track covered, every paper burnt and every letter unanswered, will, in the tower of art, stand, without a sally, the siege of years."

Most biographers of our own time, however, and certainly those dealing with public men, are more likely to complain of too much material than too little. Even Boswell, according to his own diary, was so overwhelmed by the amount of his material when he started to put it together that he would sit in London coffeehouses with tears pouring down his cheeks; Virginia Woolf was hardly less dismayed by the number of Roger Fry's papers. But what must Franklin Roosevelt's biographer have felt, surveying the forty tons of documents at his disposal?

We live in a historically minded age, and I understand that an American statesman of our time was even in the habit of having his telephone conversations recorded in large diaries. This is, surely, a formidable prospect. Moreover, in addition to the written word, it is now possible to see again our subject's face and gestures in a hundred newsreels, to hear again the very accents of his voice in recorded broadcasts. With such a plethora of material, every biography must to some extent become a selective one.

But here problems of a different nature at once arise, problems of choice: is it possible to choose without revealing a bias, to reject and not to falsify? Every biographer is familiar with the seductive tricks of the trade: the slight juggling with dates, the suppression of inconvenient letters or of remarks that are out of character or merely flat, the placing of a telling conversation or document where it is most effective, the smoothing out and the touching up. In the end a portrait is built up: slick, vivid, convincing, and false.

There are also, of course, the mistakes of sheer ignorance. I am thinking at the moment of one of my own, which was kindly pointed out to me in a letter from Rebecca West. I had mentioned, as an example of Mrs. Carlyle's touchiness, the disastrous Christmas party at the Grange, at which Lady Ashburton presented her, from the Christmas tree, with a silk dress, after which Jane retired to her bedroom in tears. I thought she was making a good deal of unnecessary fuss, or rather that she was using this pretext to express a deeper resentment against her hostess. Rebecca West, however, pointed out my mistake. Her great-aunt Isabella Campbell, who belonged to the Carlyle period, had often spoken of the episode and thought it "a most extraordinary thing for Lady Ashburton to have done, as a silk dress was the recognized present for a housekeeper, and a friend of the family would have felt bewildered at receiving it. To wear a dress which one had not ordered from the start and had fitted according to one's own measures was a sign of social inferiority." Plainly, therefore, on this occasion Jane was right to be offended, and I did not know what I was talking about. I still think, however, that Mrs. Carlyle was glad of so good an excuse to express her irritation with the woman whom her husband described as having "the soul of a princess and a captainess" and whom he considered, which was worse, as witty as herself.

One way of guarding against making too many such mistakes is to write only about those times and places with which one is familiar. Another safeguard is to become acquainted with the whole surrounding scene. I remember, for instance, once reading a translation of Leopardi's "Sabato del Villaggio" in which the *fascio dell' erba,* the bundle of grass, which the girl in the poem is carrying is translated as "a truss of hay." The image brought to mind is one of green hayfields and wagons and pitchforks and buxom country girls—an Austrian scene, or an English. But there are no hayfields near Recanati. There are only steep, dun-colored hills on which olive trees grow, with wheat beneath them and perhaps a few vines, and by the edge of the road there are sometimes tufts of grass, of which town dwellers cut an armful to feed their rabbits. This was the bundle of grass brought home by Leopardi's *donzelletta*. A single misleading sentence—written not because the translator did not know Italian but because he did not know Leopardi's birthplace—conjured up a whole nonexistent world.

Three insidious temptations assail the biographer: to suppress, to invent, and to sit in judgment, and of these the earliest and most frequent is suppression. In the Middle Ages, indeed, it was rendered inevitable by the purpose which biography was intended to fulfill: to produce a noble example. The medieval view of history was that of a drama enacted within an established pattern—God's pattern for mankind. The lives of the men who came nearest to conforming with this pattern were related as an example to other, lesser men, and consequently a disproportionate number of medieval biographies are concerned with the lives of saints, while others are about rulers or leaders rather larger than life size.

The first English author who admitted that a biography might also aim at what he calls "lawful delight" was Thomas Fuller, who in the introduction to his *History of the Worthies of England* (in 1662) places this as the fourth and last of his purposes in writing: "First, to gain some glory to God. Secondly, to preserve the manoeuvres of the Devil. Thirdly, to present examples to the Living." And only fourthly, "to Entertain the reader with Delight."

In this respect, the attitude of classical biography was much nearer to our own. It was by the example of Plutarch that writers justified themselves when taste began to turn, in the seventeenth century, from what Dr. Johnson later called "honeysuckle lives" to a more varied, livelier curiosity. Dryden, for instance, admired Plutarch precisely because he had dared to show his heroes in undress. "You may behold," he said, "Scipio and Laelius gathering cockle shells on the shore, Augustus playing at bounding-stones, and Agesilaus riding on a hobbyhorse, among his children. The pageantry of life is taken away: you see the poor reasonable animal as naked as ever nature made him; are acquainted with his follies, and find the demi-god, a man."

Here, surely, is the prelude to modern biography; but with the admission that heroes, too, should be shown as naked and fallible, the problem arose as to whether this true picture was likely to dismay or to corrupt the reader. And if this danger existed, had the biographer the right to speak the truth?

The problem was set by Boswell to Dr. Johnson. Was it right to relate that Addison, having lent a hundred pounds to Steele, recovered his loan by sending an officer to remove his friend's furniture? Dr. Johnson charitably speculated that perhaps Addison had done this with the intention of reforming Steele, but he also declared that, whether this kind of interpretation was true or not, the facts should be told. "Of such speculations," he said, "there is no end; we cannot see into the hearts of men, but their actions are open to observation." And he added that another reason for telling the whole truth was that "if nothing but the bright side of characters should be shown, we should sit in despondency and think it utterly impossible to imitate them in *anything.*" He believed, in short, that the whole truth should be told, for a highly characteristic reason: "It keeps mankind from despair."

In the nineteenth century, however, the suppression of unedifying or inconvenient facts came into favor again, partly owing to Victorian reticence and prudery, and partly to the same taste which created the Albert Memorial. "Too long and too idolatrous!" was the comment of Leslie Stephen on one of the great three-volume Victorian lives, and "How delicate," exclaimed Carlyle, "how decent is English biography, bless its mealy mouth!"

There is, however, a still more serious temptation for the biographer than suppression, and that is sheer invention. A good instance is the one quoted by Professor Trevor-Roper in a somewhat merciless attack on Lytton Strachey: the length of Dr. Arnold's legs. Strachey had formed a very clear image of Dr. Arnold in his mind; he saw him as a noble, pompous figure, and—to introduce just the right additional touch of absurdity, of debunking—it was necessary that his legs should have been too short. Unfortunately, however, as Strachey himself once admitted to a friend, there is absolutely no evidence to show that Dr. Arnold's legs were shorter than any other man's.

Now the danger of this kind of invention is that, once discovered, it shakes our capacity to believe anything that its inventor has said. "Suppose we believe one half of what he tells," suggested Lord Mansfield to Boswell, about an acquaintance whose stories, he said, "we unhappily found to be very fabulous." "Yes," Dr. Johnson replied, "but we don't know *which* half to believe. By his lying we lose not only our reverence for him, but all comfort in his conversation."

In Strachey's own opinion, a biographer's equipment consists in three points: "a capacity for absorbing facts, a capacity for stating them, and a point of view." The definition is a good one, for without a point of view no history can be written, but there is also a danger that it may not only shape but distort the facts. The biographer who puts his wits above his subject will end by writing about one person only—himself. My personal complaint about *Eminent Victorians* would be not that it is inaccurate, but that it is *thin,* and that its thinness springs from condescension. If you wish to see a person, you must not start by seeing through him. Another instance of this occurs in the first sentence of a very fine biography, Harold Nicholson's *Tennyson.* "We smile today at our Victorians," it begins, "not confidently, as of old, but with a shade of hesitation: a note of perplexity, a note of anger, sometimes a note of wistfulness, has come to mingle with our laughter."

The fatal words are, of course, the first ones, "We smile today." The biographer has started by putting up a barrier—and even if, in the next few words, he suggests that it is beginning to crumble, he is still writing from the other side. He has, in short, succumbed to yet another of the biographer's temptations: the desire to sit in judgment. "To penetrate," wrote the French historian Marc Bloch, "into the unknown being of a man separated from us by a long stretch of generations, one must almost cast off one's own self. To pull him to pieces, one need only remain oneself. The effort is undeniably less strenuous."

Every work of art, of course, implies a previous process of assessment, and it is the writer's implicit view of life that gives style and flavor to his work. Even though the assessment and criticism of manners and morals which were once assumed by the biographer and the novelist have now largely been handed over to the psychologist, the judgment of character still remains the central problem of biography. But insofar as a biographer is also a historian, he should, I think, be very careful not to drown his subject's voice with his own. One peculiar function of biography is to show history as it was to the participant, to observe for a moment *das Gewordene als Werdendes,* what has come to pass, while it is still occurring. Through the man whose life we are describing, we can see history in the course of being lived. In one sense, all organized histories are unsatisfactory, because they are written with the wisdom of the future. But in individual lives we can seize, if nothing else, a vivid sense of actuality; it is a pity to blur it.

Besides, our own judgments are surely not immune from change. We shall not, at the age of fifty, judge a man in the same way as we did at twenty-five. Ten days before his death, Dr. Johnson asserted that he was "ready now to call a man a *good* man, on much easier terms than formerly." With the passing of the years, the muscles of moral indignation sometimes begin to sag and the voice becomes less sharp, and this is true even in the field of abstract thought. I remember asking George Santayana, in his old age—when he was preparing an abridged edition of the great work of his youth, *The Life of Reason*—whether there were many things that he would now like to change. "No," he gently replied, "I feel I have much the same things to say—but I wish to say them in a different tone of voice."

Recently the psychologists have invented some ingenious devices which, they claim, will provide short cuts to assessing a man's character and state of mind. A German called Busemann advises us to count, in a man's letters and journals, the relative number of adjectives and of active verbs, thus obtaining what he calls his A/Q or Action Quotient. A prevalence of adjectives, he says, indicates a state of emotional tension. The process has even been applied to William James's letters, showing that between the ages of forty and fifty his letters to women were more emotional, and after sixty, those to men. Two American psychologists have invented a more complicated device. By counting, in interviews

with people suffering from emotional problems, the words expressing some form of discomfort, which they call D, and those expressing relief, which they call R, they obtain what they call a
DR Quotient, which, when set down on a graph, accurately reflects
their clients' states of mind at the time. They therefore suggest that
the same method should be applied by biographers. We might
ask ourselves, for instance, what Churchill's Discomfort Relief
Quotient was when he offered the British nation blood, sweat, and
tears.

I am myself not very good at counting, but even if I were, I do
not think that either A/Q or DR/Q is going to take us much further in the complicated task of assessing human personality. They
will hardly take the place of those unscientific, uncertain old instruments: intelligence and intuition. Yet how often even these
fail us! We can hang mirrors, as Virginia Woolf advised, at every
corner; we can look at our subject's face at every angle and in
every light. We can discover strange and curious pieces of information: that Aristotle had a hot-water bottle made of leather,
filled with hot oil, and that Leopardi, in the winter in Bologna,
spent his days in a bag lined with feathers, from which he emerged
looking like Papageno. But never, never do we see enough. Beneath the conscious personality, the purposing man, there is in
each of us an underworld of discarded characters who have still
some life in them. These, too, the biographer must seek. "In every
fat man," said Cyril Connolly, "there is a thin man, trying to get
out."

To Virginia Woolf the central problem of biography was how to
mold "into one seamless whole" the "granite-like solidity" of truth
and "the rainbow-like intangibility" of personality. It is, surely,
impossible—but few writers have come closer to it than she did.
The problem was one that fascinated her, not only in literature but
in life. "Go on, this is enthralling," she would say, when her friends
brought her an exciting piece of gossip. "I feel as if a buried statue
were being dug up, piece by piece."

One of her friends once told me that on a cold November evening, as he was making his way to her house, he came upon Virginia Woolf standing in the fog beside an apple barrow and asking
the old apple woman, in her deep, throaty, compelling voice: "Tell

me, what does it *feel* like to stand here in the fog on a dark evening, selling apples?" I cannot vouch for the truth of this story, but certainly the question was one she often asked. "What does it feel like," she would say to me, "to wake up in the morning on a Tuscan farm?" And once I heard her say, perhaps not wholly without malice, to a disconcerted young peer: "Tell me, what does it feel like to be a lord?"

Yet when, in later years, she came to write a life of Roger Fry, who had been one of her closest friends, the book was curiously less vivid, more conventional, than the etchings in her essays. She found, indeed, the sheer effort of putting together the material for a full biography almost unbearably tedious. "Donkey work," she recorded in *A Writer's Diary,* "sober drudgery, appalling grind." And when at last the book was finished, there was a most revealing final note: "What a curious relation is mine with Roger at this moment—I who have given him a kind of shape after his death. Was he like that? I feel very much in his presence at the moment, as if I were intimately connected with him: as if we together had given birth to this vision of him; a child born of us. Yet he had no power to alter it. And yet for some years it will represent him."

Is biography, then, worth attempting at all? Where there are so many snares, would we do better to be silent? I think not. Many critics would deny to any biographical portrait the essential reality, the truth that is truer than truth, of the novelist's or dramatist's creations, but I do not think that this need be so. The biographer has, of course, a fixed pattern; he is, as Desmond MacCarthy once said, "an artist upon oath." But the calls upon his imagination and intuition are hardly less exacting than the novelist's. The novelist and dramatist, after all, do not create their characters in a void, but out of experience informed and illuminated by the imagination. And this is the only stuff that all art is made of.

Shakespeare himself invented hardly any of his plots, but, having accepted a ready-made pattern for the actions of his characters, was then free to give his whole attention to bringing them to life. And so surely, too, the biographer's true function—the transmission of personality—may also be, within its own pattern, an act of creation, giving shape, in Virginia Woolf's phrase, to a man after his death and endowing him with what is, when we come to think of it, a very odd form of immortality. For of many great men of the past we know only what their biographers or portrait painters saw. Just as we know no other face for Pope Julius II than Raphael's, no other Federico da Montefeltro than Piero della Francesca's, so Strachey's *Queen Victoria* will probably become for many the only Queen Victoria, and it is Boswell's *Johnson* whom most people call Dr. Johnson. All that the biographer did not see or could not fit conveniently into his picture has faded into mist.

What, however, it is possible to wonder is whether in the near future there will be any demand for biography at all. Reading is a private pleasure, and not only is privacy disappearing from a world of ready-made designs for living, in which men are looking not so much for individuality as for protective coloring, but people's curiosity about other people's lives can now be satisfied in more dramatic ways than any book can offer. The radio and television now enable every man to interpret for himself, without the filter of another man's mind, the character and actions of his contemporaries.

I do not really believe this. The story of public exploits may become, to some extent, the field of the radio and of television, but the slow development of character, the processes of thought of the writer and the artist, and above all the relation of human beings to each other—these are things that cannot be simplified and that will always have to be set down, however imperfectly, in words.

"The true history of the human race," wrote E. M. Forster in a recent article, "is the story of human affections. In comparison with it all other histories—even economic history—are false." He goes on to say that owing to its reticent nature it can never be written down completely, and this of course is true, yet what little we do know of this aspect of history has come to us through biography or autobiography. And as long as human beings go on feeling affection for each other, this material will be renewed—material as complicated and yet simple, intense and yet intermittent, various and yet unchanging, as the human heart. In this sense biography is, or should be, a *completion* of life, giving a shape and a significance to the humblest, most pedestrian existence, seeing in the routine and triviality of common experience the universal pattern which gives it harmony and meaning. Every individual life is also the story of Everyman, and while it is the biographer's business to describe the passions, foibles, and idiosyncrasies which make his subject a person, his work will be very thin if these individual traits are not also seen as part of a universal drama. "A man's life of any worth," said Keats, "is a continual allegory, and very few eyes can see the Mystery."

There is an image in Pasternak's great novel, *Doctor Zhivago,* which has moved me very much—of a candle, which has melted a little patch in the icy crust on a windowpane, through which the candle's light is seen by Yura from the dark street below. "Its light seemed to fall into the street as deliberately as a glance, as if the flame were keeping a watch on the passing carriages, and waiting for someone." Perhaps that is the most that a biographer can ever hope to do: to clear, in the icy crust of each man's incomprehension of other men, a little patch, through which a faint, intermittent light can shine. But at the best, it will always be a very little patch of light, in a great sea of darkness—and it is wiser not to be too solemn about what we are doing, since the life that we are describing, like our own, is brittle and shadowy, and it is surely very arrogant to try to give it a set form. All that needs to be said about this was said by Sir William Temple in his essay on poetry, in a single, perfect sentence: "Human life is, at the greatest and the best, but like a froward child, that must be played with and humored a little to keep it quiet till it falls asleep—and then the care is over."

I do not think of truth as being made of granite, but rather as resembling a note in music, a note which we instantly recognize as the right one as soon as it is struck. Proust, the great master of the art of memory, describes in a famous passage in *Swann's Way* how in later life he was sometimes able to hear again certain sounds which, he wrote, "in reality had never stopped": the sobs which had shaken him at a crucial moment of his childhood. "It is only because life is now growing silent about me," he said, "that I hear them afresh, like convent bells which one might believe were not rung nowadays, because during the day they are drowned by the city hubbub, but which may be heard clearly enough in the stillness of the evening."

The biographer with a similar awareness of the continuity of emotion may realize at certain moments, "when life is silent about him," that he has suddenly become aware of something about his subject for which he could not give chapter and verse but which he now knows to be true. For all genuine emotion leaves behind it an eternal reverberation. Whether it is always possible for the biographer to hear and to reproduce it is another matter, unless indeed he has at his disposal such material as Keats's *Letters*— and even then, even then . . . But certainly even the faintest echo can only be heard by temporarily casting aside one's own self and one's own opinions. For this reason I would say to the young biographer who has upon his desk his first, intriguing file of papers to examine them, if he can, with an almost blank mind: to let them produce their own effect. Later on, the time will come to compare, to sift, and to draw conclusions; but first he should listen without interrupting. Sometimes then, as he deciphers the faded ink, a phrase will stand out which reveals the hand that wrote it. He may see—as suddenly as, at the turn of a passage, one comes upon one's own image in a mirror—a living face. It is then, in this fleeting moment, that he may perhaps have a faint apprehension—as near to the truth as we are ever likely to get—of what another man was like.

## Study suggestions

1. How does the author relate his allusion to Judas with the problems a biographer faces? Identify other allusions in this article.

2. Explain Boswell's contention that biography is but "the duplication of an image in the mind." Why does his biography of Dr. Johnson stand unique and convincing? Read his biography, or sample it, for his method.

3. Do you agree with Dr. Johnson that one must know his subject personally? Discover how Sandburg made the Lincoln conversation in his biography seem true to time and place. What are the many sources that a biographer writing of the past would tap? In selecting details why is it necessary to learn about the times?

4.    Analyze the two methods the biographer has, according to the author, and also three temptations he faces. Which does the author deem most serious?

5.    "We cannot see into the hearts of men, but their actions are open to observation." Discuss this as a medium for judgment.

6.    What is the author's criticism of Strachey's opinion concerning a biographer? How does age affect the opinions of people?

7.    Explain: "Every individual life is also the story of Everyman."

8.    Summarize her advice to a biographer. Compare the biographer's problem with that of the novelist and the dramatist.

9.    Discuss these directives: "Zeal in discovering evidence, faithfulness in reporting it, skill in presenting it."

10.    Compare this article with "The Art of Biography," by Virginia Woolf.

11.    Study this article for qualities of style. Refer to general helps.

12.    Explore two biographies, or more, written about the same person, yet with different interpretations and emphasis. Try to discover reasons for the diversity of opinions. Here are a suggested few, chosen for varying viewpoints.

*Calvin Coolidge,* by Claude Fuess (a family friend)
*A Puritan in Babylon,* by William Allen White
*Grace Coolidge and Her Era,* by Ishbel Ross

*Lead, Kindly Light* (Biography of Mahatma Gandhi), by Vincent Sheean
*Life of Mahatma Gandhi: His Life and Message for the World,* by Louis Fischer

Also Robert E. Lee, Franklin Delano Roosevelt, Walt Whitman, Abraham Lincoln, Theodore Roosevelt, Benjamin Disraeli, Emily Dickinson, and others.

# NOBEL, THE PRIZE GIVER

*Harland Manchester*

One day in 1861 a group of Paris bankers gave impatient audience to a young man who said he had a big idea. Neither he nor his hearers connected his idea with an annual accolade to distinguished writers, yet today his name looms large in the field of literature. He was a Swede; a thin, sickly, nervous chap, with penetrating blue eyes and plenty of assurance.

"Messieurs," he announced dramatically, "I have an oil that will blow up the globe!"

The bankers jumped, but he produced no infernal machine, and calmly went on to explain his new explosive. Shortly his hearers cut him off. The whole thing was impossible, and anyway, who wanted the globe blown up?

When Napoleon III heard about the young Swede, however, he spoke to a financier, and Alfred Nobel went back to Stockholm with a draft for 100,000 francs. Within a year, he and his father were manufacturing nitroglycerin for commercial use. Soon the world was startled by a new word: dynamite. And the foundation was laid for the Nobel fortune, the income of which is now distributed annually to workers for peace, to scientists, and to gifted writers.

To Alfred Nobel, there was nothing sinister about powerful explosives. His father, Emmanuel Nobel, an architect turned inventor, had been tinkering with them for years, and had invented a naval mine used by Russia in the Crimean War.

Emmanuel's income varied as much as his ideas. Despite the patient efforts of Mrs. Nobel, the family was often in hot water. They moved a great deal, and not by choice. When the landlord wanted cash, Emmanuel showed him blueprints. His enthusiasm was contagious, and sometimes the landlord forgot that the sketches were not legal tender. The year Alfred was born—1833—was one of those times when his father couldn't pay the rent. This time the creditors were not beguiled, and Emmanuel was thrown into bankruptcy.

Alfred was the third of four brothers, and the puniest of the lot. As a baby, he had convulsions, and for years his mother fought a constant battle to keep him alive. He had a weak spine, and when other children were playing, he sat on the sidelines and envied them. He had nervous headaches and a poor digestion, and was extremely sensitive to criticism.

Ludwig, the second son, was the apple of the old man's eye. Ludwig had genius, said Emmanuel, but Alfred worked harder. This talk got under Alfred's skin when at the age of seventeen his father sent him to New York to study a new heat engine invented by John Ericsson, who had migrated to New York and who was soon to revolutionize the world's navies with his ironclad *Monitor*. He sailed willingly, but no one knows how long he stayed in the United States or what he did. Soon he was back in Europe, rambling aimlessly here and there. He explored Paris night life, turned from it in disgust, and met a young girl with whom he fell desperately in love. She died, and he walked the streets all night, saw the sun rise, and wrote a long, introspective poem which he was to treasure all his life and to read to people who seemed sympathetic.

At the age of twenty-one the prodigal returned to his father's factory. Bitter, disillusioned, and hardened, but cherishing secret ideals which seemed impossible of realization, he went resolutely to work, for work, he decided, was all that life held for him.

Emmanuel Nobel was already convinced that nitroglycerin had great possibilities as an explosive, though it was used then chiefly as a stimulant in heart ailments. Under certain conditions it would explode, but no one knew just what these conditions were. Sometimes a container of the stuff would fall to the ground with a thud, and nothing would happen; sometimes a small jolt would cause a shattering explosion.

Some time during Alfred's four unexplained years, he had picked up a good working knowledge of chemistry, draftsmanship, and mechanical engineering. Gradually he took the lead in the experiments and arrived at the theory that the only sure way of exploding this soupish liquid was to confine it in a stout container and set it off with a sharp primary explosion. A match wouldn't explode nitroglycerin; it took force. He evolved the blasting cap —an invention still the basis of the whole nitroglycerin and dynamite industry.

After securing Louis Napoleon's help, Alfred and his father went hopefully to work, but nitroglycerin still would not behave. Neither Emmanuel nor Alfred was in the shop one morning in May 1864. The youngest son, Emil, and four workmen were there. An explosion killed everyone in the room instantly. Old Emmanuel was prostrated; he had a paralytic stroke from which he never recovered. He lingered for years, and from his bed or wheelchair continued to turn out "inventions," which Mrs. Nobel faithfully recorded. Stockholm shook with terror at the news of the explosion. The Nobels had no permit to work with explosives, and the authorities cracked down. But meanwhile, engineers and miners everywhere heard of the new time-saving, money-saving blasting oil. Orders and inquiries came in from all over the world.

Alfred Nobel moved his plant to a barge moored in a lake. Within a year he had launched manufacturing companies in Sweden, Finland, Norway, and Germany, and the Swedish government was using his "soup" to blast a terminal railway tunnel under Stockholm. Chemist, manufacturer, bookkeeper, and salesman all in one, he hardly took time to eat, and succeeded in ruining his digestion for life. Men with money to invest wanted demonstrations. Handling nitroglycerin often gives people headaches, and it affected Nobel violently, but he would allow no one else to run the risk. He would show them, he said, that his blasting oil was safe.

He was too optimistic; nitroglycerin's reign of terror was about to begin. One morning in November 1865, a Westphalian miner went to a store and asked for two pounds of blasting oil. The clerk started to pour it out, and that was the last of the clerk, the miner, and the store. At about the same time, Nobel's nitroglycerin plant in Norway soared skyward. A few weeks later, a railroad worker in Silesia tried to cut frozen blasting oil with an ax. They found his legs half a mile away.

The next April, nitroglycerin blew up aboard a ship docked in Panama. Even the wharf and freight house nearby were wrecked, and another ship badly disabled. Sixty people were killed, and the damage came to $1,000,000. Seventy cases of the stuff, marked for San Francisco, had blown up in the *European*'s hold.

A few days later a freight wagon, bearing several oil-stained wooden boxes, blew up before the express office in San Francisco. The driver said, "Whoa!" and that was his farewell to life. Fifteen persons were killed, many were injured, and a $200,000 block of buildings was wrecked. The shipment of nitroglycerin was traced to Nobel's New York agents. Other nitroglycerin catastrophes followed.

Alfred Nobel arrived in New York on a business trip a few days after the San Francisco blast, bearing some boxes of "soup." He was about as welcome as the plague. The newspapers had aroused the public, and Fire Marshal Baker was chasing down rumors that parcels of the "murderous compound" were stored in lofts and warehouses. People avoided Nobel, and hotels turned him away. When he announced that he would give a public demonstration at a quarry on Eighty-third Street, only about twenty men came to see the fireworks, and even they kept their distance. Nobel brought out a flat piece of iron and laid it on a rock. He poured a little of the terrible oil on the iron, and then raised a hammer. The spectators ducked for cover as the hammer descended. There was a sharp report, but Nobel was unharmed. He coaxed them nearer, and in a dry, scientific manner explained that only the oil struck by the hammer exploded. There was the rest of the puddle, undisturbed. You couldn't blow off the lot, he said, without confining it. Then he touched a match to the puddle. It burned, but didn't explode.

For two hours Nobel put the mysterious giant through its paces. He finished the performance with some real blasts, to show what the giant would do when you gave him his head. The crowd went away convinced.

But governments were not convinced, and neither were transportation companies. Although Nobel's office was swamped with orders and a fortune was within his reach, he almost failed that year. Several countries passed laws forbidding the use of Nobel's "soup," and ships refused to carry it. A safe nitroglycerin had to be invented. So Alfred Nobel invented it, though some say it was an accident. In Northern Germany there is a light, absorbent earth called *Kieselguhr*. Nobel's workers ran out of sawdust and used it in packing nitroglycerin cans. The story is that one of the cans leaked, and Nobel noticed that the *Kieselguhr* drank it up like blotting paper. He mixed three parts of "soup" with one part of *Kieselguhr* and his prayers were answered. The stuff could be kneaded like putty and packed in cartridges, it could be exploded with a blasting cap, and it was safe to chip. Nobel called it dynamite. Within a decade, fifteen Nobel plants were turning out six million pounds annually of the new explosive.

At forty, Nobel found himself a lonely, exhausted, melancholy man, with no interests outside his work, and few acquaintances outside his companies. He had money enough to satisfy any taste, but he couldn't relax and didn't know how to go about enjoying himself. He didn't even have a home. They called him "the richest vagabond in Europe."

He tried to make himself over. He bought a fine house in Paris and lived there most of the time. There were few things he could eat because of his stomach trouble, but he installed a good cook, began to entertain, and took great pride in his cellar and table appointments. He turned to Shelley, the god of his boyhood, and had an idea of writing something worth while. But he was equally at home in six languages and never could make up his mind which to use. Even in conversation he wandered from one to another, unconsciously slipping into the language which the topic suggested.

He had written great quantities of blank verse in his youth, but late in life he burned the lot, except for the gloomy, introspective, autobiographical poem, a hundred pages long, in which he had traced his life from infancy through his unhappy love affair, concluding in a tone of self-dedication to a life of work. He wrote the poem in English, later translating it into Swedish.

Nobel was a prodigious reader, not only of technical books but of poetry, philosophy, and, in general, what he called "ideal literature." He sternly disapproved of Zola and the realists, and greatly admired the work of Bjørnson and Selma Lagerlöf (who were both to receive the Nobel prize in literature) and the Swedish poet, Viktor Rydberg, romantic idealist. Many of his letters—he often wrote fifty a day—were exhaustive discussions of new novels, plays, and books of verse. He liked those writers who bolstered his belief in the constant progress of humanity. He had a lofty vision of a time when "people would come into the world with better-developed brains." Yet, paradoxically, he scoffed at man's meanness and insignificance, and called himself a "benevolent misanthrope."

For a time Nobel frequented the salon of Madame Juliette Adam, editor of the *Nouvelle Revue,* whose influence on politics and literature was considerable. Authors read from their books there, and actresses recited poems. He also went occasionally to Victor Hugo's house. These meetings spurred him to resume writing, and two unfinished novels resulted. *Brothers and Sisters* dealt skeptically with religion; *In Lightest Africa* was not a travel book but a vehicle for Nobel's political attitude, which may be described as a kind of socialism modified by distrust of the mass mind. In both attempts the characters are mere mouthpieces, and there are long, involved dialogues suggestive of duller passages of Ibsen or Shaw.

He also tried playwriting. Bitter at the loss of a patent suit in England, he wrote a satirical play about it which could interest no one except those involved in the litigation, and he worked for a time at a trivial domestic comedy which he called *A Victim of Imagination.* The year of his death, he turned out a four-act tragedy, in which he became completely absorbed. He went to London for a business conference, talked business for five minutes, then brought out his play and read it.

The play was called *Nemesis,* and it was based upon the same theme as Shelley's tragedy, *The Cenci.* It was full of tedious declamation and was too close to Shelley for comfort. Nobel's writing friends suggested changes, but he refused to alter a word, saying that he would rather "flutter with his own wings than fly with those of others." The play was about to be published when he died. His executors looked it over and thought it best to burn the edition, saving only three copies for the files. They said that the memory of a great man should not be dimmed by a poor play.

It would have pleased Nobel to make his house a meeting place for intellectuals; and because he wanted to entertain, he considered marriage, but since his early love affair he hadn't met a woman he thought he could get along with. He made cynical remarks about women, for he was desperately shy and believed himself so repulsive that no woman would marry him except for his money. Yet he could be very entertaining, and whenever an attractive woman made a determined attempt to be nice to him, he opened up like a peony.

It was his loneliness, in fact, that led to the establishment of the prizes. In his study there was a secretary's desk, but it was usually vacant. His correspondence was in six languages, and it was not easy to find a good secretary and an accomplished linguist in one person. He knew that he was asking a lot and got so that he hated to hire secretaries because he dreaded dismissing them.

In 1876 he tried once more, with this notice: "A very wealthy, cultured, elderly gentleman desires to find a lady also of mature years, familiar with languages, as secretary and manager of his household." He probably thought it discreet to call himself "elderly." He was only forty-three.

Bertha Kinsky, a Bohemian countess, answered this advertisement. She was an attractive woman of thirty, well educated, charming in manner, and a good listener. Nobel's gloomy, kindly, and occasionally sarcastic manner appealed to her. He, in turn, was much impressed but before she had actually entered upon her duties, she eloped with young Baron von Suttner.

The young couple worked for the Red Cross during the Russo-Turkish War. The Baroness came back appalled by what she had seen and wrote a passionate antiwar novel. The Baroness and Alfred Nobel had remained firm friends, and now she appealed to him to help in the movement. He was skeptical, but asked her to send him reading matter and keep him informed. She bombarded him with pamphlets, and they had long debates.

The Baroness had approached Nobel at exactly the right time. With leisure to think, he had made up his mind that many things needed changing. He became opposed to the inheritance of large fortunes. He provided for his mother handsomely but told the rest of the family not to expect anything when he died.

Nobel was undoubtedly moved by Bertha von Suttner's enthusiasm, although he sometimes poked a little fun at her. What she needed was not money, he told her, but a workable plan. There were too many "gas bags" in the movement, he told her, and some of their schemes were ridiculous. He predicted that his high explosives would put an end to war sooner than her peace meetings, because as military weapons became more deadly, horrified nations would disband their troops.

In spite of his doubts, Nobel made up his mind that he would leave his fortune, which amounted to about nine million dollars at his death—to found a prize for distinguished peace workers. Later he included the prizes for science and literature. It is interesting that he intended these money awards not as crowns for the eminent and successful but as lifebelts for sinking geniuses, which would save them from financial anxiety while they went on to new achievements. He said that he wished to help dreamers who have a hard time getting a living, and once, when asked to contribute to a Rydberg memorial, he said he preferred "to consider the bellies of the living." Yet the terms of his loosely drawn will have made it impossible for the award committees to consider the financial status of the recipients.

All this was not exactly what the Baroness had in mind, but her part in bringing it about was widely recognized. When the first Nobel Peace Prize was awarded in 1901, Henri Dunant, co-winner, wrote to thank Bertha von Suttner. The prize was her work, he said. It seems fitting that four years later the peace prize went to the Baroness herself.

Alfred Nobel ended his days in austere solitude in his luxurious villa at San Remo, Italy. He had turned his back on Paris when the French government, alarmed because he had sold his smokeless powder to Italy, placed restrictions upon his work. When his brother Ludwig, who had made a fortune in oil, died, the French papers thought it was Alfred; and he had the peculiar satisfaction of reading his own obituaries. They were not complimentary.

At San Remo he spent most of the time in his laboratory working on synthetic rubber and artificial silk. His heart began to give out, and he went to specialists. He laughed when they prescribed nitroglycerin. He bought a sphygmograph, watched the line which showed the irregularity of his pulse, and pointed out to friends the degree of variation that would kill him. On December 10, 1896, he died.

Before his death Alfred Nobel abandoned the idea that more powerful killing agents would frighten the nations into peace. He pinned his faith on something very much like the League of Nations. "The only true solution," he wrote, "would be a convention under which all the governments would bind themselves to defend collectively any country that was attacked."

At first, Nobel did not intend to found a perpetual peace prize. He suggested that it be discontinued at the end of thirty years, for he believed that if international peace were not assured by then, the world would relapse into barbarism. He said that in 1893. It was just thirty years later that an Austrian house painter led a *Putsch* in Munich.

## Study suggestions

1.   What seems ironical in the story of Alfred Nobel?

2.   Discuss the problems which he had to overcome and the effect of these on his personality and social life.

3.   Collect phrases and words that reveal his character.

4.   How was the original purpose of his prize awards changed?

5.   Near the end of his life what was his belief about peace in the world?

6.   Find the five areas for which Nobel Prizes are awarded. From the list of recipients, what Americans have received this award? How many of these were for literature?

7.   Read the acceptance speeches and compare them for the philosophy, but, too, for the person behind the words and thoughts.

# ALBERT CAMUS: A GOOD MAN

*Charles Rolo*

"My liberty is absolute," said the nihilist to the Englishman. "There is nothing which prevents me from punching you in the nose if I wish to." "Oh, yes, there is," replied the Englishman. "Your liberty ends where my nose begins." That each man's liberty has as its frontier the liberty of others is the hub of the humanist values which Albert Camus has been restating and revitalizing in terms of the intellectual framework of contemporary Europe. First known to us as a novelist vaguely associated with the French literature of despair, he is today Europe's foremost critic of ideologies which he finds rooted in despair—ideologies which treat man as the slave of abstractions such as history, the state, or the class struggle.

Born and raised in Algeria "on the shores of a happy sea," Camus opposes to the frenzied North and its demons of the absolute the *pensée solaire* or solar thought of the Mediterranean tradition: the Hellenic notions of measure, proportion, and limits. For Camus, the most instructive of the ancient deities, Nemesis, is the Goddess not of Vengeance but of Moderation. "There can be no attitude so free from error," Camus holds, that men should give it their total allegiance. "I've had enough," he says, "of people who die for an idea. What interests me is to live and die because of what one loves."

Albert Camus is the second youngest man ever to have been awarded the Nobel Prize; Kipling received it at forty-three, Camus at forty-four. The generation to which he belongs "grew up to the drumbeat of the First World War, and [its] history has not ceased to be murder, injustice, and violence." The European intellectuals most intimately involved in this history have been exposed to a host of corruptions—fascism, Communism, defeatism, collaborationism, reactionary nationalism—and few have emerged wholly uncompromised. One of the few is Albert Camus. He stands out, as did the late George Orwell, as a resonant spokesman for decency, a thinker of intransigent integrity and bracing independence—in sum, a good man.

Camus, who abhors self-righteousness and refuses to be counted among the moralizers, dislikes being called a moral force. However uncomfortable it may make him he has come to represent, to his numerous admirers on the Continent, the conscience of his age. In the Nobel Prize citation, even that circumspect body, the Swedish Academy, honored Camus—ostensibly an atheist—not only for "his important literary production," but also for illuminating "the problems of the human conscience in our time." Some years earlier, when *The Rebel* first appeared in Europe, Sir Herbert Read wrote: "With the publication of this book, a cloud that has oppressed the European mind for more than a century begins to lift."

Another token of Camus's importance is that at least six critical studies of his work have already been published. The two written in English—*The Thought and Art of Albert Camus* by Thomas Hanna and Philip Thody's *Albert Camus*—are excellent jobs of interpretation, which should help to make Camus better understood on this side of the Atlantic.

An American novelist said to me recently: "If a Frenchman was in line for the Nobel Prize, why didn't it go to Malraux or Sartre? I can't see what's so great about Camus." That a number of American readers should have doubts about Camus's stature is hardly surprising. To begin with, one of the things that is great about him is his handling of the French language, and fine stylists lose in translation. With its combination of lucidity and lyricism, its controlled passion, its flashing turn of phrase, and its arresting aphorisms, Camus's prose presents almost as many difficulties to the translator as poetry. Justin O'Brien has been scrupulously faithful (too faithful at times) to the wording and sentence structure of the original, but inevitably some of the luster has been rubbed off in the transition into a foreign language.

Although all of Camus's most important books have been published in English, six volumes of nonfiction and two plays—roughly half of his output—remain untranslated; and they reveal attractive aspects of the man and of his thought which are not familiar to us. Camus is best known to Americans through his fiction, and in his fiction he is sometimes highly enigmatic. One of America's best critics failed so completely to understand *The Stranger* that he sized up Camus as a hard-boiled writer of the stripe of James M. Cain. And most reviewers candidly admitted that they found *The Fall* something of a riddle. The trouble is that Camus's imaginative work is partly incomprehensible without a grasp of his philosophic thought, which he has expounded in two books of nonfiction, *The Myth of Sisyphus* and *The Rebel,* not widely read by Americans, and in essays and editorials which remain untranslated. Camus, who regards himself as "an artist, not a philosopher," may be said to have *felt his way* into philosophy guided by the emotions which govern him as a creative artist. Thomas Hanna rightly emphasizes in his study of Camus that the "interplay between [his] philosophical and literary concerns is largely responsible for the richness and value of his writings."

Like so many twentieth-century writers, Camus accepted, yet was anguished by, the picture of a world without God or justifiable values that was handed down by nineteenth-century science. The absurdity of this universe was heightened for Camus by the very bounties of nature and the keen physical joys amid which he grew up. To the youthful Camus—as he has told us in his first two books, *L'Envers et L'Endroit* and *Noces*—the sun and the sea were an insistent invitation to happiness. The bodies on the beach, the young couples in the dance halls—everything around him, in fact—celebrated the physical life as the sole reality and simultaneously proclaimed its brevity. "I learn," he wrote in his early twenties, "that there is no super-human happiness. . . . The world is beautiful, and beyond it there is no salvation. . . . Not that one must be an animal, but I find no meaning in the happiness of angels." Faithful to this experience, Camus has refused to seek meaning on any suprahuman plane. He has summed up his quest in a single, telling sentence: "I want to know if I can live with what I know, and only with that." What makes his conduct of this quest so original is that, as Phillip Thody has acutely noted, Camus has "the feelings of the common man and the mind of an intellectual." In his feelings there is a distinct penchant toward the normal, in his mind an abnormal rage for lucidity.

When Camus came of age, the European Zeitgeist was steeped in despair, and in the years that followed he "lived nihilism, contradiction, violence and dizzying destruction"; he shared the prevailing sense that man is a spiritual exile in a hostile world. Thus he found it necessary to create from scratch his own logical foundation for an ethic which was, so to speak, somewhere in his blood. "It is always easy to be logical," he has said. "It is almost impossible to be logical all the way to the end." Carrying logic all the way to the end, he posed in its most radical form the problem of *la non-garantie des valeurs*—the impossibility of justifying moral values; and on this foundation of systematic doubt, he started to erect a humanism of his own, akin to the lost humanist tradition.

Painfully involved in the dilemmas of his age, Camus is an artist in whose fiction and theater there is certainly a strong personal element. He has warned us, however, against identifying him with his protagonists or taking their reasoning as a literal transcription of his thought. In an essay published in the *Atlantic,* he wrote: "I am not a painter of the Absurd. . . . What else have I done but reflect on an idea I found current in the streets? That I nourished this idea, like the rest of my generation, goes without saying. But I have kept my distance in order to treat it and determine its logic. . . . A man often retraces the history of his nostalgias or temptations—almost never his own biography." Here Camus furnishes us with an important clue to an understanding of his work. His method as an artist, like Gide's, might be described as the experimental method: he takes an idea (which holds for him an element of "nostalgia" or "temptation"), carries it, fictionally or theatrically, to its logical conclusion, and leaves the reader to judge it by its consequences. Thus the whole body of Camus's literary creation has a well-defined pattern of exploration and evolution, which can best be charted by chronicling his life together with the development of his work.

Albert Camus was born in the Algerian town of Mondovi on November 7, 1913, the son of a Spanish mother and of an Alsatian agricultural worker who was killed in the Battle of the Marne. In the preface to his first book, Camus wrote: "Poverty was not a calamity for me. It was always balanced by the richness of light. . . . Circumstances helped me. To correct a natural in-difference I was placed half-way between misery and the sun. Mis-ery kept me from believing that all was well under the sun, and the sun taught me that history wasn't everything." Camus has re-mained strongly attached to his origins: North Africa, the world of the underdog, and his mother's country, Spain. He felt passionately involved in the Spanish Civil War, and long after it, in 1952, he resigned from UNESCO as a protest against the admission of Franco's dictatorship.

A teacher helped Camus to win a scholarship to secondary school, and he financed his university education with a variety of jobs. He stamped driving licenses for the Préfecture, checked baro-metric pressures for the Meteorological Institute, sold automobile parts, and worked for a ship broker. A newspaper advertisement led him into what was to become one of the great passions of his life, the theater. He applied for the job of male lead in a touring company, got it, and for two-week stretches traveled around Al-geria playing the French classics. Fortified by this experience, he formed his own theater group, L'Equipe, and adapted for the stage *The Brothers Karamazov* and Aeschylus's *Prometheus*. He has since written four plays of his own, and he has translated and adapted works by Calderon, Lope de Vega, and William Faulkner —his version of *Requiem for a Nun* ran for three hundred per-formances in Paris. Camus usually directs his own plays and adaptations—he greatly enjoys the camaraderie with actors at re-hearsal—and when one of the performers in *Requiem* had an ac-cident, Camus stepped into the part himself. All of his plays have been performed in Paris; but only one of them, *Caligula,* has proved effective on the stage. Critics have complained that Camus's theater is "too intelligent" and that it sacrifices showmanship to content.

Another enduring legacy of his youth is Camus's enthusiasm for football (soccer), which he played for many years. He still goes regularly to soccer matches on Sundays, and he believes that the code of good sportsmanship is a fine teacher of decency. "It was on the playing fields," he once said, "that I learned my only lessons in moral ethics."

While he was at the University of Algiers, Camus had a serious attack of tuberculosis. He completed his studies, however, and obtained a master's degree with a thesis relating Hellenism and Christianity. His first book was the fruit of travels, hobo style, to Italy, Austria, and Czechoslovakia. It was quickly followed by *Noces,* essays about the Mediterranean world whose themes were referred to earlier. At the outbreak of war Camus was engaged in crusading journalism in Algiers as a supporter of the rights of the Arabs. He went to Paris in 1940 and later founded the underground paper, *Combat,* which became one of the leading voices of the Resistance. Meanwhile, in 1942, Gallimard had published in Paris the two books that were to establish Camus's reputation: *The Stranger* and *The Myth of Sisyphus.* These works—together with *Caligula* and another play, *The Misunderstanding* (written, respectively, in 1938 and 1942)—represent a phase in Camus's career which might be summed up as the exploration of the Absurd.

Camus's analysis of the Absurd begins by noting that normally man finds it easy enough to accept his daily routine, but one day there arises a "why," a questioning of whether life has any meaning. One finds oneself "in a universe suddenly divested of illusions and lights . . . an alien, a stranger." Nature, even other men appear hostile and inhuman. Ordinary gestures, the soundless movements of a man's lips behind the glass door of a telephone booth, assume the aspect of a "meaningless pantomime." Finally, one is filled with a horrifying awareness of death as a mathematical certainty. The source of this malaise is that, in an irrational world, reason cannot satisfy man's "wild longing" for meaning—"and beyond reason there is nothing." The Absurd, then, is the result of thinking about the human condition. The impossibility of reconciling death and the desire for eternity, misery and the desire for happiness, separateness and the desire for union, the mystery of all existence and the desire for clarity—all this is the Absurd.

Malraux, Sartre, and others had developed this line of thought before Camus. His originality lay firstly in finding the world's absurdity not a cause for despair but, paradoxically, a spur to happiness. In his eyes, mortality and senseless suffering—perhaps his most haunting preoccupation—actually enhance the value of life: they invite men to live it more intensely.

Camus also refused to draw the nihilist conclusion that because the world is irrational, the irrational is the only logical principle of conduct. This is the theme of *Caligula*. Discovering that the world is absurd, the emperor imagines that he can somehow transform it for the better by becoming the prophet of absolute absurdity. He inaugurates a capricious reign of terror and topsy-turvy morality, rewarding crime and debauchery and punishing innocence. What gives the play its disturbing tension is that Caligula, in his dreadful way, is awakening his subjects to a truth: life is absurd; and at this stage in his career, Camus can invoke no values by which Caligula could be condemned. Nevertheless Caligula is destroyed by a revolt, prompted by the instinctive recognition that his conduct has *exceeded* life's absurdity.

Both in *Caligula* and in *The Misunderstanding*—the most somber of Camus's works—there is a spirit of revolt against the hostile aspects of the world's absurdity. In *The Stranger,* the revolt is against man-made standards of absolute morality. This short novel is written in a style which owes something to the early Hemingway. Each spare sentence forms a self-enclosed whole, with the result that life is registered as a succession of perceptions with no meaning beyond themselves. Camus's goal is to reproduce a *feeling* of the Absurd: nothing is explained.

Meursault, the hero of *The Stranger,* a clerk in an Algiers office, is a man completely indifferent to everything except his immediate physical sensations: he has the Absurd in his blood but no awareness of it. The death of his mother, the offer of a promotion, the love of the girl he is sleeping with—they have "no importance" to him. In due course he drifts into a situation in which, dazed by the blazing sun, he kills an Arab who seems to be menacing him with a knife. His lawyer assures him of an acquittal if he pleads self-defense and expresses the right sentiments. But Meursault is incapable of pretending to emotions he does not possess. His complete honesty at his trial makes him appear a monster, and he is sentenced to be guillotined. The imminence of death makes him conscious of what he had always taken for granted: life is meaningless. "Emptied of hope," he realizes that he had been happy and "was happy still." Meursault is an improbable, at times an exasperating character, but the ironic tenderness with which Camus has portrayed him subtly wins our sympathy.

A masterly piece of storytelling—every detail has impact—*The Stranger* satirizes the concept that human conduct can be judged by fixed moral standards. It is not the killing of the Arab which dooms Meursault. He is found guilty because he is a stranger to the ethical absolutes of the court, and by this token all men are guilty.

*The Myth of Sisyphus* likens man's fate to that of the myth's hero, doomed forever to push a heavy stone up a hillside with the certainty that it will roll down again. "There is but one truly serious philosophical problem," Camus states at the outset, "and that is suicide." He finds the answer to it in the attitude of Sisyphus, who confronts his condition without illusions yet without despair. Sisyphus surmounts the Absurd through a rebellious defiance which brings with it passion and freedom. The essay ends: "The struggle toward the heights is enough to fill a man's heart. One must imagine Sisyphus happy."

This treatment of the myth is Camus's rough draft of a doctrine of metaphysical revolt, rooted in the spirit of the average man who, always and everywhere, has braced himself against his fate with injunctions not to "take it lying down." In his preface to the American edition of *Sisyphus,* which did not appear until 1955, Camus observes: "Written . . . in 1940, amid the French and European disaster, this book declares that even within the limits of nihilism, it is possible to proceed beyond nihilism." Despair, to Camus, has always been the ultimate sin, and he argues this point stirringly in *Lettres à un Ami Allemand.* These letters to an imaginary German friend—originally published in the underground press—develop the viewpoint, nourished by Camus's experiences in the Resistance, that by revolting against oppression men affirm that they have a value in common, thereby establishing human "solidarity." This outlook is dramatized in *The Plague*.

Camus's major novel to date, *The Plague*, describes an epidemic that ravages Oran. It is an allegory of man's fate—"plague . . . is just life"—and each character represents a way of responding to the problem of misery and evil. The physician Rieux (who is not disclosed to be the narrator until the end—Camus delights in a touch of mystification) devotes all of his energies to fighting the epidemic, as does Tarrou, a former revolutionary whose insights anticipate the criticism of violence in *The Rebel*. Other characters illustrate how bourgeois complacency, or cowardice, or greed aid and abet scourges. And the Christian acceptance of suffering as the wages of sin is fiercely repudiated in a scene in which, after seeing an infant tortured to death by the plague, Rieux rails against Father Paneloux for preaching resignation to God's will.

Rieux acknowledges, however, that he and the priest are on the same side, the side of "victims." Camus has said that what concerns him most is, "How should one behave?" and *The Plague* gives what thereafter remains his answer: we cannot be sure of doing good, but we can exercise the utmost vigilance not to do anything which increases suffering, and this involves tolerance for everything except suffering itself. The temper of *The Plague* is resolutely anti-heroic. Rieux and Tarrou, in exposing themselves to exceptional risks, are "merely logical"—they have understood that resisting scourges is "everybody's business." The man referred to at one point as the story's hero is a minor municipal clerk who keeps the statistics of the epidemic and spends his spare time endlessly writing the first sentence of a novel. Through this slightly daft character—his name, Grand, is both ironic and suggestive, as are others in Camus's work—Camus expresses his affection and regard for the ordinary man whose eccentricities are harmless and whose devotion to his job makes him, in effect, a mute, inglorious Sisyphus.

*The Plague* is a bit too obviously a bearer of messages to be an artistic masterpiece, but it is certainly one of the half-dozen most important and finest novels published since World War II. The writing is crisp and vivid, the narrative tone quietly absorbing: a singular fusion of curiosity, emotion, and intense irony. And the novel's moral urgencies are communicated with an eloquent sobriety.

A play based on *The Plague, État de Siège,* and another play, *Les Justes,* preceded *The Rebel,* Camus's fullest statement of the doctrine of metaphysical revolt and of its application to politics and art. He had already progressed from the lonely and somewhat sterile revolt of Sisyphus to the affirmation that through revolt (against tyranny or simply fate) men lose their spiritual isolation and achieve that sense of unity and meaning which the world's absurdity denies them. He concludes, now, that man is by nature a rebellious animal—"the only creature who refuses to be what he is"—and that metaphysical revolt is synonymous with freedom and creativity. The supreme example of the metaphysical rebel is the creative artist; he is continually engaged in confronting the Absurd—the world is his raw material—and in rebelling against it through the imposition of form.

The political analysis sets out to inquire why a century of revolt has produced tyrannies and rationalizations of tyranny more vicious than the original evils it refused to accept. Camus's explanation is that Hegel and other apostles of absolutist thought transformed the spirit of revolt into its opposite, revolution. Revolt is a protest against unlimited power, and its moderate goal is to diminish the sum total of suffering. Revolution seeks unlimited power, and it claims absolute freedom to inflict suffering in order to gain its immoderate ends. The spirit of revolt requires that every man retain the freedom to revolt; and under no circumstances will it legitimize violence. If the rebel is forced to kill, even a tyrant, he must be willing to lose his own life in order to demonstrate that murder is a limit which can only be transgressed once.

The conviction that reverberates throughout the essay is that men cannot live by abstractions conned out of history: ideology corrupts, and absolutist ideologies corrupt absolutely. Not history, which makes men drunk with dreams, but nature, which sobers them with reminders of their limits, is the proper study of mankind. Today's political ills are the logical result of a despairing Utopianism, which finds life so horribly wrong that it shrinks from no horror to change it and is blind to the truth that nothing can transform the world into the earthly paradise. Because it is so profoundly opposed in spirit to resignation, so richly infused with the spirit of revolt, *The Rebel* is a singularly stirring statement of a philosophy of moderation.

Shortly after the publication of *The Rebel,* there occurred a break between Camus and Sartre, who had become close friends during the war. While insisting that he differed from the Communists, Sartre had for some time been taking a parallel stand to them on most issues, including the criminality of criticizing Russia. His journal, *Les Tempts Modernes,* published an attack on *The Rebel* by one of Sartre's disciples, and Sartre later seconded it himself. Camus, they said, was an escapist who would not risk sullying his purity by contact with history; and they accused him of giving aid and comfort to the reactionaries. Camus rejoined that the Existentialists claimed to exalt liberty, and "today they exalt servitude . . . [saying] it is the same thing, which is a lie." Privately he added: "To me they have always been like the planet Mars." The break between Camus and Sartre was bitter and violent, and now they never meet.

The nature of Camus's enemies is a measure of his decency: he is as angrily attacked by the former Vichyites and other reactionaries as he is by the totalitarian Left and its followers. Responsible critics, however, have noted that it is easy to find contradictions and troublesome omissions in his thought; for example, the American Revolution, which did not give birth to tyranny, is not referred to in his discussion of revolutions, and it is difficult to square his refusal to sanction killing under any circumstances with his statement, "I am not a pacifist." Another objection is that his philosophy of political action might serve as a charter for the International Red Cross, but has little application to the political arena, which seldom presents a clear-cut choice between adding to or diminishing suffering. Camus could justly meet the first criticism by pointing out that he has never claimed to be a systematic thinker; and the second by arguing (as indeed he did in *The Plague*) that, in the present state of world affairs, there is a side which consists in *not* taking sides.

Nine years elapsed between *The Plague* and Camus's next novel, *The Fall* (1956), which readers have found the most ambiguous of his books. The only work by Camus with a northern setting (Amsterdam), it is the confession of a Parisian lawyer, brilliantly unfolded as a philosophical suspense story. The narrator has resolved a spiritual crisis by becoming what he calls a "judge-penitent." He has regained his sense of superiority, and is able to indulge his need to dominate others, by going around confessing that he is the lowest of the low, thereby provoking his listeners into judging and abasing themselves. Camus has described the narrator—Jean-Baptiste Clamence (John the Baptist, *vox clamans*) —as "the hero of today," and his summation of the novel is as follows: "Europeans are no longer believers; they are agnostics or atheists. (I have nothing against that. I am more or less a pagan.) But they have retained their sense of sin. They can't unburden themselves by going to confession. So they feel the need to act. They start passing severe judgments, putting people in concentration camps, killing. My 'hero' is the exact illustration of a guilty conscience. He has the European resignation to a feeling of sin." The "fall" referred to in the title is failure to rebel, and it makes Clamence a disseminator of corruption. Since Camus himself has warned against putting too simple an interpretation on the novel, it seems probable that, for all his ironic detachment, Camus is expressing "nostalgias" and "temptations" he has known.

His latest book, *Exile and the Kingdom,* is a collection of six stories strikingly varied in style and subject, but with a common theme: all are concerned in some way with man's sense of exile and yearning for unity. "The Renegade" is an allegory of the power-worship which makes men converts to philosophies of nihilism. It is cast in the form of a horrifying monologue by a dying man, a power-obsessed missionary who has set out to convert fearsome barbarians and who, reveling in the tortures inflicted on him in the name of their idol, becomes its abject slave. "The Guest" reflects Camus's feelings about the Algerian tragedy. A schoolmaster who represents the civilizing and humane aspects of the French administration—he loves the country and feels he belongs to it— tries unsuccessfully to save an Arab murderer from being handed over to the police. In the climate of fanaticism, his effort is tragically misunderstood, and the Arab's associates announce their intention to wreak vengeance. "Artist at Work" amusingly charts the progressive demoralization of a dedicated painter, assailed by the intrusions and distractions that attend success. Its point is that it is through solitude that the artist achieves solidarity with his time: a dig at Sartre's insistence on "commitment."

Camus lives in Paris now, in an apartment near the Luxembourg gardens. He does his writing in the morning—always either standing at an upright desk or lying down—and in the afternoons works at Gallimard as editor of a series of books introducing young writers. He is married (to a pianist) and has twins, a boy and a girl. Like Faulkner, he resents intrusions into his privacy, and he refuses to be lionized or to play the social role expected of a leading intellectual in Paris. Paris is a bad place for an artist, he says, because it is a stage: it forces him to assume a posture. Though inaccessible to celebrity hunters and busybodies, Camus welcomes visitors from Algeria and keeps his door open to students.

A man of medium height, slim, dark, and muscular, he has an intense but controlled vitality which gives him an outward appearance of calm. He is capable of sitting silent in a group for long stretches or of seducing a room full of people with his gaiety and charm. His trench coat, habitual slouch, and cigarette dangling from the corner of his mouth give him a slightly proletarian air, which accords with his sympathies.

The event that has most moved Camus since the war was the Hungarian Revolt—"It blew to bits the biggest lie of the century" —and it will serve as the concluding point of the novel on which he has started work: an account of a man's life, tentatively entitled *The First Man*. It warrants the highest expectations. Still relatively young, Camus already has to his credit fine achievements as an artist, and as a thinker he has traveled far. He wrestled long and hard with nihilism, and cannot be accused of facile optimism when he says, "There is more to admire than to despise in men"; when he talks of the prospects of a European "renaissance"; when he declares, "In the midst of winter, I discovered that there was in me an invincible summer."

Albert Camus has found his real voice.

## Study suggestions

1.    From this appraisal of Camus list the characteristics of him as a man; also his qualities as a writer. Why is he called "the conscience of his age"?

2.    Paraphrase the statement, "Each man's liberty has as its frontier the liberty of others." What is the significance of *frontier?*

3.    In what sort of atmosphere did Camus grow up? In the midst of all the *isms* mentioned, for what did Camus stand?

4.    What do "fine stylists" lose in translation? According to Hanna what is responsible for the richness and value of Camus's writings?

5.    Camus was concerned with how one should behave. Do you gain an impression that he has fixed ideas or that he is groping for answers, that his writings help to crystallize his thinking? Give examples to support your opinion.

6.    What is the clue to an understanding of his work? Explain his pattern of exploration and evolution. How does he define the Absurd?

7.    Camus comments on Sisyphus, "The struggle toward the heights is enough to fill a man's heart." How does this coincide with his belief that despair is sin? Where did he learn his lessons in moral ethics?

8.    How does he define the spirit of revolt? Political ills he felt are the result of what?

9.    In what ways can the nature of Camus's enemies be a measure of his decency?

10.    Explain in some detail the concluding sentence.

11.    Compare his death, by accident, related in the *Atlantic Monthly,* February 1961, with that of his hero in *The Stranger.*

12.    Read *The Thought and Art of Albert Camus,* by Thomas Hanna.

# REMARKS ON RECEIVING THE NOBEL PRIZE

*William Faulkner*

I feel that this award was not made to me as a man but to my work—a life's work in the agony and sweat of the human spirit, not for glory and least of all for profit, but to create out of the materials of the human spirit something which did not exist before. So this award is only mine in trust. It will not be difficult to find a dedication for the money part of it commensurate with the purpose and significance of its origin. But I would like to do the same with the acclaim too, by using this moment as a pinnacle from which I might be listened to by the young men and women already dedicated to the same anguish and travail, among whom is already that one who will some day stand here where I am standing.

Our tragedy today is a general and universal physical fear so long sustained by now that we can even bear it. There are no longer problems of the spirit. There is only the question: when will I be blown up? Because of this, the young man or woman writing today has forgotten the problems of the human heart in conflict with itself which alone can make good writing because only that is worth writing about, worth the agony and the sweat.

He must learn them again. He must teach himself that the basest of all things is to be afraid; and, teaching himself that, forget it forever, leaving no room in his workshop for anything but the old verities and truths of the heart, the old universal truths lacking which any story is ephemeral and doomed—love and honor and pity and pride and compassion and sacrifice. Until he does so he labors under a curse. He writes not of love but of lust, of defeats in which nobody loses anything of value, of victories without hope, and worst of all, without pity or compassion. His griefs grieve on no universal bones, leaving no scars. He writes not of the heart but of the glands.

Until he relearns these things he will write as though he stood alone and watched the end of man. I decline to accept the end of man. It is easy enough to say that man is immortal simply because he will endure; that when the last ding-dong of doom has clanged and faded from the last worthless rock hanging tideless in the last red and dying evening, that even then there will still be one more sound: that of his puny inexhaustible voice, still talking. I refuse to accept this. I believe that man will not merely endure: he will prevail. He is immortal, not because he alone among creatures has an inexhaustible voice, but because he has a soul, a spirit capable of compassion and sacrifice and endurance. The poet's, the writer's, duty is to write about these things. It is his privilege to help man endure by lifting his heart, by reminding him of the courage and honor and hope and pride and compassion and pity and sacrifice which have been the glory of his past. The poet's voice need not merely be the record of man, it can be one of the props, the pillars to help him endure and prevail.

## Study suggestions

1.    What do the phrases "in the agony and sweat of the human spirit," "anguish and travail," suggest?

2.    In his opinion on what is good writing based? Discuss some of the problems of which he speaks.

3.    How does he define the "glory of the past"?

4.    Write a précis of this brief speech.

5.    Write on "The Problems of the Human Heart in Conflict with Itself." Use illustrations from your reading to make your concept clear.

6.    Compare this speech with the other acceptance speeches; length, tone, and message.

# DAG HAMMARSKJOLD

*Andrew W. Cordier*

Dag Hammarskjold's death marks the close of an era of unparalleled richness—in the charting of new paths in diplomacy, in combining rare gifts of energy, wisdom, and intelligence to bring crises under control and to promote programs for human betterment.

Sometimes his methods had the charm and quality of a symphony, sometimes the decisive abruptness of the hammer on the anvil, but they were always calculated to gain high ends of which he never lost sight.

If he had accomplished less, his epitaph might be that in opening up bold new vistas of international cooperation he belonged to a generation yet unborn. But his accomplishments are myriad—they are like snowflakes on a dotted landscape and the glistening white on the mountain peaks—countless small, almost unnoticed achievements joined with decisively constructive results on great issues which only he could achieve by virtue of his office and of the rare natural gifts with which he was endowed.

He belongs to our generation; he has carved his name in granite upon it; but he belongs equally to those who will come after us, benefiting by the lights he lit that can illuminate their way.

He was both actor and interpreter; both history-maker and historian. With the United Nations Charter as his guide and resolutions as his directives, he mobilized and conducted the action with the scope and initiative that each situation required; his executive actions were an interpretation of the Charter which, together with his speeches and reports, gave that document a living quality of rich potentiality for the welfare of mankind.

His unflinching courage rested upon faith and his faith upon principles and ideals derived from a sturdy and valued heritage and an intellect alive with almost limitless appraisal of values with meaning for himself and humanity.

From that day—April 10, 1953—when he took his oath of office, his dedication to his task and his single-minded devotion to duty have inspired the staff and the wider world.

Although working often from dawn to midnight or in crises around the clock, he had time for wide cultural interests—in literature, drama, art, and music—which were a source of constant pleasure to his associates in the United Nations family and an inspiration to the masters in these fields.

His deep inner stillness was a mainspring of his strength—a fortress so strong that disappointments, failures, setbacks, and even personal attacks could not weaken his will or compromise his resolution to carry on his great task. His interest in the Meditation Room at the U.N. Building was deeply personal, not merely esthetic. He wrote the words on the entrance: "This is a room devoted to peace and those who are giving their lives for peace. It is a room of quiet where only thoughts should speak." He went there frequently for quiet reflection, knowing that retreats into loneliness were a source of strength for the struggle.

Our sorrow and grief for the one who led and inspired us extend equally to all of those who died with him. They were selfless in their interest, devoted to their tasks, and dedicated to the noble cause of peace which the United Nations represents. Along with him they will be hallowed in precious memory. In future it will be said of them that they died with their chief in the line of duty.

Let us not be ashamed to shed some tears over our loss, nor shrink from reflection of the void that has been created for us and the world, but let this be a part of our rededication to the task which he so nobly advanced. His concern must now be matched by our increased concern for the future of the United Nations. His greatest concern would be that we should carry on with new resolves and in a spirit of magnificent cooperation. Our greatest tribute to him will be our continuing individual and collective efforts, by following his glorious example, to strengthen the edifice of peace.

His words taken from the pamphlet that he wrote for visitors to the Meditation Room now have prophetic meaning, a charge from him to all of us: "It is for those who come here to fill the void with what they find in their center of stillness."

## Study suggestions

1.   In this brief tribute to Dag Hammarskjold, written by the Executive Assistant to the Secretary-General of the United Nations, through what qualities does the writer acquaint us more intimately with the many facets of the man? Note the writer's ability to convey many qualities in few words.

2.   Identify sentences and phrases that are packed with meaning.

3.   How effective is his use of figurative expressions?

4.   Explain the significance of his "deep inner stillness"; "retreats into loneliness were a source of strength for the struggle"; "It is a room of quiet where only thoughts should speak"; also the last sentence.

5.   *United Nations Review,* after his death, quoted his last message to the staff four days before he left for Africa. This excerpt shows the spirit of the man. "We all know that if we feel that what we do is purposeful, not to say essential, for the progress of men and human society in a broader sense—yes, even if we believe that what we do is essential only for a small group of people and its future happiness—we are willing to accept hardships and serve gladly for the value of serving."

Are these empty words or do they reflect his own goals? Justify your opinion.

"All the hundreds of tributes have a single theme: that the name of Dag Hammarskjold will live on as a symbol of peace."

Read: *Dag Hammarskjold,* by Joseph P. Lash

# SCHWEITZER AT EIGHTY-FIVE

*Norman Cousins*

Albert Schweitzer observed his eighty-fifth birthday earlier this month at his hospital in Lambarene, French Equatorial Africa. He had spent several months in Europe—at his home in the Alsace and in visiting libraries, universities, churches, and the homes of old friends. For the first time in many years he gave a formal lecture—and a few informal ones. He was in excellent health.

When the holiday season approached, he left for Africa. As usual, he traveled by surface transportation—by train and boat and native canoe. And, as is well known, he generally took third-class accommodations—because there were no fourth-class ones.

His main concern, reflected in his talks and his letters, continued to be the monstrous risks taken by nations in their nuclear affairs. He had spent more than half a century in trying to awaken and serve the creative and compassionate spirit in man. The infinite reaches of mind, the connecting power of conscience, the fragility of human tissue—these were the main strands of his life and work. But now, in his harvest years, his thoughts and energies are turned also to the uncertainty that has clouded over the prospects for civilized man.

There was nourishment and hope for him in the decision of the United States and the Soviet Union to suspend their atomic experiments pending an attempt to work out effective control of nuclear weapons in the world. But the lack of urgency in these attempts, the spread of nuclear capability in the world, and the absence of wisdom in the collective conduct of human society—these concerns have become his close and prodding companions. Something else concerns him these days—the feeling of helplessness that has settled over men and women all over the world. He believes that governments will become responsible and sane in large affairs only as people create a mandate for them to do so. But individuals everywhere seem to him to be defaulting; they do not appear to have confidence in themselves to take hold, nor do they accept the absolute need to do so.

Does Dr. Schweitzer have any specific prescription or formula he would have individuals follow? He does not. Is there a specific line of action he would have them take? There is not. All he asks, or rather hopes for, is that the individual will be able to peel off the layers of hardened artificialities that separate him from his real self. He hopes that the individual in the twentieth century will somehow be able to cut through to the original purity inside him. Man's resources do not exist outside him. His responses must come from within. A thinking and feeling man is not a helpless man. The sense of paralysis proceeds not so much out of the mammoth size of the problem but out of the puniness of purpose.

Nothing is more universal today than the tragic question: "What can a man do?" If the purpose is strong enough, the question will answer itself. When Schweitzer first came to Africa, he was not frozen because thousands of doctors were required. The infinity of the need did not produce in Schweitzer either awe or surrender. In the very act of accepting a responsibility a single doctor could make it visible to others. Besides, to deprive one man of help because a multitude were calling for it was a design for a morally feeble society.

"A single doctor in Africa," he has said, "even with the most modest equipment, can mean very much for very many. The good which he can accomplish surpasses by a hundredfold what he gives of his own life and the cost of material support he must have. Just with a few medicines and with sufficient skills he can in a single year free hundreds of men from the grip of suffering and death."

It may be said that only a Schweitzer has the knowledge and personal power to answer satisfactorily the question: "What can one man do?" Certainly we can't all be Schweitzers. But what should concern us is not what it takes to be a Schweitzer but what it takes to be a man. Nature has not been equally lavish with her endowments, but each man has his own potential in terms of achievement and service. The awareness of that potential is the discovery of purpose: the fulfillment of that potential is the discovery of strength.

For Albert Schweitzer, the assertion of this potential was not directed to charity but to justice. Also, moral reparations. He had always been troubled by the fact that the white man, carrying with him the cross of Jesus, not infrequently also carried the means of cheapening the lives of people he sought to change or dominate.

"Ever since the world's far-off lands were discovered, what has been the relationship of the white people to the colored?" he has asked. "What is the meaning of the simple fact that this and that people have died out, and that the condition of others is getting worse because they were 'discovered' by men who professed to be followers of Jesus? Who can measure the misery produced by the fiery liquids and hideous diseases we have brought to them?

"We are burdened with a great debt. We are not free to confer benefits on these people, or not confer them, as we please. It is our duty. Anything we give them is not benevolence but atonement. That is the foundation from which all deliberations about 'works of mercy' must begin."

As for the right time to act? The time, inevitably, is now. It can only be now. "Truth has no special time of its own," he has said. When circumstances seem least propitious, that is the correct time.

Much of the ache and the brooding unhappiness in modern man is the result of his difficulty in using himself fully. He performs compartmentalized tasks in a compartmentalized world. He is reined in—physically, socially, spiritually. Only rarely does he have a sense of fulfilling himself through total contact with a total challenge. He finds it difficult to make real connection even with those who are near him. But there are vast urges of conscience, natural purpose, and goodness inside him demanding air and release. He has the capacity for moral response. And he has his own potential, the regions of which are far broader than he can even guess at—a potential that keeps nagging at him to be fully used.

This is not to say that Albert Schweitzer has achieved "happiness" in meeting his potential. He is less concerned with happiness than with purpose. What is it that has to be done? What is the best way of doing it? How does a man go about developing an inner awareness of important needs outside himself? How does he attach himself to those needs? Is he able to recognize the moral summons within him? To the extent that the individual is unconcerned about these questions, or lives apart from them, he is unfulfilled and only partly alive.

One night at the hospital in Lambarene, long after most of the oil lamps had been turned out, I walked down towards the river. It was a sticky night and I couldn't sleep. As I passed the compound near Dr. Schweitzer's quarters, I could hear the rapid piano movement of a Bach toccata. The doctor was playing on the upright piano next to his bedside.

I approached the doctor's bungalow and stood for perhaps five minutes outside the latticed window, through which I could see his silhouette in the dimly lit room. The piano had an organ footboard attachment so that he could keep his feet in musical condition. While he played the toccata his feet moved over the footboard with speed and certainty. His powerful hands were in total control of the piano as he met Bach's demands for complete definition of each note—each with its own weight and value, yet all of them laced intimately together to create an ordered whole.

I had a stronger sense of listening to a great console than if I had been in the world's largest cathedral. The yearning for an ordered beauty; the search for a creative abandonment—yet an abandonment inside a disciplined artistry; the desire to re-create a meaningful past; the need for outpouring and release, catharsis— all these things inside Albert Schweitzer spoke in his playing. And when he was through, he sat with his hands resting lightly on the keys, his great head bent forward as though to catch any echoes.

He was now freed of the pressures and tensions of the hospital, with its forms to fill out in triplicate; freed of the mounds of unanswered mail; freed of the heat and the saturating moisture of the Equator; freed of the insects and the ants that would invade the costly medicines. Johann Sebastian Bach had made it possible for Albert Schweitzer to come to Lambarene in the first place; it was Schweitzer's books on Bach that provided royalties to support the hospital in the early years. Now Bach was restoring him to a world of creative and ordered splendor.

The doctor knew in some way that I was standing outside, listening to him play, for when he finished the toccata, he called out to me by name and asked me to come in. For one half-hour or so, we chatted in the thin light of the oil lamp near the piano. He was speaking personally now—about his hopes mostly. First, he would like to see his hospital in complete running order. Second, he would like to be able to train others to run the hospital after he is gone. Third, he would like to have just a little time—to work quietly and finish his two books. One is his major theological work, "The Kingdom of God." The other is his final volume on "The Philosophy of Civilization."

He did not wish these longings of his to give the impression he was unhappy in his work. Now and then something would happen that would give him a sense of fulfillment and deep reward. Only a few days earlier, for example, he received a letter from a professorial colleague in France about an examination paper turned in by a nineteen-year-old boy. One of the questions on the examination was worded: "How would you define the best hope for the culture of Europe?" The boy had written: "It is not in any part of Europe. It is in a small African village and it belongs to a man in his eighties."

Dr. Schweitzer looked up from the letter. "At times like this, when the hospital has gone to sleep and everything is at peace, it makes me proud that a young man would think as he does, whether what he thinks is true or not. But in the morning, when the sun is up and the cries from the hospital are sounded, I do not think of such fancy ideas. I have all I can do to sit still while reality stares me in the face. And sometimes, if I am lucky, I can stare back."

## Study suggestions

1. Discuss Schweitzer's main concerns in these days, of peoples and of individuals.

2. Explain: "Each man has his own potential in terms of achievement and service." What injustices have disturbed him?

3.   Does the author feel that Schweitzer believes in compartmentalized task in a compartmentalized world? Discuss your opinion.

4.   How does he exemplify the statement: "He is less concerned with happiness than with purpose"? To what does he attribute most of man's unhappiness?

5.   How did he "speak" in his music? Note the talents of this
man.

6.   What qualities are revealed in Schweitzer's personal hopes?

7.   Summarize your impression of this man "in his harvest
years."

8.   Theme subjects:
      What Can One Man Do?
      A Man (or Woman) I Admire
      Read *Dr. Schweitzer of Lambarene,* by Norman Cousins

# THE MASS MIND

*Joyce Cary*

Every age, they say, has its special bit of nonsense. The eighteenth
century had its noble savage, and the nineteenth, its automatic
progress. Now we have this modern nonsense about the "mass
man." We are all told constantly that people are becoming more
and more standardized. That mass education, mass amusements,
mass production, ready-made clothes, and a popular press are
destroying all individuality—turning civilization into a nice,
warmed, sterilized orphan asylum where all the little lost souls
wear the same uniforms, eat the same meals, think the same
thoughts, and play the same games.

This belief is now so completely accepted that it underlies half the writing and thinking of the time, like chalk under the downs. You don't see it but it gives shape to what you do see. If you deny it you will get exactly the same response as Galileo when he said that the earth moved through the sky. You will be told, "Use your eyes. And don't talk nonsense. Look at the crowds in the street or at any football match. Go to the films, read the newspapers. Consider the disappearance of national dress all over the world—the immense development of laws restricting individual liberty, standardizing our lives. Go on a tour to famous sights— year by year there will be bigger crowds of morons gaping at them and listening to the spiel of some bored guide—a piece nicely designed to satisfy the mass mind."

And you will be referred to history and old travel accounts to learn how various and delightful the world was, in dress and thought and individuality, one hundred or even fifty years ago.

I was convinced of all this myself till I went to administer the affairs of a primitive tribe in Africa. There I found that the tribal mind was much more truly a mass mind than anything I had known in Europe. The nearest approximation to it was among illiterate peasantry in remote country districts. Tribesmen and primitive peasants are intensely narrow and conservative. Their very simple ideas and reactions guide them in a mysterious and dangerous world.

I found that young chiefs with enterprise and ambition were keen to learn about the world outside the tribe. If they got away from it, they tended to put on European dress. To them, European dress was not a mark of the mass mind, but of the free and independent mind.

Likewise, when a European peasantry becomes educated and enterprising, it breaks away from the national dress which seems a badge of servitude and backwardness. To tourists, no doubt, this is a misfortune. As a keen tourist and sight-seer, I wish all Scotsmen would wear the kilt and all Turks the tarboosh. I'm delighted that some are beginning to do so again. But these are individualists, eccentrics, nationalists—national dress is not a tribal uniform to them, but a proclamation of difference, an assertion of self.

Education, contact with other peoples, breaks up tribal uniformity of thought and custom, brings in new ideas. That is, it makes for difference. The celebrated eccentrics of former centuries were either lunatics—or educated men.

New ideas also make for conflict. Old African chiefs hated roads and railways: they said they brought in strangers who corrupted the young people with new ideas and made them rebellious. They were quite right. It is far easier to rule a primitive tribe than a modern democracy where every individual is ready to criticize the government, where everyone has his own ideas about politics and religion, and where dozens of societies, unions, religious sects claim independence and support ambitious leaders who are ready to fight at any time for their "rights."

The more education a man has the more likely he is to be independent in his views and obstinate in sticking to them. A committee of professors, I can assure you, is much harder to manage than a council of African chiefs.

And this throws light on another argument brought forward to prove that individuality is vanishing from the world—the enormous increase of law and regulation, the growing power of the police. In my primitive African tribe, law enforcement was in the hands of village chiefs. There was very little theft. I could leave my bungalow wide open and unguarded for three weeks at a time and nothing was ever taken. We had crimes of passion and crimes of witchcraft, but no criminal class, no crooks as you know them in the big city, no cranks, no anarchists—so we did not require an elaborate structure of law.

You do not need traffic police where there is no wheeled traffic. You do not need postal bylaws where no one knows how to write. But the modern state, simply because of the independence of its citizens, the complication of their demands, needs a huge machine of law and police. This is not a proof of the mass mind but the exact opposite—of a growing number of people who think and act for themselves, and, rightly or wrongly, are ready to defy the old simple rules founded on custom.

Thus, the modern state has lost its mass mind in getting education. But, you will say, this education destroys the primitive mass mind only to replace it with a number of mob minds: in the crowds which queue for the films or a match, read the same newspapers, and shout for the same spellbinders. Mass education is driving out the sound, traditional culture to bring in a lot of half-baked slogans. It produces the shallow brain seeking only to be distracted from serious reflection.

But these "mobs" have no resemblance to those of the tribal world where every individual does the same thing at the same time—hunts, dances, drinks in the mass. Even if he had the will to do anything else, it would not be there to do. The modern individual has an immense choice of occupation and amusement. So that the "mass" of sight-seers at any show place today is actually composed of individuals who have freely chosen to join that crowd and will join a different one tomorrow. What looks like a proof of the mob mind is really evidence of spreading interests among the people and a variety of occupations. And if some of these interests are "popular," aimed at a crowd which is not very critical or reflective, they are a good deal more so than interests which were the only recourse of their ancestors—dog-fighting, bear-baiting, the fit-up melodrama or one-night stand, once a year, and booze.

In the best educated countries, you find the biggest demand for something new in amusement as well as for instruction. Education enlarges all the interests of a man. Apart from what he learns, he acquires a general curiosity and a wider taste.

Compare the press of today with that of a hundred or even fifty years ago. You will find a far greater variety of subjects appealing to a greater variety of tastes. You will find instructive articles on matters formerly dealt with only in the special magazines. Perhaps they don't aim at a learned audience, but they help the general reader to get some idea of what the experts are doing in atomic research or medicine or even astronomy. If you want to write a best seller, your best subject nowadays is probably cosmology.

But if a hundred thousand people are ready to buy a book on the nature of the universe, you have a mass demand at the bookshops. The mass demand is not a proof of falling standards: it means that millions are being educated who would formerly have been left in the illiterate mass. There are "masses" reading learned works just as there are other "masses" going to popular films. The number of people with a good university education is many hundred times what it was fifty years ago, and that explains the immense development of arts and literature in experimental forms that would have had no chance of appreciation before. And in the millions in the next category who have just become literate in the last generation, whose reactions to education have given rise to this illusion of an increasing "mass mind," what we are seeing is not a collapse of standards, but a very rapid improvement. The crowds at the cinemas and the bus loads on the sight-seeing tours are on the way up. They have already left the mass; they are individuals seeking ideas for themselves.

The mass mind idea is not only a bit of nonsense, it is a dangerous nonsense. It leads to a profound defeatism, to the secret and unacknowledged belief that the dictators hold all the trumps.

The reasoning, when you bring it to light, is something like this. There are two kinds of education in the world: the free, which develops the individual according to his nature, and the specialized, which turns out doctors, scientists, mechanics—useful servants of the state or of industry. In a democracy each individual has both types. In the Soviet he gets only the specialized—the whole plan is to make him a state slave.

But it seems that free education merely debases the standards of thought and life by producing mob minds without spiritual strength. Meanwhile the Soviet acquires millions of workers, docile as serfs, yet skillful as our own craftsmen. Aiming deliberately at the creation of a mass mind it will easily defeat the free world, where opinions are shallow and divided.

But this is based on bad psychology. The West is not producing a mass mind, but a variety of strong minds with the richest sense of adventure and will for discovery. The East is not succeeding in obtaining a mass mind either—it is going in the opposite direction. Merely by process of education, it is producing every year people who can at least think a little more freely than illiterate peasants, who are very likely therefore to think critical thoughts, however much they may hide them. That is why the task of the dictatorship becomes constantly more difficult, why it is obliged to stiffen its grip, to hire more police, to bribe more spies, and to purge its own party, every year or so, of "deviators."

What I suggest is that no kind of education, however narrow, can produce the mass mind. The reason is that minds are creative, that thoughts wander by themselves and cannot be controlled by the cleverest police. All education is free in this sense; it cannot be shut up within walls. To teach people to think, if only to make them more useful as soldiers and mechanics, is to open all thoughts to them—a whole world of new ideas. And though the dictator may wish to think of them as a proletariat they have already begun to leave the proletariat.

The "mass mind" is a delusion. How many dictators have been amazed when their rule, which seemed so strong, has collapsed in a few hours, without a friend?

## Study suggestions

1.   Identify sentences which give the keynote ideas of the paragraphs.

2.   Choose from these at least two and write paragraphs in which you agree or disagree. Give reasons.

3.   Compare the tribal mind of primitive tribes with the ideas and reactions of people in contact with others.

4.   Why is it easier to rule a primitive tribe than a modern democracy? A council of African chiefs than a committee of professors?

5.   What comparison does the writer give of education in the Soviet and in the free countries? Written some ten years ago, is this still true? Why does the task of dictatorship grow "more difficult"?

6.   "To teach people to think . . . is to open all thoughts to them—a whole world of new ideas." Write a theme illustrating from three fields of thought the truth of this.

7.   Compare the thought in this essay with that in "Compulsive Suburbia."

8.   In a paragraph illustrate the sentence, "Education enlarges all the interests of man."

9.   How has he proved the concluding thought that "The mass mind is a delusion"?

# THE EDUCATED MAN

*Jacques Barzun*

For a writer to express himself publicly about the Educated Man
is perhaps as dangerous as for a lady to bring up the topic of the
Virtuous Woman. In both cases everybody's attention immediately
shifts from the matter in hand to the person who is discussing it.
What of his or her qualifications? If a writer modestly pretends
that he does not consider himself an educated man, then what business has he to be writing on the subject? And if he does allow,
again modestly, that he *is* educated, then he is suspected of talking down to those less favored by the gods than he.

Fortunately the present mental state of the world cuts short any
shilly-shallying between true and false modesty. Modern society
is not geared to produce, receive or respect the educated man, and
it is hard to imagine anyone in his senses claiming the title as an
honor. The term is in fact seldom used. "Highbrow" has replaced
it, and since to prove that his own brow is attractively low—a thin
line of common sense between two hairy hedges denoting com-
mon-manliness. One's intellect or learned profession or habit of
self-cultivation is something to hide or live down, and this is true
even though more and more people are being schooled and col-
leged and "educationed" than ever before.

All the purposes and achievements of Western man in the
twentieth century conspire, for the time being, to blot out the
meaning of education. Looked at globally, today's task is to "edu-
cate" the peoples of the earth to mass production and national
independence. In this effort the world's work and the world's wealth

are now being redistributed among nations, classes and persons, and vast layers of mankind are slowly emerging from ancestral poverty and a sense of wrong. It is a mighty spectacle and one that the highbrow should not scorn, for the ideals and techniques which are at work come straight out of our past culture in the highbrow sense—out of the thoughts and books of educated men, from Jefferson to Bernard Shaw. But it is also true that the pace and scale of this great transformation take the heaviest toll on those best fitted to carry on the work of culture itself. Peace of mind, solitude, long stretches of concentration, have become luxuries almost beyond reach. We express this very inadequately by saying that we are "frightfully busy *just now*." Deep down we know that the condition is permanent for all those who cannot afford the blessed release of a nervous breakdown.

Now the educated man as we have known him in the past has roots in an entirely different soil and breathes a different air. He is a product of leisure and independence, of established institutions and quiet maturing. His destination is a society of his own kind, in which his role is private and his superiority welcome. He does contribute to others' enjoyment of life by sharing with them the pleasures of conversation and friendship and spoken wisdom, but the enrichment of his own mind is his chief concern. He can attend to this, not only because he has the time and the means but also because he does not have to justify his existence nor to issue progress reports on his life-long "individual project." Whatever he does to earn fame or money, from winning battles to farming estates, he is not so bedeviled by it that he lacks time to engage in the fundamental activities of the educated, which are: to read, write, talk and listen.

Actually, everybody would be happier if the plain fact were admitted (as Jefferson admitted it in his plan for public education in Virginia) that no amount of industry or even of acquired knowledge will make an educated man. The specialist knows a great deal and is not educated. The pedant knows more than enough and is not educated. Why then be ashamed of not having what comes mainly from native endowment? Is it sensible to growl about not having absolute pitch or not being a champion billiard player? To resent not being educated is particularly absurd when one con-

siders that education, like virtue, is its own reward, nothing more
—nothing, certainly, to brag about. Indeed one test of a true education is that it sits lightly on the possessor. He knows better than
anybody else how thin in spots is the mantle which others would
pluck from him.

Contrariwise, a frankly aggressive envy of the educated few by
the unlettered many is thoroughly justified. It is a fair guess that
the solid citizens who put Socrates to death said to themselves:
"Why should this outrageously ugly mug spend his days talking
with brilliant young men while we wear ourselves out in the fig
business?" And to this there is really no amiable answer. Resentment based on democratic equality and patriotism (figs are the
cornerstone of empire) is what precipitates the tragedy. Socrates
always seems to be saying, "Don't you wish you were like me!"
while pointing out that only a chance-selected few can make the
attempt. In reality Socrates is not saying or thinking any such
thing, but he is the living demonstration of an offensive truth.
Hence the accusation which leads to the hemlock cocktail.

With us, the democratic assumption works more gently. It easily
prevails by sheer force of numbers. Whatever is alarmingly different or superior is leveled off like the froth on the glass of beer. Go
to the friendliest social dinner, and the conversation will run exclusively on current events and common experiences—so much so
that after dinner the men and women form separate groups and
talk business in the one, domesticity in the other. The correct mixture of passion and detachment about beliefs, which makes of con-
viviality something more than eating and drinking together, is less
and less attainable.

Despite appearances, the common language of the educated is
neither difficult in itself nor overwhelming in extent. The well-
read have not read everything, and after a while—as somebody
said very wittily—you begin to know things ex officio. In any case
facility does not come by grinding away of nights and memorizing
obscure facts. Obscurity is the very opposite of culture as it is the
opposite of good breeding. But what is required for mastery is a
lively and insatiable interest. This is the thing that cannot be faked.
And this is also what makes it impossible to "climb" into educated
society under false pretenses as people do into snobbish, moneyed

or artistic society. The brotherhood of educated men is the one social group which our century cannot open to all by legislative fiat. The irony is that those within have no desire to keep it exclusive—the more the merrier, provided they are the genuine article.

Meantime, from another quarter, the word education has been snatched by business and government to refer to activities ranging from fire drill to political propaganda. The makers of sewing machines have educational departments where you may take lessons in hem-stitching, and so have magazines which use alluring pictures to teach how a young lady in the bath should scrub her back. These genteel accomplishments are not to be despised, but they remind us that while the faith in intellect has receded from the high places, the new thing which goes by the name of education has some distance to go before it reaches the head.

For today's young men and women who went to a genuine seat of learning and took their studies seriously, the blind forces of our society act as a barrier to further self-education. At college the chances are that they absorbed just enough to awake their mind and spur its quest for more learning. It is after college that these young people are stymied. The girl, now married, has no help and is too busy in kitchen and nursery to read a book. The man, saddled early with family responsibilities in a competitive world, must by tireless slaving "make good" in the first ten or fifteen years of his career. By taking work home every night he proves to his employers that he cares for nothing in the world but insurance or law or the prospects of natural gas. It remains a mystery how the world's work got done in the old days when college-trained beginners in business worked only from nine to five and were not deemed traitors to the firm if they were seen at a concert.

Today's beginner, it may be said, learns more about the nature of his job and its interconnections with the rest of the "economy." But what he bones up on during those career-building nights is only in part real knowledge. The rest is artificial verbiage and statistics, like so much that we are now compelled to carry in our heads— bunches of initials, trade names and telephone numbers—incoherent facts by the bushel, which are out of date almost before they are learned. Inevitably this essential rubbish soon overlays anything the young man learned to enjoy in college. At the end of a long day which never really shuts down on business, he cannot attend to that other world of which he was given a glimpse in the classroom, the laboratory or the art gallery. And thus, by a queer turn of the wheel, our present equalizing of social and economic rights, which should create a larger sense of community, actually drives people apart by narrowing the contents of their minds. Our hypothetical young couple shows this, sometimes tragically. They married on the strength of common interests, and five years out of college they have nothing to say to each other except what relates to home or office routine.

But there persists a thirst for spiritual refreshment that cannot be satisfied by the glut of "hard facts." There remains one restless want: imaginative experience. To this need our technological age responds with the most lavish provision of organized entertainment, from gambling and sports to radio and the screens. Here at last we are given a chance to be lifted out of our mechanical concerns and to take part in exciting or amusing or awe-inspiring experiences. No doubt the habit of being entertained, of letting the show come in one eye and out the other, may end by destroying one's power to enjoy such thoughts and visions as one may have. But the world owes something to the men and women who lavish their talents for our pastime, twenty-four hours a day, by sink or bedside, in the air, on the road and to the very edge of the grave. It staggers the imagination to conceive what would happen to mankind in its present state if it were left to its own resources like our forefathers, in caves without canasta and tents without television.

For some few mavericks, however, there is no alternative to despair or boredom except the pleasure of making one's life a means to one's education. Young men and women continue to be born with an insatiable desire to know, and among these not all are bent on knowing the things that are negotiable. These marked souls manage somehow, in spite of all they see around them, to make themselves into educated persons. They show a remarkable power to survive unfavorable environments, such as advertising agencies, movie studios and teachers' colleges. But the oddest thing about them is that without any clear guidance from society at large, and in the teeth of all the disturbing forces of the day, they all develop very much the same interests and rediscover for themselves the original humanities. Literature, philosophy and the arts, religion, political theory and history become staples on which they feed their minds. And with slight variations in diet expressive of different temperaments, they ultimately come into possession of the common knowledge and the common tongue.

Occasionally, of course, they are helped to enter into the Great Conversation, or to keep their footing there, by the presence of other educated men, better entrenched or sufficiently numerous to resist the tides. In one city there is a college truly committed to general education; in another there is an adult reading group; in a third the woman's club actually reads the authors whom it invites to lecture and be stared at. There is no doubt that you could fill Madison Square Garden with educated people. The species is obsolete but not extinct, and you could enlarge an admission fee without offering them anything to see or hear—except their own well-modulated voices.

Alone though they may be much of the time, they are not so much to be pitied as the sociable creatures who must have "people around" or a movie to go to. For the educated person has appropriated so much of other men's minds that he can live on his store like the camel on his reservoir. Everything can become grist to his mill, including his own misery, if he is miserable; for by association with what he knows, everything has echoes and meanings and suggestions ad infinitum. This is, in fact, the test and the use of a man's education, that he finds pleasure in the exercise of his mind.

Pascal once said that all the trouble in the world was due to the fact that man could not sit still in a room. He must hunt, flirt, gamble, chatter. That is man's destiny and it is not to be quarreled with, but the educated man has through the ages found a way to convert passionate activity into a silent and motionless pleasure. He can sit in a room and not perish.

1.  Comment on the dilemma Barzun describes in his opening paragraph as an introduction to his essay.

2.  Why do people "hide or live down" their education? Refer to an essay on "Mucker Pose" by James Truslow Adams in *Essays for Discussion,* for an excellent discussion of this.

3.  How do world conditions and past culture affect man today?

4.  Compare his mention of "peace of mind, solitude, long stretches of concentration," with Dag Hammarskjold's belief in a Meditation Room and its function.

5.  Compare the educated man of the past with one today.

6.  Define the author's requirements of mastery in an educated society. How has the word *education* been tossed around?

7.  How dependent is modern society on being entertained?

8.  In many communities what various attempts are being made to "rediscover" the humanities?

9.  Comment on the last sentence of the next to last paragraph, and the last paragraph.

10.  Suggested theme topics:
     The Art of Conversation
     My Ideas of the Educated Person
     The Use of Solitude
     "We are Frightfully Busy"

# HOW BIG IS ONE

*Edward Weeks*

My late friend, the French writer Raoul de Roussy de Sales, who knew America intimately, used to tease me about our infatuation with bigness. "It's in your blood," he would say. "When I listen to

Americans talking on shipboard, or in a Paris restaurant, or here in New York, it is only a question of time before someone will come out with that favorite boast of yours—*'the biggest in the world!'* The New York skyline, or the Washington Monument, or the Chicago Merchandise Mart—the biggest in the world. You say it without thinking what it means." How right he was, yet until he prodded me about it, I had never realized that this was indeed our national boast. We take pride in being big, and in a youthful way we used to think that bigness was our own special prerogative. But now we know better; now we find ourselves confronted with nations or with groups of nations which are quite as big as we are and which have the potential of being considerably bigger. This calls for a new orientation; indeed, I think it might be timely if we examine this concept of bigness and try to determine how it has affected our private lives and our thinking.

We have been in love with bigness ever since the adolescence of our democracy. The courtship began on the frontier: the uncut virgin forests, so dense and terrifying; the untamed flooding rivers; the limitless prairies; the almost impassable Sierras—to overcome obstacles like these, man, so puny in comparison, had to outdo himself. He had to be bigger than Hercules. The English live on a small, contained island, and English humor is naturally based on understatement; but an American when he is having fun always exaggerates.

Our first hero of the frontier was a superman, Davy Crockett, who could outshoot, outfight, and outwoo anyone. One day he sauntered into the forest for an airing but forgot to take his thunderbolt along. This made it embarrassing when he came face to face with a panther. The scene is described in the old almanac, as Howard Mumford Jones says, "in metaphoric language which has all the freshness of dawn." The panther growled and Crockett growled right back—"He grated thunder with his teeth"—and so the battle began. In the end, the panther, tamed, goes home with Davy, lights the fire on a dark night with flashes from his eyes, brushes the hearth every morning with his tail, and rakes the garden with his claws. Davy did the impossible, and listening to the legends of his prowess made it easier for the little guy on the frontier to do the possible.

Davy Crockett had a blood brother in Mike Fink, the giant of the river boatmen, and first cousins in Tony Beaver and Paul Bunyan of the North Woods and Pecos Bill of the Southwest. They were ringtailed roarers, and everything they did had an air of gigantic plausibility. Prunes are a necessary part of the lumberjack's diet, and Paul Bunyan's camp had such a zest for prunes that the prune trains which hauled the fruit came in with two engines, one before and one behind pushing. "Paul used to have twenty flunkies sweepin' the prunestones out from under the tables, but even then they'd get so thick we had to wade through 'em up over our shoes sometimes on our way in to dinner. They'd be all over the floor and in behind the stove and piled up against the windows where they'd dumped 'em outside so the cook couldn't see out at all hardly. . . . In Paul's camp back there in Wisconsin the prunestones used to get so thick they had to have twenty ox-teams haulin' 'em away, and they hauled 'em out in the woods, and the chipmunks ate 'em and grew so big the people shot 'em for tigers." Only an American could have invented that build-up, and I am grateful to Esther Shephard for having recaptured the legend so accurately in her *Paul Bunyan*.

Texas, with its fondness for bigness, preferred the living man to the legend: it provided the space for men like Richard King, the founder of the King Ranch. Richard King's story as told by Tom Lea is Horatio Alger multiplied by a thousand. The son of Irish immigrants, he ran off to sea at the age of eleven; a river boat captain in his twenties, he came ashore, married the parson's daughter, bought 15,000 acres of desert at two cents an acre, and went into the cattle business. His close friend and adviser was Lieutenant Colonel Robert E. Lee of the Second United States Cavalry, and it was Lee who gave King what has come to be the family slogan: "Buy land; and never sell." The King Ranch has grown to 700,000 acres in Texas with big offshoots in Kentucky, Pennsylvania, Australia, Cuba, and Brazil, and those of us who dwell in cities and suburbia have developed a kind of Mount Vernon reverence for this vast domain. It is just about as big, we think, as a good ranch ought to be.

I entered publishing in the summer of 1923 as a book salesman in New York. As I look back over the thirty-five years of my working life, I recognize that a significant change has taken place in our business community. The motorcars which I used to covet as a young bachelor, the Stutz Bearcat, the Mercer, the Simplex, the Locomobile, the Pierce Arrow—all these beauties and hundreds of the lesser breeds, like the Hupmobile, the Maxwell, the Franklin, the Stanley Steamer, and the Moon—are museum pieces today. The beauty and the originality which went into their design have been melted down and vulgarized in the models of the five major companies which survive.

In the days I am speaking of, Mr. Potts was our family grocer, and he knew the exact cuts of roast beef and lamb which would bring joy to my father's heart, just as he was prepared for my mother's remonstrance when there was too much gristle. There used to be a family grocer, like Mr. Potts, in every American community. Then some genius in Memphis, Tennessee, came up with the Piggly-Wiggly, the first gigantic cash and carry where the customer waited on himself, and in no time there were chains of these supermarkets stretching across the country. Such consolidation as this has been going on in every aspect of business, and at a faster and faster tempo.

When I was a book salesman, an American book publisher who sold a million dollars' worth of his books in one year was doing quite a prosperous business. Today a publisher who sells only a million dollars' worth of books a year cannot afford to remain in business; he has to join forces with another and larger publisher so that their combined production will carry them over the break-even point.

In the nineteen-twenties almost every American city had two newspapers, and the larger ones had four or five, and there is no doubt that this competition for ideas, for stories, for the truth was a healthy thing for the community. Today most American communities are being served by a single paper.

Of the daily papers that were being published in this country in 1929, 45 per cent have either perished or been consolidated. This consolidation, this process of making big ones out of little ones, is a remorseless thing, and it may be a harmful thing if it tends to regiment our thinking.

We Americans have a remarkable capacity for ambivalence.

On the one hand we like to enjoy the benefits of mass production, and on the other we like to assert our individual taste. Ever since the Civil War we have been exercising our genius to build larger and larger combines. Experience has taught us that when these consolidations grow to the size of a giant octopus, we have got to find someone to regulate them. When our railroads achieved almost insufferable power, we devised the Interstate Commerce Commission, and we eventually found in Joseph Eastman a regulator of impeccable integrity who knew as much as any railroad president. We have not had such good luck with our other regulatory agencies, as the recent ignoble record of the FCC makes clear. What troubles me even more than the pliancy of FCC commissioners to political pressure is their willingness to favor the pyramiding under a single ownership of television channels, radio stations, and newspapers. Isn't this the very monopoly they were supposed to avoid?

The empire builders, who were well on their way to a plutocracy, were brought within bounds by the first Roosevelt. Then under the second Roosevelt it was labor's turn, and in their bid for power they have raised the challenge of what regulations can be devised which will bring them to a clearer recognition of their national responsibility. In the not far future we can see another huge decision looming up: When atomic energy is harnessed for industrial use, will it be in the hands of a few private corporations or in a consolidation which the government will control? My point is that in the daily exposure to such bigness the individual is made to feel smaller than he used to be, smaller and more helpless than his father and grandfather before him.

I realize, of course, that twice in this century our capacity to arm on an enormous scale has carried us to victory with a speed which neither the Kaiser nor Hitler believed possible. But it is my anxiety that, in a cold war which may last for decades, the maintenance of bigness, which is necessary to cope with the U.S.S.R., may regiment the American spirit.

In his book, *Reflections on America,* Jacques Maritain, the French philosopher, draws a sharp distinction "between the spirit of the American people and the logic of the superimposed structure or ritual of civilization." He speaks of "the state of tension, of hidden conflict, between this spirit of the people and this logic of the structure; the steady, latent rebellion of the spirit of the people against the logic of the structure." Maritain believes that the spirit of the American people is gradually overcoming and breaking the logic of their materialistic civilization. I should like to share his optimism, but first we have some questions to answer, questions about what the pressure of bigness is doing to American integrity and to American taste.

Henry Wallace has called this the century of the Common Man. Well, the longer I live in it the more I wonder whether we are producing the Uncommon Man in sufficient quantity. No such doubts were entertained a century ago. When Ralph Waldo Emerson delivered his famous address on "The American Scholar" to the Phi Beta Kappa Society of Harvard in 1837, he was in a mood of exhilaration, not doubt, and he heralded among other things a change which had taken place in American literature. It was a change in the choice of subject matter; it was a change in approach, and it showed that we had thrown off the leading strings of Europe. Here is how he described it:

> The elevation of what was called the lowest class in the state assumed in literature a very marked and benign an aspect. Instead of the sublime and beautiful, the near, the low, the common, was explored and poetized. . . . The literature of the poor, the feelings of the child, the philosophy of the street, the meaning of household life, are the topics of the time. It is a great stride. It is a sign—is it not?—of new vigor when the extremities are made active, when currents of warm life run into the hands and the feet. . . . This writing is blood-warm. Man is surprised to find that things near are not less beautiful and wondrous than things remote. The near explains the far. The drop is a small ocean. A man is related to all nature. This perception of the worth of the vulgar is fruitful in discoveries.

This change from the appreciation of the elite to the appreciation of the commonplace, or as Emerson called it, the vulgar, has been increasingly magnified under the pressure of numbers. But were Emerson able to return to us for a short visit, I am not sure that he would be altogether happy about what we have done to elevate the vulgar in literature or in television.

In contemporary literature, new books—the best we can produce—are still published in hard covers and sold to a discriminating body of readers. If I had to guess, I should say that there are about one million discriminating readers in this country today, and what disturbs me as an editor is that this number has not increased with the population; it has not increased appreciably since the year 1920. What has increased is the public for comic books, for murder mysteries, for sex and sadism. This debasement, especially in fiction, was most noticeable in the early stages of our paperbacks, when the racks in any drugstore were crowded with lurid, large-bosomed beauties who were being either tortured or pursued. Recently there has been an improvement, both in quantity and in seriousness, thanks to the editors of Anchor Books and the New American Library, thanks also to a feeling of outrage which was expressed in many communities. But it still seems to me regrettable that after a hundred years of public education we have produced such a demand for the lowest common denominator of emotionalism.

Am I, I sometimes wonder, a minority of one when I shudder at certain photographs in our pictorial magazines? The picture of a Negro being lynched; the picture of an airliner which has crashed and burned, with that naked body to the left identified as an opera singer whose voice we have all heard and loved; the picture of a grieving mother whose child has just been crushed in an automobile accident? Am I a minority of one in thinking that these are invasions of privacy, indecent and so shocking that we cringe from the sight?

Television, for which we once had such high hope, is constantly betrayed by the same temptation. It can rise magnificently to the occasion, as when it brought home to us the tragedy in Hungary, yet time and again its sponsored programs sink to a sodden level of brutality, shooting, and torture. And is there any other country in the world which would suffer through such incredible singing commercials as are flung at us? Does the language always have to be butchered for popular appeal, as when we are adjured to "live

modern" and "smoke for real"? Am I a minority of one in thinking that the giveaway programs, by capitalizing on ignorance, poverty, and grief, are a disgrace? These are deliberate efforts to reduce a valuable medium to the level of the bobby-soxers.

There was a time when the American automobiles led the
world in their beauty, diversity, and power, but the gaudy gondolas
of today are an insult to the intelligence. In an era of close crowd-
ing when parking is an insoluble problem, it was sheer arrogance
on the part of the Detroit designers to produce a car which was
longer than the normal garage, so wasteful of gasoline, so laden
with useless chromium and fantails that it costs a small fortune to
have a rear fender repaired. I saw in a little Volkswagen not long
ago a sign in the windshield reading, "Help Stamp out Cadillacs!"
There speaks the good-natured but stubborn resistance of the
American spirit against the arrogance of Detroit.

Is it inevitable in mass production that when you cater to the
many, something has to give, and what gives is quality? I wonder if
this has to be. I wonder if the great majority of the American people do not have more taste than they are credited with. The phenomenal increase in the sale of classical music recordings the moment they became available at mass production prices tells me
that Americans will support higher standards when they are given
the chance. I stress the aberration of taste in our time because I
think it is something that does not have to be. The republic deserves better standards, not only for the elect, but straight across
the board.

I wish that our directors of Hollywood, the heads of our great
networks, and those who, like the automobile designers in Detroit,
are dependent upon American taste—I wish that such arbiters
would remember what Alexis de Tocqueville wrote a hundred
and twenty-five years ago in his great book, *Democracy in America*.
"When the conditions of society are becoming more equal," said
Tocqueville, "and each individual man becomes more like all the
rest, more weak and more insignificant, a habit grows up of ceas-
ing to notice the citizens to consider only the people, and of overlooking individuals to think only of their kind."

It seems to me that our tastemakers have been guilty of this
fallacy ever since the close of World War II. They have ceased to

notice the citizens and consider only the people, just as Tocqueville warned. They no longer plan for the differences in individual taste, but think only of people in the mass.

In the years that followed the crash of 1929, Americans began to transfer their trust from big business to big government; if big business and banking, so ran the reasoning, could not be trusted to keep us out of depressions, perhaps big government could. Gradually in this emergency we began to shape up our version of the welfare state, a concept which was evolving in many parts of the Western world and to which both Democrats and Republicans are now committed.

A welfare state requires a big government with many bureaus, just as big government in its turn requires big taxes. We embarked on big government with the idea of safeguarding those segments of American society which were most in jeopardy, and now after twenty-five years of experimentation we are beginning to learn that the effects of big government upon the individual are both good and bad. It is good to provide the individual with security, and to give him the chance to adjust his special claims; another and perhaps unsuspected asset has been dramatized by Edwin O'Connor in his novel, *The Last Hurrah,* in which he showed us how President Roosevelt had diminished and destroyed the sovereignty of the city boss. It is Washington, not Ward Eight, that has the big patronage to give today.

The maleffects of big government are more subtle. Consider, for instance, the debilitating effect of heavy taxation. I remember a revealing talk I had with Samuel Zemurray when he was president of the United Fruit Company. Born in Russia, Zemurray made his start here by pushing a fruit cart through the streets of Gadsden, Alabama. Then he set up his own business as a banana jobber by selling the bunches of bananas the fruit company didn't want. He sold out to United Fruit and continued to acquire shares until he controlled the majority of the stock. In the autumn of F.D.R.'s second term, when we were sitting in adjoining Pullman seats on the long run to Washington, Mr. Zemurray began talking about the President's promises to "the forgotten man." "He made three promises," Zemurray said, "and he has kept two of them: the promise to labor and that to the farmer. The promise he has not kept is to the little businessman. Under today's taxes it would be quite impossible for a young man to do as I did—he would never be able to accumulate enough capital."

Some years after this talk, in 1946 to be exact, I was on a plane flying West from Chicago. It was a Sunday morning and the man who sat beside me at the window seat had the big bulk of the Chicago *Tribune* spread open on his knees, but out of politeness' sake he gave me the proverbial greeting, "Hello, where are you from?" And when I said, "From Boston," his face lit up. "Do they still have good food at the Automat?" he asked. "Boy, that's where I got my start and it certainly seems a lifetime ago." And then in a rush out poured his life story in one of those sudden confidences with which Americans turn to one another: How he had become a salesman of bedroom crockery, and how his Boston boss had refused to raise him to thirty dollars a week. In his anger he had switched to the rival company, and under their encouragement he had simply plastered Cape Cod with white washbowls, pitchers, soap dishes, and tooth mugs. "Seven carloads I sold in the first year," he told me. The company called him back to its head office in Chicago, and then came the crash. The company owned a bank and lake shore real estate, and when the smoke had cleared away and recovery was possible, he found himself running the whole shebang. His wife hadn't been able to keep up with it all, he said, shaking his head sadly. He had had his first coronary, and what kept him alive today was his hope for his two sons, who had just come out of the Navy. "But, you know," he said to me, his eyes widening, "they neither of them want to come in with me. They don't seem to want to take the chances that I took. They want to tie up with a big corporation. I just don't get it."

Security for the greatest number is a modern shibboleth, but somebody still has to set the pace and take the risk. And if we gain security, but sacrifice first venture and then initiative, we may find, as the Labor Party in England did, that we end with all too little incentive. As I travel this country since the war, I have the repeated impression that fewer and fewer young men are venturing into business on their own. More and more of them seek the safety of the big corporations. There are compelling reasons for this, the ever-shrinking margin of operating profit being the most insistent. But if we keep on trading independence and initiative for security, I wonder what kind of American enterprise will be left fifty years from now.

A subtle conditioning of the voter has been taking place during the steady build-up of big government. During the depression and recovery we took our directives from Washington almost without question; so too during the war, when we were dedicated to a single purpose and when the leadership in Washington in every department was the best the nation could supply. And for almost twenty years local authority and the ability to test our political initiative in the home county and state has dwindled. About the only common rally which is left to us is the annual drive for the community fund. Too few of our ablest young men will stand for local office. Their jobs come first, and they console themselves with the thought that if they succeed they may be called to Washington in maturity. We used to have a spontaneous capacity for rallying; we could be inflamed, and our boiling point was low. Our present state of lethargy, our tendency to let George do it in Washington, is not only regrettable, it is bad for our system.

I remember one of the last talks I had with Wendell Willkie. He was still showing the exhaustion of defeat, and he spoke with concern as he said, "One of the weaknesses in our democracy is our tendency to delegate. During an election year we will work our hearts out, and then when the returns are in, we think we have done our part. For the next three years what happens to the party is the responsibility of the national committeemen. Have you ever looked at them?"

The decision having been made to drop the atomic bomb on Hiroshima, President Truman tells us that he retired and slept soundly. But those in authority in these days are less sure. The delegation of so much authority to those in Washington and the difficulties of dealing with an opponent so ruthless and enigmatic as Russia seem to have developed in our most responsible officials a secretiveness and an uncertainty which make it hard for the citizen to follow. This administration has practiced a policy of nondisclosure toward the press and the electorate which has left the average citizen in a state of constant uncertainty. I have nothing but admiration for the dedication and stamina of Secretary Dulles, but I wish with all my heart that he had made our purpose and our commitments clearer for our allies and for our own people to understand. When we pulled that dam out from under Nasser's feet, we projected a crisis which must have come as a great shock to France and Britain. And how can we blame the young leaders of Hungary for misunderstanding the words "dynamic liberation" when we at home had no clear notion of what they meant? It was inexcusable not to have warned the American people that the Sputniks were coming and that greater exertions must be expected of us. This is no time for remoteness or for lulling slogans or for the avoidance of hard truths. The volume of material, the thousands of articles dealing with the great issues of today which are pouring into my office from unknown, unestablished writers, testifies to the conscientiousness and the courage of American thinking. The pity of it is that such people have not been taken more fully into the confidence of their own government.

I have said that the concept of bigness has been an American ideal since our earliest times. I pointed to our propensity to build larger and larger combines ever since the Civil War, and how the process of consolidation has speeded up during the past thirty-five years. I suggested that we cannot have the fruits of mass production without suffering the effects of regimentation. And I ask that we look closely at what the pressure of bigness has done to American taste and opinion. Is the individual beginning to lose self-confidence and his independence? In short, how big is one?

Surely, in an atomic age self-reliance and self-restraint are needed as they have never been before. See with what force Van Wyck Brooks expresses this truth in his *Writer's Notebook:*

> Unless humanity is intrinsically decent, heaven help the world indeed, for more and more we are going to see man naked. There is no stopping the world's tendency to throw off imposed restraints, the *religious* authority that is based on the ignorance of the many, the *political* authority that is based on the knowledge of the few. The time is coming when there will be nothing to restrain men except what they find

in their own bosoms; and what hope is there for us then unless it is true that, freed from fear, men are naturally predisposed to be upright and just?

As we look about us, what evidence can we find that in an atmosphere overshadowed by Russia and made murky by the distrust of McCarthyism there are citizens who will still stand forth, upright and ready to speak the hard truth for the public good? How big is one?

One is as big as George F. Kennan, who believes that we cannot continue to live in this state of frozen belligerency in Europe. We do not have to accept all of his proposals before applauding his thoughtful, audacious effort to break up the ice.

One is as big as Omer Carmichael, the superintendent of schools in Louisville, Kentucky, who led the movement for voluntary integration in his border state; as big as Harry Ashmore, the editor of the Little Rock, Arkansas, *Gazette,* for his fearless and reasonable coverage of the Faubus scandal.

One is as big as Frank Laubach, who believes in teaching the underdeveloped nations how to read their own languages, and then in supplying them with reading matter which will aid them to develop their farming and health.

One is as big as Linus Pauling, Harold C. Urey, Robert Oppenheimer, and the other editors and sponsors of the *Bulletin of the Atomic Scientists,* who have never underestimated Russian scientific capacities, who have always believed in the peaceful value of scientific exchange and never ceased to struggle against fanaticism in secrecy and security.

One is as big as Edith Hamilton, the classicist, the lover of Greece and of moderation; and as Alice Hamilton, her younger sister, who pioneered in the dangerous field of industrial medicine.

One is as big as Sheldon and Eleanor Glueck, who for years have been guiding lights in the resistant field of juvenile delinquency.

One is as big as Ralph Bunche and Eleanor Roosevelt.

One is as big as Louis M. Lyons, whose interpretation of the news and whose judgment of the popular press have provided, in the words of the Lauterbach Award, "a conscience for a whole profession."

One is as big as I. I. Rabi, a brilliant scientist and a passionate humanist, who, on being asked how long it would take us to catch up to Russia and to safeguard our long-range future, replied, "A generation. You know how long it takes to change a cultural pattern. The growing general awareness of this need will help us, but nevertheless we will have to work hard to succeed in a generation."

One is as big as Frederick May Eliot, president for twenty-one years of the American Unitarian Association, who worked himself to the bone for the deepening of faith and for reconciliation.

One is as big as you yourself can make it.

## Study suggestions

1.   Americans seem to have won the reputation of exaggeration and of boasting. How deserved is this? How does the writer contrast English humor with the American?

2.   Identify other folk-lore and "tall stories" typical of early humor.

3.   What trends in the country does he explore?

4.   How does he answer his question "about what the pressure of bigness is doing to American integrity and to American taste"?

5.   Why did Henry Wallace call this the century of the Common Man? How did Emerson feel and how would he feel now?

6.   Explain his use of "lowest common denominator of emotionalism" in magazines, on television—even in the automobile. How does he feel about standards today?

7.   Comment on his idea of "the mass" with that in the previous essay.

8.   In your opinion is security a "modern shibboleth"?

9.   In answering his question, "How big is one," analyze each illustration for the contributions of each. What other names would you add?

10.   Write a theme in which you answer his question, but with your illustration and opinions today.

# SPORTS AND
# THE OUT-OF-DOORS

*Man responds to challenge because that is the nature of man.*

JAMES RAMSEY ULLMAN

# WHY MEN CLIMB MOUNTAINS

*Wilfrid Noyce*

I am sitting in the little Gamba hut on Mont Blanc, the highest mountain of Western Europe. Storm has driven us down from the Peuterey Ridge. Now there is nothing for it but to return to Courmayeur and wait on the weather, which looks as though it will take some days to mend. And, as I wait, between glum inspections of the town's various barometers, I ask myself: why do I climb?

It goes back a long way. Awe and admiration of mountains are almost as old as the human race. Did not the Jews imagine Moses upon Mount Sinai, the Greeks place their gods upon Olympus? And though in the 18th Century, in Europe at any rate, mountains were disliked by many (Doctor Johnson described them as a "uniformity of barrenness"), yet in the 19th, under the guidance of prophets like Wordsworth and John Ruskin, they once more came to be regarded as beautiful and awesome, and as fit places for worship and the practice of art, for travel and recreation.

"That is all very well," the critics said, "but why pollute the sanctuary by trying to *climb* them?" In other words, why waste your time sitting in wet huts and bivouacs, when your family would much prefer you to be with them at home.

I have returned to Chamonix now, and am sitting in a little café looking out at the rain, and at the main square with its statue of Horace Benedict de Saussure. He stands there, looking up toward the summit of Mont Blanc, now covered in thick black cloud, his eyes directed by the pointing finger of a guide. Why did this young Genevese scientist come to Chamonix in 1760, and offer a reward to the first man who should stand upon that summit?

De Saussure's reason, of course, was scientific. He wanted to know what the air, the snow, the temperatures and so on were like up there, and whether the human body could stand such altitudes.

When, in 1787, he made his own ascent—it was the third successful climb of Mont Blanc—he spent four hours on the top with thermometer, hygrometer and the rest, despite acute bodily discomfort, in order to leave a detailed record. And I think that all of us,
even now, have this detached scientific interest in what it is like
"up there," in how our bodies will behave at a height or in the intricacies of rock—even though the scientific has been discarded as a
principal reason for making ascents.

It was during the 19th Century that all such pretexts were shed,
and the idea of mountaineering for its own sake evolved, hesitantly,
along with all those complex sentiments that are keeping me here,
in the rain, when I might be romping with my children beside the
blue sea of Cornwall.

I think that two strands went into the make-up of the pioneers.
First was the love of mountains. Seeing these great and beautiful
shapes before them, they wanted to reach the top, to explore, to
find in them still more hidden qualities than they could see simply
by looking from below. Having climbed them first by the easiest
way they then wanted to examine every facet, to see them from
every angle, as you would want to know fully anyone or anything
truly loved.

In the Himalaya this latter stage has not yet been reached; the
easiest way is still enough. In Britain, on the other hand, the cycle
has come so far that there are innumerable routes up mountains
from which there is a simple walk down, so that as you struggle up
some vertical crack or wall you may look up and hear a tourist
shouting: "I say, didn't you know there was an easy way round
here?"

But the point about this strand is that it is the beauty of the
mountain for its own sake that holds you in its spell: rock ridge and
snow crest, the sweep of heather and grass. Ever since, as a small
boy, I first fell in love with the outline of the North Welsh hills, I
have enjoyed every side of mountains, seeing them in different
lights, feeling their rock under my fingers and the breath of their
winds against my face.

The second strand is more personal and concerns our own
achievements. To reach most summits required no very high degree of technique. But when the summits had been reached,

and when the ridges and faces came to be explored too, men found that a higher and higher level of skill was necessary to overcome the obstacles of rock step and steeply angled ice slope. Gradually they became interested in the skill for its own sake, developing it slowly and bringing it at last to the perfection we see, for example, in a guide like Gaston Rébuffat.

Perfectly poised, hands low, Rébuffat moves up a rock face on tiny holds; he is always in balance, always looking ahead, calm and assured. Then you try it yourself, find that it's not so easy as it looks, and are absorbed by a longing to master the skill.

The second reason why I climb, therefore, is that I enjoy physical effort and directed skill. I enjoy the sensations of raising my body confidently from ledge to ledge, of swinging my ax rhythmically to form a step and of balancing myself carefully, as I place my foot on the step I have fashioned. In this strand mountaineering is a sport like other sports, and gives all the rewards of well-being and of nicely timed, co-ordinated effort—in co-operation with my companions on the rope.

For here is another reason I climb. I like doing things that demand collaboration to a degree unknown in many sports. Climbing with one or two others, you are no longer a single person, you are a "party," or, when there are a number of climbers, an "expedition." You move as one, feel as one; sometimes your very life depends on your thinking as one. I like the sensation that the rope joining me to my friend is more than a physical bond; it is the reason two small human beings are able to overcome the hugeness of the confronting mountain, and to climb together one degree nearer the stars. It was not by chance that Dante chose a guide, the poet Virgil, to assist him up the Mount of Purgatory to Heaven.

I have a friend, Alf Bridge, who used to climb for years with Colin Kirkus, one of Britain's most brilliant rock climbers between the wars. During World War II Colin was a sergeant in the Bomber Command. One night in 1944, Alf suddenly awoke at 2 A.M. and told his wife that he was going for a walk on the nearby Sheffield moors. He could not explain why he should want to walk at that unusual hour, but when he returned, at about 7 A.M., he sent a telegram to Colin's parents: "Is Colin all right?" The reply came back: "Colin reported missing over Hamburg."

The comradeship by which two men can be almost physically linked, even when the rope no longer joins them, is something worth living for.

I have felt this same comradeship, in exactly the same way, on the bigger climbs of the Himalaya, and particularly on Mount Everest in 1953. We felt that we were a team, and the important thing was not "who" got to the top but that "we" got to the top. I remember especially the afternoon of May twenty-ninth. At 12:50 I was plodding for the second time across the Geneva Spur (26,200 feet), toward the South Col, and I was going very slowly because I had no oxygen. I was carrying forty-five pounds, and would take just three steps, then I would pause. Three steps and a pause. For the moment life held no more than that. But I still remember the excitement of my Sherpa's cry, as he pointed toward the diamond-shaped tip of the south summit, two thousand feet above us. And later, when George Lowe had gone up and I met him above the col, coming down with Hillary and Tenzing, I remember with joy George's ax waving at the top and his cry: "They done it." (When I came to write *South Col* I quoted George at first as saying, "They done it." Then, since George was a teacher, I thought it might hurt him to be so ungrammatical, and I changed it in the galley proofs to a more ordinary "They've done it.")

I remember the excitement and the pleasure; and I remember that I did not think: "If only they had failed, I'd have been at the summit on the next attempt." I claim no credit for this, since I am the most jealous of persons. But it was the expedition, not our individual selves, that had succeeded. And that was how we all felt about it.

Last year I was on an ice mountain in Nepal, much harder than Everest but 6000 feet lower. It is called Machapuchare, Nepalese for "The Fish's Tail," and is said to have an inaccessible summit that is sacred to the gods. At last, after many difficulties, two of us reached a point less than 150 feet from the top and directly below it. It was snowing, and those last feet were a wall of blue ice, polished smooth. We were old friends and had climbed together often before. It hardly needed a spoken word to know that we must go down; the gods had drawn their line here and we must not transgress it.

Why do I climb? Well, if you want yet another reason, I am an escapist. Civilized man is getting farther and farther away from the world of real things, of trees and grass and rocks. He takes his meals out of a tin, a reel of celluloid brings him his amusement. But at the same time it becomes increasingly necessary for him to have an escape hole by which he can flee back to something primitive within him which, against all reason, he still finds necessary to his well-being. The two greatest and most natural escape holes are mountains and the sea.

It is interesting that those who work on the land or the sea usually do not need these escape holes. The city man, on the other hand, from time to time has an irresistible urge to tear off his stiff collar and tie, don old clothes, sweat and shiver, "dig his fingers into the wet earth" and sleep on the hard ground. All these things he can do, to his heart's content, on the untamed mountains.

In the mountains, then, I can feel free as the winds. Civilization forgotten, I can drink from the streams and eat simple food with a pleasure that I had forgotten at my desk. More than that, I can feel a sense of mastery, of new confidence, in the pure primitive joy of pitting myself against natural difficulty. This is not "conquest," and it has always seemed to me a strange misunderstanding when people talk of the "conquest of Everest"—or of any other mountain. Who can say that the Alps are conquered, when Franz Lockmatter, greatest of the Alpine guides, fell to his death from an easy ridge? When Louis Lachenal of Annapurna disappeared into a crevasse on Mont Blanc, which, with the Matterhorn, is the biggest consumer of victims in the Alps? When Tom Bourdillon, the first man to reach 28,700 feet, was killed on a 9000-foot peak in Switzerland? When even our little Welsh Snowdon of 3560 feet each year claims its toll?

The mountain is not conquered, and pray Heaven it never will be. But in measuring himself against it a man strips off the surface husks and stands there, rougher perhaps and yet more real than ever he was in business clothes. And if that goes for you, it goes no less for the friend beside you. If you would really know a person, there is no better device than to climb with him on the same rope, to be overtaken by night together on the same tiny cold ledge with no food. Then you will know better whether he is your friend than if you have spent twenty summers playing golf together, or if he is "always such good company" at cocktail parties.

This overlay of civilization, of course, peels off even more noticeably in the Himalaya, where lack of oxygen and close quarters bring out sharply the differentness of the human types. In a high camp your friend of sea level may turn into a positive ogre. Everything, from his snore to the way he licks his spoon, may so infuriate you that you desire nothing in the world so keenly as to see him fall irretrievably into the deepest crevasse. If you can go on enjoying the same person's mountain company, in any part of the world, for more than ten years, then he is your friend indeed, and in a way more satisfying than any other that I know.

But is even all this, you may ask, worth it? Is it worth sitting in a Chamonix café, in the rain, while your wife and children are waiting far away for you to join them? And suppose you don't come back? Accidents happen to the very best. And if you, too, disappear, how grave is your responsibility to your widow and your children? Is mountain beauty why you climb? You have admitted that you can get this, in a sort of way, from below. Or do you climb to develop skill? Aren't some climbers really gymnasts, and couldn't they get just as much enjoyment out of tennis, or acrobatics? Remember that sometimes you spend whole days on a cliff and never reach a summit at all. And as for escape, just work a month on the land if you want to get cured of that one.

The only way I can answer is to go back to first principles, to the principle of adventure. Everything done that is worth doing is in a sense an "adventure"; it is the human spirit pushing out into unknown regions, usually for no other purpose than to prove itself, to voyage where it has never voyaged before. Without this sense of adventure we humans would be like cows. We must travel to the ends of the earth, to the poles, to the bottom of the sea, and, yes, to the world's highest point, just "because it's there," as George Leigh-Mallory answered when someone asked why he tried to climb Everest. Mallory also has said, "If you cannot see that what we get from this adventure is pure, sheer joy—then it is no use my trying to explain. . . ."

I have said that adventure is usually a collective effort; we share and we enjoy the controlled risk and the discomfort. But the man who has never climbed alone misses something too. To lie by yourself on a high grassy ridge, cradled in the hills, with only the stars for company; to scramble up some rock buttress and be greeted by the infinite prospect of evening beyond; these are experiences we share with no one. There is nothing that will come between you and the mountain. There is no companion to obtrude his presence, however welcome. You feel that you are part of the crags and ridges; and that feeling is very worth the having.

Much that has been said of the dangers of climbing alone is true. But is it not true also of many other of the best adventures of life? Besides, precautions can be taken. The lone climber should determine, for instance, to do nothing that is not well below his normal standard. He may experience frustration, he may have moments of fear (I have been lured too often onto difficult solo climbs), but, in compensation, there will be times when the secret of the Universe will seem almost within his grasp—if he can only hang on for a few seconds more. But no. He has to think about getting down; or the wind gets chilly and he must pull on a sweater. The spell is broken. But it is a spell that he will never forget. Nor will he forget the beauty of that clouded sunset scene, and of the green valleys beyond.

The mention of beauty brings me to perhaps the deepest reason why I climb. Most of us, whether or not we are religious in the conventional sense, feel that some hidden power must be "behind it all." In our everyday lives we have little opportunity to perceive this. But when we are among mountains we are somehow closer to that unfathomable Being.

I do not mean for a moment that I started climbing for religious reasons, or that this enters the heads of many who climb. Most young men and women go to the hills because they are an obvious playground. Many never go beyond that stage but those who keep on will be rewarded with a new and especially happy mountain experience. All the wide ways of glacier and valley and snow summit will still speak to them, but with gentler, more understanding accents.

At forty I no longer feel inclined to do the extreme rock climbs. On the other hand my stamina on a big mountain is better than when I was twenty. The gnat of ambition—not to climb better than your fellows but to do better than you yourself have done before—is still there, pricking me to do what I can, while I can. That is all right, provided I realize that in a few years physical incapacity must temper my ambition. Then I shall still climb, and if the reasons I have given are sound, I shall enjoy climbing as much or even more than now.

Even as I begin this paragraph the storm is cleared. The great white dome towers in weak sunlight above the Vale of Chamonix. To the left, the gaunt Aiguilles in their armor of new snow seem to frown their challenge upon me. I must hurry and get provisions . . . rucksack . . . up to a hut. For in a day or two we may be able to see once again whether we cannot climb the Peuterey Ridge of Mont Blanc.

### Study suggestions

1.  How does the author, an experienced climber, answer his own question?

2.  Explain his feeling that the two greatest and most natural escape holes are mountains and the sea.

3.  Phrases, such as "sense of mastery," "new confidence," "pure primitive joy," give what tone to the essay? Find others.

4.  What sort of companion would he make? Why does he feel climbing together a test of friendship? Yet why does he enjoy climbing alone?

5.  How does beauty affect him?

6.  Comment on his conclusion.

7.  Theme suggestions:
    Mountains I have Climbed
    Youth Hosteling
    Living in the Open
    I am an Escapist
    Facing Dangers
    Exploration

# WE'VE MADE IT!

*Maurice Herzog*

On the third of June, 1950, the first light of dawn found us still clinging to the tent poles at Camp V. Gradually the wind abated, and with daylight, died away altogether. I made desperate attempts to push back the soft, icy stuff which stifled me, but every movement became an act of heroism. My mental powers were numbed: thinking was an effort, and we did not exchange a single word.

What a repellent place it was! To everyone who reached it, Camp V became one of the worst memories of their lives. We had only one thought—to get away. We should have waited for the first rays of the sun, but at half-past five we felt we couldn't stick it any longer.

"Let's go, Biscante," I muttered. "Can't stay here a minute longer."

"Yes, let's go," repeated Lachenal.

Which of us would have the energy to make tea? Although our minds worked slowly we were quite able to envisage all the movements that would be necessary—and neither of us could face up to it. It couldn't be helped—we would just have to go without. It was quite hard enough work to get ourselves and our boots out of our sleeping-bags—and the boots were frozen stiff so that we got them on only with the greatest difficulty. Every movement made us terribly breathless. We felt as if we were being stifled. Our gaiters were as stiff as a board, and I succeeded in lacing mine up; Lachenal couldn't manage his.

"No need for the rope, eh, Biscante?"

"No need," replied Lachenal laconically.

That was two pounds saved. I pushed a tube of condensed milk, some nougat and a pair of socks into my sack; one never knew, the socks might come in useful—they might even do as Balaclavas. For the time being I stuffed them with first-aid equipment. The camera was loaded with a black and white film; I had a color film in reserve. I pulled the movie-camera out from the bottom of my sleeping-bag, wound it up and tried letting it run without film. There was a little click, then it stopped and jammed.

"Bad luck after bringing it so far," said Lachenal.

In spite of our photographer, Ichac's, precautions taken to lubricate it with special grease, the intense cold, even inside the sleeping-bag, had frozen it. I left it at the camp rather sadly: I had looked forward to taking it to the top. I had used it up to 24,000 feet.

We went outside and put on our crampons, which we kept on all day. We wore as many clothes as possible; our sacks were very light. At six o'clock we started off. It was brilliantly fine, but also very cold. Our super-lightweight crampons bit deep into the steep slopes of ice and hard snow up which lay the first stage of our climb.

Later the slope became slightly less steep and more uniform. Sometimes the hard crust bore our weight, but at others we broke through and sank into soft powder snow which made progress exhausting. We took turns in making the track and often stopped without any word having passed between us. Each of us lived in a closed and private world of his own. I was suspicious of my mental processes; my mind was working very slowly and I was perfectly aware of the low state of my intelligence. It was easiest just to stick to one thought at a time—safest, too. The cold was penetrating; for all our special eiderdown clothing we felt as if we'd nothing on. Whenever we halted, we stamped our feet hard. Lachenal went as far as to take off one boot which was a bit tight; he was in terror of frostbite.

"I don't want to be like Lambert," he said. Raymond Lambert, a Geneva guide, had to have all his toes amputated after an eventful climb during which he got his feet frostbitten. While Lachenal rubbed himself hard, I looked at the summits all around us; already we overtopped them all except the distant Dhaulagiri. The complicated structure of these mountains, with which our many laborious exploration had made us familiar, was now spread out plainly at our feet.

The going was incredibly exhausting, and every step was a struggle of mind over matter. We came out into the sunlight, and by way of marking the occasion made yet another halt. Lachenal continued to complain of his feet. "I can't feel anything. I think I'm beginning to get frostbite." And once again he undid his boot.

I began to be seriously worried. I realized very well the risk we were running. I knew from experience how insidiously and quickly frostbite can set in if one is not extremely careful. Nor was Lachenal under any illusions. "We're in danger of having frozen feet. Do you think it's worth it?"

This was most disturbing. It was my responsibility as leader to think of the others. There was no doubt about frostbite being a very real danger. Did Annapurna justify such risks? That was the question I asked myself; it continued to worry me.

Lachenal had laced his boots up again, and once more we continued to force our way through the exhausting snow. The whole of the Sickle glacier was now in view, bathed in light. We still had a long way to go to cross it, and then there was that rock band—would we find a gap in it?

My feet, like Lachenal's, were very cold and I continued to wriggle my toes, even when we were moving, I could not feel them, but that was nothing new in the mountains, and if I kept on moving them it would keep the circulation going.

Lachenal appeared to me as a sort of specter—he was alone in his world, I in mine. But—and this was odd enough—any effort was slightly *less* exhausting than lower down. Perhaps it was hope lending us wings. Even through dark glasses the snow was blinding—the sun beating straight down on the ice. We looked down upon precipitous ridges which dropped away into space, and upon tiny glaciers far, far below. Familiar peaks soared arrow-like into the sky. Suddenly Lachenal grabbed me:

"If I go back, what will you do?"

A whole sequence of pictures flashed through my head: the days of marching in sweltering heat, the hard pitches we had overcome, the tremendous efforts we had all made to lay siege to the mountain, the daily heroism of all my friends in establishing the camps. Now we were nearing our goal. In an hour or two, perhaps, victory would be ours. Must we give up? Impossible! My whole being revolted against the idea. I had made up my mind, irrevocably. Today we were consecrating an ideal, and no sacrifice was too great. I heard my voice clearly:

"I should go on by myself."

I would go on alone. If he wished to go down it was not for me to stop him. He must make his own choice freely.

"Then I'll follow you."

The die was cast. I was no longer anxious. Nothing could stop us now from getting to the top. The psychological atmosphere changed with these few words, and we went forward now as brothers.

I felt as though I were plunging into something new and quite abnormal. I had the strangest and most vivid impressions, such as I had never before known in the mountains. There was something unnatural in the way I saw Lachenal and everything around us. I smiled to myself at the paltriness of our efforts, for I could stand apart and watch myself making these efforts. But all sense of exertion was gone, as though there were no longer any gravity. This diaphanous landscape, this quintessence of purity—these were not the mountains I knew: they were the mountains of my dreams.

The snow, sprinkled over every rock and gleaming in the sun, was of a radiant beauty that touched me to the heart. I had never seen such complete transparency, and I was living in a world of crystal. Sounds were indistinct, the atmosphere like cotton wool.

An astonishing happiness welled up in me, but I could not define it. Everything was so new, so utterly unprecedented. It was not in the least like anything I had known in the Alps, where one feels buoyed up by the presence of others—by people of whom one is vaguely aware, or even by the dwellings one can see in the far distance.

This was quite different. An enormous gulf was between me and the world. This was a different universe—withered, desert, lifeless;

a fantastic universe where the presence of man was not foreseen, perhaps not desired. We were braving an interdict, overstepping a boundary, and yet we had no fear as we continued upward. I thought of the famous ladder of St. Theresa of Avila. Something clutched at my heart.

Did Lachenal share these feelings? The summit ridge drew nearer, and we reached the foot of the ultimate rock band. The slope was very steep and the snow interspersed with rocks.

"Couloir!"

A finger pointed. The whispered word from one to another indicated the key to the rocks—the last line of defense.

"What luck!"

The couloir up the rocks though steep was feasible.

The sky was a deep sapphire blue. With a great effort we edged over to the right, avoiding the rocks; we preferred to keep to the snow on account of our crampons and it was not long before we set foot in the couloir. It was fairly steep, and we had a minute's hesitation. Should we have enough strength left to overcome this final obstacle?

Fortunately the snow was hard, and by kicking steps we were able to manage, thanks to our crampons. A false move would have been fatal. There was no need to make hand-holds—our axes, driven in as far as possible, served us for an anchor.

Lachenal went splendidly. What a wonderful contrast to the early days! It was a hard struggle here, but he kept going. Lifting our eyes occasionally from the slope, we saw the couloir opening out on to . . . well, we didn't quite know, probably a ridge. But where was the top—left or right? Stopping at every step, leaning on our axes we tried to recover our breath and to calm down our racing hearts, which were thumping as though they would burst. We knew we were there now—that nothing could stop us. No need to exchange looks—each of us would have read the same determination in the other's eyes. A slight detour to the left, a few more steps—the summit ridge came gradually nearer—a few rocks to avoid. We dragged ourselves up. Could we possibly be there?

Yes!

A fierce and savage wind tore at us.

We were on top of Annapurna! 8,075 meters, 26,493 feet.

Our hearts overflowed with an unspeakable happiness.

"If only the others could know. . . ."

If only everyone could know!

The summit was a corniced crest of ice, and the precipices on the far side which plunged vertically down beneath us, were terrifying, unfathomable. There could be few other mountains in the world like this. Clouds floated halfway down, concealing the gentle, fertile valley of Pokhara, 23,000 feet below. Above us there was nothing!

Our mission was accomplished. But at the same time we had accomplished something infinitely greater. How wonderful life would now become! What an inconceivable experience it is to attain one's ideal and, at the very same moment, to fulfill oneself. I was stirred to the depths of my being. Never had I felt happiness like this—so intense and yet so pure. That brown rock, the highest of them all, that ridge of ice—were these the goals of a lifetime? Or were they, rather, the limits of man's pride?

"Well, what about going down?"

Lachenal shook me. What were his own feelings? Did he simply think he had finished another climb, as in the Alps? Did he think one could just go down again like that, with nothing more to it?

"One minute, I must take some photographs."

"Hurry up!"

I fumbled feverishly in my sack, pulled out the camera, took out the little French flag which was right at the bottom, and the pennants. Useless gestures, no doubt, but something more than symbols—eloquent tokens of affection and goodwill. I tied the strips of material—stained by sweat and by the food in the sacks—to the shaft of my ice-axe, the only flagstaff at hand. Then I focused my camera on Lachenal.

"Now, will you take me?"

"Hand it over—hurry up!" said Lachenal.

He took several pictures and then handed me back the camera. I loaded a color-film and we repeated the process to be certain of bringing back records to be cherished in the future.

"Are you mad?" asked Lachenal. "We haven't a minute to lose: we must go down at once."

And in fact a glance round showed me that the weather was no longer gloriously fine as it had been in the morning. Lachenal was becoming impatient.

"We must go down!"

He was right. His was the reaction of the mountaineer who knows his own domain. But I just could not accustom myself to the idea that we had won our victory. It seemed inconceivable that we should have trodden those summit snows.

It was impossible to build a cairn; there were no stones; everything was frozen. Lachenal stamped his feet; he felt them freezing. I felt mine freezing too, but paid little attention. The highest mountain to be climbed by man lay under our feet! The names of our predecessors on these heights raced through my mind: Mummery, Mallory and Irvine, Bauer, Welzenbach, Tilman, Shipton. How many of them were dead—how many had found on these mountains what, to them, was the finest end of all?

My joy was touched with humility. It was not just one party that had climbed Annapurna today, but a whole expedition. I thought of all the others in the camps perched on the slopes at our feet, and I knew it was because of their efforts and their sacrifices that we had succeeded. There are times when the most complicated actions are suddenly summed up, distilled, and strike you with illuminating clarity: so it was with this irresistible upward surge which had landed us two here.

Pictures passed through my mind—the Chamonix valley, where I had spent the most marvelous moments of my childhood; Mont Blanc, which so tremendously impressed me! I was a child when I first saw "the Mont Blanc people" coming home, and to me there was a queer look about them; a strange light shone in their eyes.

"Come on, straight down," called Lachenal.

He had already done up his sack and started going down. I took out my pocket aneroid: 8,500 meters. I smiled. I swallowed a little condensed milk and left the tube behind—the only trace of our passage. I did up my sack, put on my gloves and my glasses, seized my ice-axe; one look around and I, too, hurried down the slope. Before disappearing into the couloir I gave one last look at the summit which would henceforth be all our joy and all our consolation.

Lachenal was already far below; he had reached the foot of the couloir. I hurried down in his tracks. I went as fast as I could, but it was dangerous going. At every step one had to take care that the snow did not break away beneath one's weight. Lachenal, going faster than I thought he was capable of, was now on the long traverse. It was my turn to cross the area of mixed rock and snow. At last I reached the foot of the rock-band. I had hurried and I was out of breath. I undid my sack. What had I been going to do? I couldn't say.

"My gloves!"

Before I had time to bend over, I saw them slide and roll. They went further and further straight down the slope. I remained where I was, quite stunned. I watched them rolling down slowly, with no appearance of stopping. The movement of those gloves was engraved in my sight as something irredeemable, against which I was powerless. The consequences might be most serious. What was I to do?

"Quickly, down to Camp V."

Rébuffat and Terray would be there. My concern dissolved like magic. I now had a fixed objective again: to reach the camp. Never for a minute did it occur to me to use as gloves the socks which I always carry in reserve for just such a mishap as this.

On I went, trying to catch up with Lachenal. It had been two o'clock when we reached the summit; we had started out at six in the morning, but I had to admit that I had lost all sense of time. I felt as if I were running, whereas in actual fact I was walking normally, perhaps rather slowly, and I had to keep stopping to get my breath. The sky was now covered with clouds, everything had become gray and dirty looking. An icy wind sprang up, boding no good. We must push on! But where was Lachenal? I spotted him a couple of hundred yards away, looking as if he was never going to stop. And I had thought he was in indifferent form!

The clouds grew thicker and came right down over us; the wind blew stronger, but I did not suffer from the cold. Perhaps the descent had restored my circulation. Should I be able to find the tents in the mist? I watched the rib ending in the beak-like point which overlooked the camp. It was gradually swallowed up by the clouds, but I was able to make out the spearhead rib lower down. If the mist should thicken I would make straight for that rib and follow it down, and in this way I should be bound to come upon the tent.

Lachenal disappeared from time to time, and then the mist was so thick that I lost sight of him altogether. I kept going at the same speed, as fast as my breathing would allow.

The slope was now steeper; a few patches of bare ice followed the smooth stretches of snow. A good sign—I was nearing camp. How difficult to find one's way in thick mist! I kept the course which I had set by the steepest angle of the slope. The ground was broken; with my crampons I went straight down walls of bare ice. There were some patches ahead—a few more steps. It was the camp all right, but there were *two tents!*

So Rébuffat and Terray had come up. What a mercy! I should be able to tell them that we had been successful, that we were returning from the top. How thrilled they would be!

I got there, dropping down from above. The platform had been extended, and the two tents were facing each other. I tripped over one of the guy-ropes of the first tent; there was movement inside, they had heard me. Rébuffat and Terray put their heads out.

"We've made it. We're back from Annapurna!"

## Study suggestions

1.  How are we made aware of the hazards, the problems, and the heroism of these mountain climbers?

2.  In this essay identify the varied types of style: narrative, description, flashback, reflective thinking. How does the writer blend these so that the reader shares his thought and excitement almost as if a member of the party?

3.  Note the simplicity of style and his use of the short sentences, which increase the excitement, as "Above us there was nothing!" The utterly brief fragments of conversation make us, too, breathless—why?

4.  Why were his impressions the strangest he had ever known?

5.  Study the paragraph beginning, "Our mission was accomplished—" the very core of the essay—why was he loath to go down?

6.  Compare the two parts, the climb and the descent, for hazard and problems.

7.   Why have critics called this "one of the best accounts of mountain climbing in the modern literature of adventure"?

8.   Read from *The National Geographic,* January 1961, "A New Look at Everest," by Dag Hammarskjold, who was an avid climber of mountains. From what focus did he write? In the last paragraph how does he reveal his feelings for mountains?

9.   From *United Nations Review:* "Mr. Hammarskjold questioned by newsmen about his interest in mountaineering, among other things said, "What I know about the sport is that the qualities it requires are just those which I feel we all need today—perseverance and patience, a firm grip on realities, careful but imaginative planning, a clear awareness of the dangers but also of the fact that fate is what we make it and—the safest climber is he who never questions his ability to overcome all difficulties."

In these essays how would this statement coincide with the feelings of each writer?

10.   Compare these three essays on mountain climbing for focus, for style, for the writers' attitudes and feelings for mountains.

# IN ANCIENT DAYS

*John Kieran and*
*Arthur Daley*

At the time of the full moon of the month of Apollonius, in the year that we now reckon as 776 B.C., there was a great foot race in a meadow beside the river Alpheus at Olympia, and one Coroebus was the winner. He was crowned with a wreath of wild olive, a garland woven from the twigs and leaves of the tree that Hercules —so sang the ancient poets—had sought in the lands of the Hyperboreans and planted in the sacred grove near the Temple of

Zeus at Olympia. Thus Coroebus, a youth of Elis, was the first
Olympic victor of whom we have anything more than legendary
record.

Yet the festival, religious and athletic, held in the vale of Olympia below the heights of Cyllene and Erymanthus, goes back beyond the recorded triumph of Coroebus. It goes back to the twilight
of legend. Pindar and other Greek poets have told the tale in varying form and metre. Some say that Zeus and Kronos, the mightiest
of the gods, wrestled for possession of the earth on the high peaks
above and that the games and religious celebrations held later in
the valley below were in commemoration of the victory of Zeus.
Some tell the tale of King Œnomaus, his beautiful daughter Hipo-
damia, the fatal chariot races, the thirteen slain suitors for her
royal hand and the ultimate triumph of Pelops.

Olympia lies in Elis in the southwestern part of Greece. The Alpheus River of old, now the Ruphia, rises in Arcadia, flows peace-
fully through the valley past Olympia and empties into an arm of
the Ionian Sea. On the north bank of the river at Olympia there was
a wide meadow, a plain; beyond that, hills covered with trees; beyond that, guarding the horizon in every direction except the west-
ward vista toward the Ionian Sea, tall and rugged peaks, snow-
covered through most of the year.

The legend of Pelops is that King Œnomaus ruled this land and
enjoyed himself at the expense of those suitors who came from afar
to seek the hand of his beautiful daughter, Hippodamia. For Œnomaus had decreed that Hippodamia was to be gained as a bride
only by taking her in a chariot and escaping from the pursuit of
her majestic father in a similar vehicle. The pursuit was carried on
with homicidal intent and, upon overhauling the pursued, it was the
custom of good King Œnomaus to transfix the unlucky suitor with
his royal spear.

Thirteen times did suitors appear and run the risk of gaining a
royal bride or meeting a sudden and painful death. Thirteen
times did the spear of Œnomaus rid him of a prospective son-in-
law. But the fourteenth aspirant was Pelops, a youthful warrior of
fine presence and great courage. Pelops, so runs the tale, used guile
in outwitting his amiable royal friend and bribed the charioteer
of King Œnomaus to tinker with the axle of the regal chariot. The

pursuit race started and when the swift mares of Œnomaus were, as usual, overhauling the swaying chariot of the pair ahead, the wheel of the regal car came off and good King Œnomaus fortunately broke his neck in the ensuing crash. Thus Pelops won himself a bride and rid himself of a father-in-law in a chariot race at Olympia in Elis, and on that hallowed ground he instituted the games and religious rites in celebration of this double triumph.

So runs the legend. But it is testified by archeologists that the Temple of Hera and perhaps some other edifices standing within the original enclosure for games and religious celebrations at Olympia were erected centuries before Coroebus won the 200-yard dash (approximate distance) in 776 B.C. Probably there were earlier games, but it was starting with the recorded triumph of Coroebus that the Greeks began to reckon time by Olympiads, the four-year spans between the celebrations of the games. That the First Olympiad started in 776 B.C. is history. What lies in antiquity beyond that is myth or mystery.

The ancient Greeks, with their worship of beauty, so mingled religious observances with their athletic demonstrations that it is difficult to define where one left off and the other began. The Olympic victors were more than athletic heroes: they were local and even national idols. In some cases they had, after death, almost the worship of minor gods. The approach to the games, for spectators and competitors, was largely religious in character. All competitors had to swear, with fitting ceremonies, that they were free-born Greeks and without taint or suspicion of sacrilege against the gods. With the priests at the opening of the games, they sacrificed a pig to Zeus and a black ram to Pelops. The olive grove north of the Temple of Hera was sacred territory and the whole Olympic enclosure was dotted with shrines, in some of which there were sacred fires that were never allowed to die out. Even in the great era of the Olympic Games, they never extended beyond five days for athletic performances. But for religious purposes the temples and altars were kept open all through the year.

When an athlete triumphed in the stadium, he gave public thanks to Zeus and the other deities who ruled the destinies of those old days in Greece. The town or territory in which an Olympic victor lived was considered in high favor with the gods. The city walls were breached to welcome home the athlete bearing the wreath of wild olive from the sacred tree. There is the story of Œbotas of Achaia, winner in the Sixth Olympic Games, who was received home with what he deemed insufficient honors and who, in revenge, put a curse upon the town. For seventy-four Olympiads the town never welcomed home another Olympic victor. Messengers were sent to ask the Oracle of Delphia for advice. Word came back to the citizens to raise a belated statue to Œbotas. This was done and, at the next Olympic Games, Sostratas of Achaia won the foot race for boys.

When Coroebus ran, there was only one event on the Olympic athletic program. That was the foot race of approximately 200 yards, straightaway, this being the length of the athletic ground minus the marginal requirements for starting and finishing. The athletic field inside the stadium itself was 234 yards long and 35 yards wide. In this earliest of recorded Olympic events there were trials—or heats—run, of course, the survivor in each trial moving ahead to the next test and ultimately to the final and deciding sprint. After the 13th Olympiad other events were added, and in time there were races at different distances, races for boys, boxing, wrestling and discus competitions and chariot racing in the hippodrome erected just beyond the south wall of the stadium. The program became so crowded at the 77th Games that Callias, the Athenian boxer, protested that the chariot racing had so held up the games that the boxers were compelled to fight by the light of the moon.

For all this increase in athletic activity, the games never lost their religious significance. Rather it grew with the widening of the athletic program. The athletes performed scheduled religious duties. The holding of the games was a religious feast for all Greece. Though those were the days of almost incessant warring among neighboring towns and states, hostilities were suspended during the "Hieromenia," the sacred month during which athletes and spectators were allowed to journey to and from the games with safety under the protection of tradition and the watchful eyes of the gods.

Poets and sculptors were called upon to immortalize the figures and feats of the Olympic field and to fill the Olympic edifices with statues of the powerful and protective gods. Herodotus read parts of his history to the spectators at the games. Pindar celebrated the victors in odes. On the base of the great statue of Zeus in the Temple of Zeus at Olympia were chiseled the words: "Phidias the Athenian, the son of Charmides, made me." Indeed, the great sculptor had a workshop within the walls that bounded the Olympic grounds proper.

The great gymnasium, a masterpiece of architecture, had attached to it a colonnade of Doric columns with a roof that covered a practice running track almost the length of the Olympic field itself. It was used by the athletes for practice, especially in bad weather or when the turf in the stadium had been drenched with rain. There were hot and cold baths in various buildings; steam and vapor baths. There were drying-rooms, rest-rooms and luxuries that few modern athletic plants can boast. The training of the Olympic athletes was very strict. All competitors had to swear that they had undergone a period of ten months of training before appearing at Olympia. On the ground they went through a thirty-day period of training under the eyes of Olympic instructors and officials. They were fed and exercised according to rigid rules. At one stage in the early Olympic development the training table diet for athletes was fresh cheese at all meals—and nothing else except water! And all this was 2500 years ago.

At the beginning and for some centuries thereafter, the games —from the sporting standpoint—were strictly amateur. The prizes were wreaths. The expenses incident to competing were borne by the competitor or his family. A certain amount of leisure and a definite amount of money was needed to support the athlete through the long period of training and the subsequent trip to and from the games. The competitors in the chariot races had to furnish their own chariots and horses. An Olympic victor was supposed to foot the bill for a banquet in celebration of his triumph. This somewhat narrowed the competitive field of early days to those who could spare the time and who had—or whose families had—the money.

Some of the contests in the ancient games were brutal. The "pancratium," a combination of boxing and wrestling, resulted in several deaths. One boxer in a final bout killed his opponent by a deliberate trick, whereupon the judges ruled him in disgrace and the dead man was crowned the winner, if that was any post-mortem satisfaction to him. Theagenes, son of Timosthenes, a priest of Hercules, was a great all-around champion, but he remained out of several Olympic Games when it was alleged that he had unfairly triumphed over his rival in a boxing match. His fame was so great that his fellow townsmen raised a statue to Theagenes. A rival and unsuccessful boxer, coming at night, belabored the statue until it toppled over and fell upon him, killing the envious athlete on the spot. Thus it appeared that Theagenes could deal a fatal blow, even by proxy. Yet the surviving records indicate that the best of a long line of Olympic boxers was Glaucus of Arthedon in Boeotia. His feats with his mailed fists are celebrated in Olympic annals.

In the 98th Olympic Games a note of scandal crept in and, in the light of modern athletic history, it is worthy of note that the scandal grew out of the boxing part of the program. Eupolus of Thessaly was convicted of bribing three opponents to let him win at boxing. He was disgraced and fined; but this was not the last of such happenings, for in the course of time a whole line of statues called "Zanes" was erected with the money collected as fines from erring athletes who violated the Olympic code of honor in competition. These "Zanes" were placed so that they marched into the stadium to take part in the games. The statues were a reminder and a warning "in terrorem."

Just how many spectators watched the ancient games we do not know. The tiers of the Olympic stadium were built to accommodate between 45,000 and 50,000 spectators, but whether or not they were ever filled or overflowing, history does not tell. Women were barred from the early Olympic Games, even as spectators. Thus there was an uproar when it was discovered that the mother of Pisidorus, a winning runner, was in the stadium and watching the race. His father having died while training him, the mother of Pisidorus took charge of the training of her son and attended the race in disguise. Her joy at his victory was so great that her disguise was detected. The penalty for such an offense was death, the victim being tossed off a huge rock in the vicinity. But in this special case the penalty was not inflicted and eventually women were admitted to the Olympic Games as spectators and even on the field as contestants. In the race for chariots drawn by pairs of colts at the

128th Olympic Games, the winning driver was Belisiche, a woman of Macedonia.

For centuries the Olympic Games were the great peaceful events of the civilization that centered around the Mediterranean Sea. Then the glory that was Greece began to fade before the grandeur that was Rome. As Greece lost power and prestige, the games lost their ancient significance. They lost the spirit of the older days. They lost the religious atmosphere. Aliens entered the lists. Winners were no longer contented with a simple olive wreath as a prize. They sought gifts and money. The ebb-tide had set in. The games, instead of being patriotic and religious festivals, became carnivals, routs, circuses. The Emperor Nero appeared as a swaggering competitor and built himself a house by the Olympic hippodrome. The games dragged on intermittently to a lingering death and were finally halted by decree of Emperor Theodosius I of Rome in 394 A.D. The Olympic temples were pillaged by barbarian invaders. Theodosius II, in 426 A.D., ordered the razing of the old boundary walls around the Olympic enclosure. About a century later earthquakes completed the ruin of the historic edifices and the Alpheus River rose to cover the hallowed plain on which the Olympic Games had started.

The records of the later Olympic Games have been lost. Probably they were not worth keeping. The glory had departed and only the husk remained. The last victor whose name was preserved was Varasdates, an Armenian prince, who triumphed in a boxing match. Prince or pauper, in the high tide of the ancient Greek games his profane foot never would have been allowed to tread the sacred turf of the Olympic arena.

**Study suggestions**

1.   From this portrayal of the earliest athletic contests compare the type of sports, the purpose, the preparations and training, the human elements with those of our contests today.

2.   Compare the gymnasium with that of today.

3.   Explain myth, legend, and history. Why were these contests named Olympics? Why did they decline?

4.    Compare the àttitude of the people toward the athletes with that of today.

5.    When were these Olympics revived and how are they run today?

The book from which this was taken deals with the Olympic Games from 776 B.C. to 1960 A.D.

# COLLEGE ATHLETICS
## Their Pressure on High Schools

*Eugene Youngert*

A university professor was talking to some people from a town in the Middle West. He said with asperity, "Your high school does not prepare its students for college work." Then, he used as an example in proof of his statement a boy who had gone to the university from that high school and been flunked out for poor academic work. But the professor did not put the blame where it belonged—namely, on his own university.

What were the facts in the case? In a high school graduating class of 157, the boy in question was number 155, third from the bottom of the class. In high school, the lad had neither intention nor desire to go to college. He had no business to go to college. He had not taken a college preparatory course. He could not get a college entrance recommendation from his high school. But he was a superb athlete, and that meant that he was desirable to many colleges. He was "worked on" by representatives from several universities, and the one lucky enough to get him was the professor's university.

However, in his freshman year it became clear that the boy was not up to university football. Therefore he was dropped from the freshman squad. The athletics officers demonstrated that they had no further use for him, so he was flunked out of college, and soon after that the professor was using the boy as illustration for his statement that "your high school does not prepare its students for college work."

This incident is taken from an official report of a committee of one of our regional associations that accredits colleges and secondary schools. Now, let me relate a case told to me in a letter that I have just received from the principal of a high school in the Eastern part of our country. I shall tell the story directly from the letter, but omitting names of colleges and calling the boy Sonny.

"Until Sonny came along, our quiet little school was virtually unknown to the great majority of collegiate institutions. However, thanks to this lad, we became the crossroads meeting place for college admissions officers and coaches.

"Sonny was a lad whose I.Q. remained a steadfast 92-95, and we never considered him of college caliber. But what an athlete he was! It was a shame to see the devices a host of coaches and some admissions officers used to try to buy this boy. College people came, literally, from all over the country to get Sonny for dear old Alma Mater. There were free round trips to visit campuses, with parties thrown in for atmosphere. Appropriately enough, the representatives of one university interviewed Sonny in a famous New York night club.

"Sonny finally went to a university where he received a full 'free ride' scholarship, plus the following perquisites: private tutors to keep him passing in his courses, a campus job for his father and a low-rent apartment for the family, and spending money for Sonny. But Sonny lost interest in trying to study even the diluted program he was asked to follow, and early in the second year he left college and joined the army.

"The sad part of this tale is that we had to work like the dickens to get highly qualified, intelligent boys into the very colleges and universities that were vying with one another for our Sonny and his 92-95 I.Q."

If these cases were exceptions there would be little point in telling them here. But they are not, as the evidence on my desk bears out. Nor were the colleges that sought the boys only those known popularly as "athletic mills." In fact, among them were some that are distinguished for academic excellence. The recruiting letters of athletic departments of some of the universities would be good models for the admissions offices of those same universities. I wish that admissions officers would as assiduously seek information about academic ability as athletics officers seek information about athletic ability. I have before me some recruiting letters turned over to me by the boys who received them. The information requested about athletic prowess is fascinating, as is also the extent to which the recruiting goes: "List names and addresses of football players whom [sic] you feel would make good university prospects"; "Name the most outstanding linemen and backs against whom you played last fall." Incidentally, the boys who received these letters had not asked for them.

There are two major ways in which high schools are hurt by the athletic pressure in colleges and universities. First there are the recruiting and scholarship procedures, and secondly the practices of professionalized athletics that are carried into high schools by coaches who have used professional tactics in college.

A young boy in his senior year in high school received twenty-six scholarship offers to play football in colleges and universities. One of the offers, which I saw, was a telegram so funny as to be laughable, and yet so honest in its commercial appeal as to be highly interesting: "Accept no offers until you see ours." This telegram was from a university that year in and year out fields one of the formidable football machines of our country. Think what that kind of recruitment can do to a seventeen-year-old's sense of values, especially when the offers are followed by persistent visits from college representatives, who avidly seek the boy's favor through financial lures far greater than those offered to the academically talented students in the class.

Here is a quotation from a letter to a high school principal. "We should like to have the boy come to our campus for a weekend and get the feel of our athletic facilities. If you will bring him to us, we will invite you and your wife, your athletic director and his wife, and the boy's mother and father to spend the weekend here as our guests. We shall provide first-class transportation and campus hospitality." A seventeen-year-old would have to have his feet pretty firmly planted not to have his common sense warped by that kind of talk.

Is an institution interested in a boy's sense of values when it engages in this sort of recruiting activity? Or, isn't the interest in what the boy can do for the institution and for those who are seeking his services? I remember a basketball coach from a college whose basketball team is always one of the pacesetters. He was out on his annual talent search and had stopped in at the school I long served as principal to ask whether the athletics department had any prospects to suggest. In fun, one of our men asked whether he would like the name of a strong football star, to which he replied, "Well, look, after all, I've got my own job to protect." There is about as casual a definition of exploitation as we could hope to see!

I do not mean that coaches do not have strong feelings of affection for the boys who make their teams. Quite to the contrary, I know that they often do have those feelings. But in the recruiting activity I see nothing but exploitation. Furthermore, I believe that that is what a college faculty would call it had it the courage to make an independent study of athletic recruitment, beginning with the machinery for uncovering prospects and proceeding to the recruitment letters, interviews, and the pressure that eventually bring the boys to the campus and its teams.

It has been my privilege to talk with a large number of men broadly experienced in college athletics administration. Without exception they have said that recruitment and its scholarship bait are by all odds the major problem in college athletics practice. All that one needs to do is follow the disciplining procedure of the NCAA to realize that this expert judgment of the serious nature of the recruitment problem is correct. In the face of this fact, it is hard to understand how college faculties—the most powerful single force in a college—can ignore athletic recruiting and scholarships as though they were not their problems but only the president's. Certainly, they are the faculty's problems, since all admissions must go through the admissions office and since the admissions office is responsible to the faculty for those whom it submits for instruction and whom it recommends for scholarship aid because of ability to perform at a level worthy of scholarship aid.

College recruitment of athletes is hurtful to the high schools because of its effect both on the athletes and on the student body. I have spoken about what the bidding for boys must do to their sense of values. I could write at some length of what athletic scholarships cause high school athletes to do when they know they must get the attention of the talent scouts. But I want here to include a word about the cynicism that infects the students as a whole when they see favoritism and free ride scholarships bestowed on boys whose classroom work has been mediocre. Under such circumstances, high school students cannot be blamed if they think that we are shedding crocodile tears today in our wailing about the lack of intellectual vigor in our secondary schools.

The argument commonly advanced in defense of free ride athletic scholarships is that modern football is so complex a game, and must be so perfectly learned in order to meet normal competition, that players have no time in which to earn any of the money needed to cover their college expenses. This argument assumes that players and their families have no means of their own and that it is *good practice* that a college recreational game be so professionalized as to need all of an athlete's spare time and even some that he might well be giving to his classes (presumably his principal reason for being in college). So generally accepted is this notion that college athletics should be on a professional level that a wag has said, "No self-respecting college coach or alumnus, and not many college presidents, would be satisfied with a college football team that played like a bunch of amateurs."

It is this professionalization of college athletics, and the elimination of the amateur spirit from the college game, that brings me to the second way in which I believe that intercollegiate athletics are having a harmful influence upon high schools and high school sport. What I am thinking of now is the infusion of the "pro" attitude and spirit into high school athletics, and the shady practices that such infusion carries in its wake—practices that are shady from the point of view of the amateur's sportsmanship code. To quite an extent, high school coaches are the product of professionalized college sport, and they tend to coach as they were coached. Here, I do not write disparagingly of coaches as men. I have known a lot of them, and with few exceptions they are fine men personally. But I agree with what G. W. (Sec) Taylor said of them when he made his presidential address to the Football Writers Association: "Coaches have their job to do, and for the most part they do those jobs exactly the way that is expected of them by the president, the faculty, and the public. They are simply caught in the whirlpool of pressure athletics and are helpless to do anything about it until the college presidents and faculties give them some help." In this quotation, Mr. Taylor explained the situation, but he did not condone it.

Very few remember the sportsmanship code: "Honorable victory; respect for a worthy opponent; no personal or team advantage, and no disadvantage to the opponents, through dishonorable and unfair means." Ideally, this should be the heart of the athletics program in college and school. It is the reflection of the purpose of an educational institution—of the integrity upon which the entire program of a college or school must rest if society is to be served well. It is the greatest lesson that college and school athletics can teach. But the code is breaking down, first on the college level, and then, by the example of the colleges, on the high school level. When victory is demanded at any price, the means to victory, whether honorable or dishonorable, sportsmanlike or unsportsmanlike, becomes a matter of relative indifference.

A well-known college basketball coach was lecturing to high school basketball coaches. Among other things, he told how his team defeated one of the highest-rated teams of the year. He said that his real obstacle was the star forward on the opposing team and that the route to victory lay in tempting that man into the fouls necessary to cause his ejection from the game. And he taught it as sound game tactics that although it took deliberate fouling by four successive players, they tricked their victim into the necessary fouls, got rid of him, and then won the game. Now, I suspect that that could be called a species of respect for a worthy opponent, but I doubt that it is the kind of respect envisaged in the code. Furthermore, it conflicts pretty directly with the clause that forbids "dishonorable and unfair means." It is the kind of bad practice that under the pro spirit is transmuted into "smart ball," and I submit that it has no place in college or high school sport.

Another illustration of bad practice is the injury feigned in order to get another time-out period to give more time for the one additional play that may win the game or at least stave off defeat. After one well-remembered college game in which that device was used, cries of "smart football" were legion, although some angered sports writers called it dirty ball. We in the high schools do not want this kind of play in our games, or anything in the spirit of "win at any price, by any means," even though our elders by example portray it as sensible play. But it is hard to resist the pressure of intercollegiate sport, which we sometimes have to do if we are to convince new coaches that we actually want our high school teams coached to revere the sportsmanship code.

A third bad practice is one that some of us in high schools call "the exalted spotter." Some years ago, a professional football league coach placed an assistant on top of the stands to telephone reports to the bench on the formations of the opponent and how to outmaneuver them. Were I in the professional league, I'd do the same thing, for I would have to win games in order to attract a heavy gate. Many college coaches who needed to draw heavy gates quickly adopted the exalted spotter technique. Apparently, they have little respect for the ability of quarterbacks to assess the field and call the plays; or perhaps the pressure is so great that they dare not release to an underling the pivotal responsibility of calling plays. But now the exalted spotter has entered the high school lists, and in high school and college the game is taken away from the players and directed by the tactician on the bench. Thus a boy is denied one of the main benefits of athletics: the opportunity, on his own, to think fast and independently and to make decisions as the game develops on the field.

These three examples, out of many, are not isolated instances of pro college practices that are hurting high school athletics; they are illustrations of a *spirit* that is inimical to the sportsmanship code. Particularly objectionable is the insistence that every team must win all of its games, and that the coach who cannot achieve that result should be fired. Bad team practices are bound to result from such an impossible condition.

"Caught in the whirlpool of pressure athletics," as Mr. Taylor expressed it, coaches have done what they might have been expected to do. Asked to win or leave, they have demanded more money, both to compensate for strain and to serve as insurance between hirings and firings. Furthermore, they have gone out to find or buy players with whom to win. The strange thing is that some bad athletics policies have become so respectable with use that the subsidization of college athletes, to such an extent as almost to constitute their *employment* as athletes, is often defended as the bedrock prerequisite of amateur sport!

Is there any hope in the college athletics situation? Yes, there is a lot of hope, if the one force capable of doing something about the situation will stop ignoring it and actively insist upon its correction. That force is the college faculty. The athletics situation is primarily a faculty situation. As I said earlier, it is agreed that recruitment and subsidization constitute the major problems in college athletics, and these eventually are matters for the admissions office. Here is where the faculty comes in, for it is to the faculty that the admissions office is responsible for those whom it recommends, both for instruction and for scholarship aid. The NCAA and some athletic conferences are doing what they can, but they face two hard facts: 1) some colleges do not want reform, and will cheat; 2) bad practices have been frozen into conference codes. The real cure must take place in the individual college.

What can the faculty do? It can do what it should have done long ago. It can adopt a resolution, the enforcement of which it can demand and, if necessary, police. The resolution would say about six things. There should be no substandard admissions. All scholarships should be granted on the one basis of apparent ability to do college work on the scholarship level recommended by the faculty. Scholarship amounts should be based on need. Job opportunities should be genuine jobs, and pay should be regulated according to the accepted local scale. There should be no snap courses designed to favor any particular group of students. All students should be evaluated on the same general basis: their course work in classes. Of course, the resolution can say whatever else needs to be said to cure the local situation. If a college faculty really means business, administrative officers will think hard before they will deny a resolution of the faculty. But the catch is that the faculty must mean business.

In my experience, athletes in general are an intelligent group of boys. They would not and they should not be discriminated against under the recommended resolution. On their merit as students, they would win their fair share of scholarships and other financial help. I know that college athletics, if they were fairly and firmly handled, would become highly respected as a student activity. They would no longer be an enterprise run for financial profit, public relations, protection of vested interests, and as a sop for the alumni.

## Study suggestions

The author, recently working with Dr. James Bryant Conant on the study of the American High School, became more alerted to these pressures when he, superintendent of the Oak Park and River Forest High School, was a member of the Intercollegiate Athletic Committee of the North Central Association of Colleges and Secondary Schools. This information shows that he is not quoting hearsay.

1.   How do the two illustrations in the first section focus the reader's mind on a wrong emphasis?

2.   Discuss the two major ways in which high schools are hurt by the athletic pressures.

3.   What three bad practices does the writer illustrate? What is the dilemma of the coach?

4.   On whom does the author place the responsibility of this situation? List the six items he suggests for a cure of these bad practices.

5.   Make an outline of this to show the organization.

6.   Write a criticism of this article from your point of view and prove by examples.

7.   Write a football story in which a major player is asked to make a play which he feels would not be a credit to him or his school. Show his reasoning and the manner by which he works out his problem.

# EVERYBODY'S SPORT

*John Knowles*

Swimming is a very unnatural sport. Since our ancestors gave up life in the water some time ago, we have lost almost everything aquatic creatures need. We aren't streamlined or finned or gilled, we have no webbing left anywhere. Even our bouyancy is wrong. If we try to lie on the surface we sink, if we try to lie on the bottom we rise. Our natural level is somewhere in between, where we can't breathe.

But animals, which haven't evolved so far from water, take to it far more naturally. I remember the time a boy I was teaching to swim lifted his waterlogged head from the depths one day and glared in rage as his cocker spaniel walked to the water's edge and then, simply by making walking motions, swam out far over his depth, gliding along with his head disdainfully above the surface and his silly ears trailing behind. Dogs know they can swim; or rather they know they can walk, and swimming is the same thing, for them. Only a few creatures can't swim, and they don't make very flattering colleagues for us humans—the giraffe, the ant, the ape.

Our alienation from water makes it a flat challenge, and from that comes the great joy of swimming. We set out to subdue this hostile element, to somersault into it, to stay up when it wants us to go down, stay down when it tries to push us up, loll in it, be refreshed by it—and then walk away from it unharmed, victorious.

Yet for much of recorded history, "civilized" people declined to take up the challenge. The real creators of modern swimming were the natives of warm tropical islands and jungle coasts, who lived so intimately with water, using it as a hunting preserve, thoroughfare and playground, that they had to love it. The first true swimmers probably appeared somewhere in the islands stretching from Hawaii southwest to Indonesia; and very likely, sprinting for the fun of it across coral lagoons, they established the first world records without knowing or caring. They swam as they walked, as a matter of course: the great Hawaiian swimmer Duke Kahanamoku said he picked up his record-shattering crawl stroke simply by watching older boys; no one stopped to teach him anything as natural as swimming.

Civilization did notice native swimming at last, but slowly. Western explorers in the Solomons, Ceylon, West Africa, Hawaii, observed the aborigines doing a fast unknown stroke—and paid little attention.

London got a look at this stroke, the crawl, when two American Indians, Flying Gull and Tobacco, raced there in 1844. They were much faster than the breast-stroking English, but the *Times* summed up the general impression by calling their style "grotesque" and "totally un-European."

Not until the latter part of the 19th Century did the crawl come to be recognized as the most efficient stroke ever devised. The first to pick it up was J. Arthur Trudgen, an English traveler who learned it from South American Indians. He overlooked the flutter kick that went with it, but this was noticed a little later, on the other side of the world, when the English-born Australian Frederick Cavill paid a visit to the South Pacific islands. Cavill combined the overhand stroke with the up-and-down kick to produce the famous Australian crawl. Its first adepts were his six sons, who left both breast-strokers and "Trudgen" strokers behind to establish the Australian technique as the supreme swimming style at the turn of the present century.

So we have taken up swimming late but enthusiastically. Thanks to our new travel habits, more and more people are crossing water or living beside it; and like Polynesians, we are fast growing to love it.

Having gone in for swimming, we naturally develop it with every trick we can think of. A good swim is fine, invigorating, refreshing.

But after you have made the trip to the raft and back a dozen times, you look around for a little variety. A pair of kick fins will change everything; wearing them you plow out to the raft like a Johnnie Weissmuller, or shoot along under the surface as though you were one of the fish. But you can't see very well down there, so a pair of goggles is added. Now you can see the vegetation on the bottom, glimpse some unimpressed fish. You can't catch them, so you get a spear gun and spend hours tracking them from above. Next you get a mouth tube with a vent sticking up in the air, so you can swim on the surface with your face continually under water, watching the fish below. But you still can't go down for any length of time, so you get a mechanical lung and a skin diver's outfit, and with the goggles and the spear gun and the kick fins you are completely outfitted as a hunter of the deep.

All this equipment makes swimming more adventurous than ever. It opens an underwater world of sport, with the freedom to move and explore and hunt in a region we could only peer into before, and reach only with a blindly lowered hook.

We have also trumped the warm-water natives in what can be done on the surface. They devised the surfboard for a thrilling ride along the crest of a wave rolling toward shore. We adopted it. Then we shortened it, attached it by a long rope to the rear of a speedboat, and produced the aquaplane to make the ride continuous and faster. Then we split it in two and fashioned skis. With them all kinds of new maneuvers became possible; by putting a ramp in the water we could even have an aquatic ski jump.

By this time the great hostile challenge of water was so diminished that we began to jump clownishly all over it. Men in baggy clothes threw themselves into epic belly-floppers from thirty-meter towers; a comedian in comic *fin de siècle* bathing costumes swam with one foot stuck rigidly up in the air, like a lunatic periscope; others moved with dignity to the end of the diving board, missed their final spring, somehow avoided fracturing their skulls on the board, and entered the water chin first, grinning. Nothing was sacred about water any more. It was so thoroughly tamed that we could send out young girls to adorn it, forming pretty patterns; it was a stage for Aquacades and water carnivals.

Considering water as the tremendous popular playground it is today, it is curious how slow people were to admit that swimming is good for the health. Benjamin Franklin, who wrote the best book on the sport down almost to our own time, insisted on this in a period when bathing was often classed with black magic. Franklin himself swam so well he could cut his toenails in the water. He paralleled his famous electricity experiment by letting a kite pull him across a lake. But few people followed his lead. Swimming was still considered bad for the health.

Besides, it didn't seem decent. From pre-Victorian times, when boys and girls swam naked in a fountain in Zurich, and Paris dismissed bathing suits as "vain ornament," the few bathers there were had gotten continually dressier, until by the middle of the 19th Century a woman venturing into the surf at Biarritz resembled a Moslem lady among the Infidels. She wore capacious *pantalons* reaching to the ankle, boots, a kind of tailored waistcoat with long sleeves, and a brimmed hat.

Her counterpart today wears a Bikini, without a vain ornament anywhere—perhaps the final evolution in a process that has been going on since the turn of the century. At the same time that the crawl stroke began drawing more people to the water, tastes and moral standards also began to change. An exposed ankle ceased to be inflammatory. Women's clothes were allowed to hint that there was a woman inside. Fresh air, sunshine, and finally exercise in the water were accepted as beneficial to health.

And the crawl stroke, which Australia has named after itself, is now recognized as a peerless source of muscular development. Bob Kiphuth, coach of the Yale University and U.S. Olympic swimming teams, *knew* that a swimmer uses all muscles in his body, but he couldn't really see this until he went down in a diving helmet. From there, without the distortion of looking at swimmers from above the surface, he could study the rippling play of muscles from the forearm down the trunk to the calves and ankles, all of them coordinated in the rhythmic power which drives the body forward.

Even tropical swimmers were only indifferent stylists in the water; they had endurance and a good stroke but they didn't bother to refine it. Within the last fifty years, trained minds have studied the best position of the arms, the optimum number of kicks to accompany each stroke, the fastest racing turn (currently a kind of twisted somersault)—and racing swimmers today are the finest exponents of a new bodily technique. No one has ever approached their speed before.

This can sometimes be a mixed pleasure for the competitor though. Swimming a mile or two up and down a pool every day gives you eventually a surprised feeling of durability. But there is monotony and there is eventually a sense that you've had too much water, you're simply tired of the stuff.

Comes the race, and you are likely to arrive at the pool feeling inexplicably weak. You put on your trunks and go out to the pool. The temperature here is colder than usual to accommodate the spectators. This will certainly put you off your best performance. You dive in for some warm-up laps, and because the air was colder the water seems hospitably warm. You lounge lazily through a few lengths, exaggerating, even burlesquing good swimming style, fooling with this skill of yours. You suddenly recall that after all you are pretty good at it.

The meet begins, your race approaches. The muscles of your abdomen begin to tingle. So do your hands and feet.

You take your place on the starting box. There is a roaring in your ears, everything looks blurred, and you have just time to think, "What in the world am I doing here?" when the gun goes off.

When you hit the water, lightheadedness, tinglings, doubts and regrets are all torn off you. The outcome now depends on your ability to think under pressure about how to do it right, your condition, your technique, and how fully you can put your heart into it. Those things, plus native strength and luck.

Almost immediately, if it is a sprinting event, it is over. Whether you have won or not, you're elated to have made yourself go through with it. There was no one but you, no teamwork, no one to blame or congratulate but yourself.

These are the special pleasures and pains of the competitive swimmer. In many ways a pool is the best place to do real swimming. Free water tends to be too tempestuous, while in a pool it is tamed and imprisoned; the challenge has been filtered out of it along with the bacteria.

I did my first swimming in a pool, and have tried pools in many places since then. The most glittering was the Eden Roc pool of the Hotel du Cap d'Antibes, and the most enjoyable was at a kind of oasis in Texas where I was stationed with the Air Force. Here, a swimming pool was a real blessing, for this part of Texas lacked water to drink, let alone to swim in. Many days a cloud of dust—"Oklahoma!" the Texans called it—blew over and settled down upon us, our cots, and everything else. Finally we learned that water had been struck nearby and that two crude swimming pools had been built.

One of the pools was very cold, and the other was colder. To us in Texas in July, they had the power to exhilarate, to free us from the sunlight which fell like metal from the blank sky. They offered all you could ask of water, all you could wish for in swimming. No indoor pool could rival them.

Nevertheless, indoor pools excel in one way—in the use of artifice to enhance the pleasure of swimming. The best artificial effects I have seen are in the Exhibition Pool at Yale University.

It is surrounded by a large, dark green amphitheater which slopes steeply upward. Shining in the center of this somber oval is the pool, its white tile deck and pastel blue water glittering frivolously away. If you stand beside it alone, with no one in the water or the seats, you become aware of an august silence, as though you were in a mechanized cathedral.

I was there alone one day when someone began throwing control switches. Banks of lights overhead and along the sides went out and only the pool remained lighted, from below the surface, glowing like a luminous, smoky, green-blue cloud suspended in a black cavern. I dived in. The light seemed amazingly to increase my buoyancy; the water bore me up as though I were made of cork and could float forever.

In fierce contrast to such peace and glamour is the surf, which is charged with challenge. Surf swimming is much better managed now, of course; in the old days people who had come near drowning were revived by being hanged from the heels, or bled, or rolled over a barrel, or, as sometimes happened, pushed back into the water lest God consider it impious for men to bring back someone so close to eternity. We know better now, but even so, the surf's disturbing undercurrent is there for every swimmer to feel, and on rough days the warnings go up and the swimmers are restricted to a particular area or kept out of the water altogether.

The surf at such moments is not to be trifled with. In fact you never trifle with the surf; when it is in a playful mood, the surf trifles with you. That's the joy of swimming in it. Along comes a large playful wave. It rises up and smacks you, shoves you along, knocks you off your feet like a big clumsy dog trying to ingratiate itself with a child. You are the child. It doesn't matter if you hold an Olympic gold medal; in the surf you wallow and are knocked around like any dog-paddler.

Another wave swells up, growing more intimidating by the moment. As it nears you, the great crest breaks, an immense amount of rushing water is about to crash over your head. You are just a morsel of flotsam, but you happen to be human and you have the ingenuity which raised your ancestors out of the water in the first place. You put your arms in front of you, your head between them, and dive through the wave. Despite its tremendous force, it hurtles harmlessly over you and smashes its energy ineffectually against the shore.

A new swell approaches, and you decide to ride it in. This is a much trickier feat. You turn your body toward shore and glance coolly over your shoulder to note how big the wave is, how fast it is coming and, most crucially of all, when it will break. Your judgment, let's say, is just right. You are already planing toward the beach when the wave reaches you. It bears you surgingly up and forward, and just then the threatening tracery along its crest breaks, not over you but under you. You can feel its chaotic turbulence beating all along your body. It goes on and on, like some rolling hydraulic engine beneath you, shooting you wildly toward shore. At last it beaches you, with a certain grudging gentleness. Victory.

More usually, you are too far from shore and begin to plane too soon, so that the wave lifts you up briefly, like King Kong balancing a match box, then contemptuously lets you fall and sweeps on. Or worse, you are too close to shore, and as you watch the approach of the wave with that cool glance over your shoulder, you notice that the foam is thickening too soon along its crest. The wave suddenly transforms itself into a top-heavy, rushing wall; it's too late to turn and dive into it, too late to run, too late to duck. The wave breaks on top of you. Now you're helpless; the breaker embroils you, grinds you in its vortex, somersaults you six or eight times and then tosses you up on the shore like a piece of spent seaweed. Surf swimming is perhaps the most experimental of all athletic experiences; you give over your being to the action of waves, currents, tides—things titanic and even cosmic.

These are some of the joys of swimming. In all its forms, even in competitive swimming, the source of our pleasure is facing and conquering the challenge of water. Watch any child, after he has been alarmed by a ducking or two, gingerly find his way to a delighted confidence when he learns that water will actually support him. As he learns to deal with it, the water will become the best playground he ever had, with just enough echo of the challenge left in it to keep him always stimulated.

Swimming is essentially a simple and even a humble sport. It inspires none of the mass adulation of baseball, or the protocol of tennis or the folklore of fishing or the *esprit de corps* of skiing. Most sports require equipment ranging from a ball to a bull, but swimming is independent even of the fins and goggles and other innovations that have brought so much new fun in the water. This is the sport of commoners. All you need to enjoy it is a certain amount of water—the most abundant substance on earth.

### Study suggestions

1.  The first sentence catches the reader's attention immediately for what reasons—especially if the reader is an expert swimmer?

2.  In what various ways has man met the *challenge* of the water?

3.  What reasons does the writer give for the slowness of people in seeing any health advantage in swimming?

4.  What is the great joy of swimming? Compare this feeling with that of the mountain climber.

5.  From this article what seems to be his attitude toward all forms of water sports? Does he prefer the pool or the ocean?

6.  Study the orderly structure of his writing. Why does he change the focus from the first person *we* to the *second* person *you* as he describes the different water activities?

Theme suggestions:
Fun with Water Skis
Learning to Swim and Dive
Studying Life on the Ocean Floor
Skin Diving—Its Pleasures and Uses
A Swimming Race
The Surf and I

# WE PLAY TO WIN, THEY PLAY
# FOR FUN

*Peter M. Dawkins*

It is interesting indeed to investigate the different positions sport occupies in the lives of people of varying backgrounds and standards of living. For purposes of convenience, let us consider three basic kinds of society.

In the first kind the entire mental and physical capabilities of the people are dedicated to maintaining a tolerable existence. It is natural that these people will not have the interest or energy to participate in sport, since they are working ten or twelve hours a day, six or seven days a week. They may enjoy a vicarious attachment to a winning soccer team (compensating for the relative lack of success in their lives) or they may associate themselves with the drama and glamour of the bullfighter (to substitute for the lack of glamour in their own existence) but sport is not a particularly significant factor for them.

In the second society the standard of living is such that the people do have a certain amount of time to themselves, but only a limited budget to exploit their leisure. In these circumstances sport seems to become an important part of their lives. This is because they have the interest and enthusiasm for sport, and yet not enough money to be enticed into the multitude of non-athletic (and generally more expensive) forms of diversion.

The third category comprises those societies in which the general public can afford leisure-time activities. In this situation, there are many means by which one can occupy his leisure time, and sport, being but one of many such avenues, naturally becomes less important.

This analysis may help explain the difference in the approach to sport in America and in Britain. I think most people would agree that British society belongs to the second group, while the United States falls into the third.

One of the things that first impresses an American at a British university is the great number of people who personally participate in athletics. One encounters all conceivable sizes, shapes, forms and figures; but they are sportsmen all, and their games are an essential part of their lives. This is in graphic contrast to the scene at the American university, where there seems to be an increasingly discernible gulf between the student and the athlete.

In America the "professionalism" of high school and college athletics focuses upon excelling. The sole objective in participating is to win and, as a result, the average or mediocre athlete is discouraged from participating. In Britain there does not seem to be this same concern with excelling. The important thing seems to be playing the games, and enjoying one's self in the process.

The contrast springs too, from the different place sport occupies in the educational patterns of the two countries. In the average high school or university in the United States (my alma mater, West Point, being a pointed exception) athletics are not considered to be an integral part of the educational process. It is true that there are physical-education programs, but these are normally not taken very seriously by the students. In the main, athletics are considered to be an extracurricular diversion for those people who are adept while the vast majority of students are mere spectators.

The British viewpoint, on the other hand, is that athletics are an integral part of the educational process; the emphasis is not upon perfection but upon seeing that every student should have the experience of participating in some sort of competitive sport. The attitude exists primarily at the high school level, but it becomes almost habitual and its influence is clearly reflected in university sport.

There is as much difference—again in the context of university sport—between the meaning of amateurism in Britain and its meaning in the United States as there is between the concept in the United States and in Russia. Where amateurism in America simply means that the players are not paid, in Britain it is extended to the entire sports establishment.

As a result, the professional coaching staff, the offices of the university director of athletics and the elaborate public information organization are non-existent in British university athletics. Instead, each sport is represented by a club, with members of the team occupying the positions of president, secretary, treasurer, etc.; then people carry the responsibilities of the professional establishment that accompanies American university athletics.

The president of the club is the man who determines what teams will be included on the schedule, what techniques will be utilized by the squad, what training procedures will be employed, and who will actually represent the club in a given match. This experience is considered one of the benefits to be derived from sport, and I must admit that the captaincy of an American team, though a truly rewarding experience, has much less scope.

The sports themselves are affected by this difference in approach. In the matter of training, the British veer away from the many hours of drill on fundamentals that are the backboard of practice in American sports, and are apt to play the game itself for practice. The organization of a practice session, in contrast to the efficient succession of planned activities in America, is normally a rather casual procedure.

I am not intimating that the British athlete is less enthusiastic about his sport or less energetic in his participation. Although he may not spend as much time in anticipation or in "post-mortems," once the game is in progress the Briton wants to win just as badly as his American counterpart.

He approaches training in a much less businesslike manner primarily because the person organizing the practice is a student himself and simply does not have the time for practice that the full-time professional coaching staff of an American university has. In general, much less time is spent in practice in Britain, with only the rare exception approaching the daily schedule that is almost universal in the United States.

Whether the diversity of participation in British sports results *in* or results *from* this British approach to training is uncertain, but in any case the British student is able to participate in quite a number of sports at the same time. Whereas the American athlete is almost always limited to one sport per season, it is not at all unusual for the British student to play soccer, field hockey, squash and Rugby all in the same week.

With the multitude of games going on daily, representing a vast range in both type and standard of excellence, any student, regardless of his athletic limitations, can play on a team if he wants to. This, to me, is a wonderful thing.

Here, I don't mean to condemn American sports in any way. The maintenance of paid coaching staffs, long and arduous hours of practice, and devotion to one sport at a time, produce a standard of excellence that could never be realized with the British approach. My memories of American football I cherish highly, and of all my experiences in sport none has given me a greater sense of satisfaction than did college football.

The feeling of accomplishment that comes from knowing you assaulted the peak and were successful is one that is rarely equaled, and the ties of fellowship and comradeship thus developed may be lifelong. The dedication and singleness of purpose that permeates a group like the Corps of Cadets in anticipation of an Army-Navy game is one that brings with victory the extremely rewarding satisfaction of a momentous challenge having been accepted and met— of a job well done.

In a British university there is no such point of focus. The Oxford-Cambridge boat race would be the closest comparison I can think of—and this is very much an exception rather than the rule. Although the university Rugby team is well supported, there are many people who feel far more strongly about their college teams within the university than they do about the university side as a whole; and even on the occasion of the Oxford-Cambridge Rugby match there is nothing of the intense feeling among the student body that there is in America.

There are many occasions when the game itself—while played in earnest—is almost incidental. The entire experience, with tea and beer afterward, followed perhaps by a banquet and dance, is a most enjoyable social event, and no one is terribly upset by the results of the game one way or the other.

The British have a fine thing in their attitude toward sport. They derive great pleasure and satisfaction out of personally taking part. The student whose athletic activity at an American university would be limited to the occasional game of Frisbee for Phi Delta Theta can be a member of four or five college athletic clubs at a British university and experience all the pleasures and satisfactions of competitive sport. The student who has never seen a lacrosse game can, with a few short weeks' work, represent his college in competition—and he can also play soccer, Rugby, tennis and cricket, and enjoy them all equally.

Sport in America is wonderful; I would not change it drastically, even if I could. But sport in Britain is wonderful also—in a very different way—and I wonder whether we could not benefit by the British approach in certain respects. The vigor and enthusiasm of youth is not satisfied by the vicarious "athletics" of the spectator. Television and the Yankee Stadium, enjoyable though they be, are no substitute for energetic competitive play, whether the playing field is at Oxford, West Point or on the sandlot around the corner.

### Study suggestions

1.    The author of this article was captain of the football team at West Point in 1958 and a unanimous all-America choice at halfback. A Phi Beta Kappa student, he became a Rhodes scholar at Oxford where he has played Rugby and hockey. From this background what conclusions does he draw concerning the attitudes toward collegiate sports in the two countries?

2.    For purpose of analysis how does he classify people?

3.    In what specific ways does he contrast university athletics of America and England? Note his title.

4.   Again compare his focus on *challenge* with that in mountain climbing and swimming in the two preceding articles.
5.   What impression does he give concerning his choice of systems?

Theme suggestions:
The Place of a Sports Program
Baseball versus Football
Leisure-time Activities
My Favorite Sports

# AMERICANS ARE MOLLYCODDLES

*Herb Elliott* (*with Alan Trengove*)

When I say that I'm glad I was born Australian, not American, I hope all my American friends will not be offended. But I believe in frankness. And it's a fact that the warm, soft, synthetic existence Americans lead poses a real doubt about their future. A people who so thoroughly mollycoddle themselves must steadily become weaker, physically and spiritually. The Americans are not the only people who are insulating themselves from their environment; the tendency exists even in my own country. I shudder to think what would happen to some of these pampered people who've separated themselves from nature if suddenly they were thrown back into the natural environment that God provides. How many would survive?

My first taste of American life came at the end of the 1957-58 Australian season when Merv Lincoln and I were invited there to compete in a series of races prior to our appearance in the Empire Games in Wales. It was an experience I wouldn't have missed for the world, though I was shocked by some of the things I saw. No sooner had the invitation arrived than I was alerted for a radiotelephone call from Villanova University. It was Ron Delany, the young gentleman who 18 months before had expressed doubts about the wisdom of my tough training schedules. He wanted to know what races were planned for me.

"You know, my bhoy, Oi don't mind admittin' you've got me a bit worried now," said Ron. And he tried to pump me on my plans—without success.

The plane trip from Sydney to Honolulu left me so tired and sick that I viewed my scheduled 880-yard race in Hawaii's Punahou Relays with some apprehension. The Hawaiian champion, Chauncey Pa, provided fierce opposition until well into the second lap. If he'd known how awful I felt he might not have cracked when he did, allowing me to win in 1:53.1.

It was at Waikiki Beach that I became aware how many wealthy Americans lose interest in their physical condition. There is no point in using euphemisms; they were fat and they were flabby. Even the kids. I saw a boy of no more than 8 whose muscle tissue hung on him limply like pieces of sacking—the end result, I was sure, of two generations of soft living. Unlike Australian beachgoers, the frequenters of Waikiki couldn't swim 10 yards to save themselves. Two other facets that intrigued me were the way the women bossed their menfolk and the vanity of almost all of them, men and women. I took great delight in sprinting through the water, splashing bald heads and white, puffy legs.

Ironically, amid this apparent decadence I was introduced to one of the most masculine characters I've been fortunate enough to meet. George Downing was in his late 30s or early 40s, superbly fit, easygoing and adventurous, and the greatest surfer in the world—a fact that I realized as soon as I was informed that each day he went out on a surfboard to crack the huge waves north of Honolulu. One day, while out on a catamaran, we discussed the possibility of touring the world together on such a small but sturdy craft. A reckless mood came over me in which impetuously I decided to toss in my job, retire from running and live under sail. The mood wore off sufficiently for me to continue my tour, though I'm not sure to this day whether there's a more appealing life than the rugged outdoor existence, close to water, that George leads.

Another pleasant experience in Honolulu was discovering such a harmonious intermingling of so many races. Japanese, Chinese, Indians, British, Portuguese and French intermarried, sang, danced and ate together, played together and prayed together. Their uninhibited happiness was to me an encouraging symbol in today's troubled world.

When my coach, Percy Cerutty, and I flew into Los Angeles we felt very much like innocents abroad. We were installed at the Sheraton Hotel in a suite of rooms bigger than my home in Perth.

"Hey, Percy," I joked when the porter opened our door. "You go in that direction and I'll go in this and if we lose contact I'll see you tomorrow morning at breakfast."

We were dined and feted in America until we felt like wealthy potentates; yet I found the surfeit of luxury so tedious that I was soon craving my normal routine of plain living. American food is soft, mushy and much too highly seasoned. I was confronted with about 10 different varieties of dressing for my salads and the potatoes were mixed with so many other foods that they were unrecognizable, and, in my opinion, ruined. I lost count of the number of times I was offered hot doughnuts, waffles and cakes for breakfast when all I wanted was honest-to-goodness ham and eggs.

My admiration for the average American's big thinking, initiative, commercial enthusiasm and charm is boundless. In so many spheres he is decades ahead of his Australian counterpart, but in the basic things he has lost his sense of proportion. Modern society revolves around the family; in America, because family life is unsound, the whole society is sick. Overemphasis is given to luxury. The women want their own cars; they want all the household gear that opens and shuts by pushbutton control. If their men can't earn enough to give them these amenities the women hire someone to look after their kids and go out to make the necessary money themselves. As a consequence, women tend to regard themselves as equals in the American home. In most homes they appear almost to be the bosses. But nobody is really happy. The women are not happy because they are not being slightly dominated, as nature ordained they should be. The men are not happy because they *are* being dominated, also defying nature's law. When a wife is completely dependent upon her husband, their marriage is more likely to succeed.

It is difficult trying to impress upon Americans that money is not so important in this life as the simple pleasures that generally cost nothing. They have lost touch with the simple pleasures. An Australian family will go to the beach and be content to eat sandwiches on the sand; a European will take his family bicycling in the country with a hamper of bread and cheese and a bottle of wine. An American, after taking his family to the beach, climbs into a flashy late-model car and drives them to a luxury restaurant for a meal! Does he enjoy his outing as much as the Australian and European?

Few American men, once they leave college, bother about physical exercise, in marked contrast to Australian men, who are sport-conscious from cradle to grave. I was disturbed also by the quantity of rye and bourbon that the Americans drink, which must be symptomatic of their discontent. Now I believe that you can tell a tree by its fruits. And the fact that the Americans in recent years have not produced many outstanding distance runners is directly attributable to their soft way of life. They are not a hardy race of people, whereas the Australians, Norwegians, Russians and English are.

In facilities, few nations can match America. No matter how complete these facilities, though, they cannot offset the national characteristics of softness and complacency. In some ways America's outlook reminds me of those personal tendencies I try to guard against. To reach that pinnacle of achievement where you're accepted as a leader you must be tenacious and determined. Once there, it's natural to relax and rest on your laurels. Having reached its pinnacle, as it were, America lacks the aggression and initiative of smaller countries, who love nothing better than succeeding occasionally in knocking her off her perch. The fact that America still produces over-all the world's best sprinters, high jumpers, pole vaulters and shotputters shows that her people are capable of explosive bursts of energy and enthusiasm, qualities that make her businessmen so effective. But sprinters and field-games men do not have to train as grueling as middle-distance and distance runners. Twenty 100- or 200-yard bursts in a night may tire a sprinter; they don't wring his lungs out as a 10-mile run would. On the whole, Americans are not suited temperamentally to race beyond the 880 yards.

Early in February 1959 I made another trip to America and Canada to collect several trophies commemorating 1958 performances. I returned from America after this fleeting visit with three of my earlier impressions confirmed. The average American, even more than the average Australian, can never sit back and say to his wife, "Well, at last everything is ours." He's constantly in debt to the hire-purchase companies. He cannot bear anything to be old-fashioned, and once he thinks it is he'll trade it in for a more modern version. I cannot believe that this unrelenting urge to possess newer, shinier chattels—encouraged by big business—makes him happy. Most Americans know little about Australia, and the knowledge they do have they've gleaned through the exploits of such sportsmen as Frank Sedgman, Lew Hoad, John Konrads and Jack Brabham. If you were to tell them that the traffic in Collins Street was halted occasionally by a stray kangaroo they'd believe you. As the world shrinks with jet travel, they will learn more.

In hospitality the Americans can't be matched by any people in the world; they overwhelm you with kindness, overawe you with extravagance. Yet sometimes there's an insincere veneer to all their polished charm. They're almost too sweet to be true. On this particular visit it was remarkable how few of the smiling, back-slapping Americans who'd greeted me in 1958 bothered to see me. Naturally, I'm not vain enough to think they should have met me, except that in 1958, when I was competing, they made such a fuss it was embarrassing. "Golly," I would think, "this bloke is so wonderful he'll go through hell and high water to see me the next time I'm here. Maybe we'll have a meal together." And then he doesn't even show up! When someone smiles and shakes my hand as though he means it, I take him for a friend, but in America it merely seems to be the correct thing to do.

## Study suggestions

1.   Why does the writer, the Australian four-minute miler, call American life "warm, soft, synthetic" and "insulating themselves from their enviroment"?

2.   What is your defense for his statement, "A people who so thoroughly mollycoddle themselves must steadily become weaker, physically and spiritually"?

3.   Why does he believe Americans have lost their sense of proportion?

4.   Have all Americans "lost touch with simple pleasure," or are "constantly in debt"?

5.   List the adverse criticisms together; then the favorable. What is the balance? How thoroughly has he studied America?

6.   Write a reply to this article with proof to support your opinions.

# THE MARGINAL WORLD

### *Rachel Carson*

The edge of the sea is a strange and beautiful place. All through the long history of Earth it has been an area of unrest where waves have broken heavily against the land, where the tides have pressed forward over the continents, receded, and then returned. For no two successive days is the shore line precisely the same.

Not only do the tides advance and retreat in their eternal rhythms, but the level of the sea itself is never at rest. It rises or falls as the glaciers melt or grow, as the floor of the deep ocean basins shifts under its increasing load of sediments, or as the earth's crust along the continental margins warps up or down in adjustment to strain and tension. Today a little more land may belong to the sea, tomorrow a little less. Always the edge of the sea remains an elusive and indefinable boundary.

The shore has a dual nature, changing with the swing of the tides, belonging now to the land, now to the sea. On the ebb tide it knows the harsh extremes of the land world, being exposed to heat and cold, to wind, to rain and drying sun. On the flood tide it is a water world, returning briefly to the relative stability of the open sea.

Only the most hardy and adaptable can survive in a region so mutable, yet the area between the tide lines is crowded with plants and animals. In this difficult world of the shore, life displays its enormous toughness and vitality by occupying almost every conceivable niche. Visibly, it carpets the intertidal rocks; or half hidden, it descends into fissures and crevices, or hides under boulders, or lurks in the wet gloom of sea caves. Invisibly, where the casual observer would say there is no life, it lies deep in the sand, in burrows and tubes and passageways. It tunnels into solid rock and bores into peat and clay. It encrusts weeds or drifting spars or the hard, chitinous shell of a lobster. It exists minutely, as the film of bacteria that spreads over a rock surface or a wharf piling; as spheres of protozoa, small as pinpricks, sparkling at the surface of the sea; and as Lilliputian beings swimming through dark pools that lie between the grains of sand.

The shore is an ancient world, for as long as there has been an earth and sea there has been this place of the meeting of land and water. Yet it is a world that keeps alive the sense of continuing creation and of the relentless drive of life. Each time that I enter it, I gain some new awareness of its beauty and its deeper meanings, sensing that intricate fabric of life by which one creature is linked with another, and each with its surroundings.

In my thoughts of the shore, one place stands apart for its revelation of exquisite beauty. It is a pool hidden within a cave that one can visit only rarely and briefly when the lowest of the year's low tides fall below it, and perhaps from that very fact it acquires some of its special beauty. Choosing such a time, I hoped for a glimpse of the pool. The ebb was to fall early in the morning. I knew that if the wind held from the northwest and no interfering swell ran in from a distant storm the level of the sea should drop below the entrance to the pool. There had been sudden ominous showers in the night, with rain like handfuls of gravel flung on the roof. When I looked out into the early morning the sky was full of a gray dawn light but the sun had not yet risen. Water and air were pallid. Across the bay the moon was a luminous disc in the western sky, suspended above the dim line of distant shore—the full August moon, drawing the tide to the low, low levels of the threshold of the alien sea world. As I watched, a gull flew by, above the spruces. Its breast was rosy with the light of the unrisen sun. The day was, after all, to be fair.

Later, as I stood above the tide near the entrance to the pool, the promise of that rosy light was sustained. From the base of the steep wall of rock on which I stood, a moss-covered ledge jutted seaward into deep water. In the surge at the rim of the ledge the dark fronds of oarweeds swayed, smooth and gleaming as leather. The projecting ledge was the path to the small hidden cave and its pool. Occasionally a swell, stronger than the rest, rolled smoothly over the rim and broke in foam against the cliff. But the intervals between such swells were long enough to admit me to the ledge and long enough for a glimpse of that fairy pool, so seldom and so briefly exposed.

And so I knelt on the wet carpet of sea moss and looked back into the dark cavern that held the pool in a shallow basin. The floor of the cave was only a few inches below the roof, and a mirror had been created in which all that grew on the ceiling was reflected in the still water below.

Under water that was clear as glass the pool was carpeted with green sponge. Gray patches of sea squirts glistened on the ceiling and colonies of soft coral were a pale apricot color. In the moment when I looked into the cave a little elfin starfish hung down, suspended by the merest thread, perhaps only by a single tube foot. It reached down to touch its own reflection, so perfectly delineated that there might have been, not one starfish, but two. The beauty of the reflected images and of the limpid pool itself was the poignant beauty of things that are ephemeral, existing only until the sea should return to fill the little cave.

Whenever I go down into this magical zone of the low water of the spring tides, I look for the most delicately beautiful of all the shore's inhabitants—flowers that are not plant but animal, blooming on the threshold of the deeper sea. In that fairy cave I was not disappointed. Hanging from its roof were the pendent flowers of the hydroid Tubularia, pale pink, fringed and delicate as the wind flower. Here were creatures so exquisitely fashioned that they seemed unreal, their beauty too fragile to exist in a world of crushing force. Yet every detail was functionally useful, every stalk and hydranth and petal-like tentacle fashioned for dealing with the realities of existence. I knew that they were merely waiting, in that moment of the tide's ebbing, for the return of the sea. Then in the rush of water, in the surge of surf and the pressure of the incoming tide, the delicate flower heads would stir with life. They would sway on their slender stalks, and their long tentacles would sweep the returning water, finding in it all that they needed for life.

And so in that enchanted place on the threshold of the sea the realities that possessed my mind were far from those of the land world I had left an hour before. In a different way the same sense of remoteness and of a world apart came to me in a twilight hour on a great beach on the coast of Georgia. I had come down after sunset and walked far out over sands that lay wet and gleaming, to the very edge of the retreating sea. Looking back across that immense flat, crossed by winding, water-filled gullies and here and there holding shallow pools left by the tide, I was filled with awareness that this intertidal area, although abandoned briefly and rhythmically by the sea, is always reclaimed by the rising tide. There at the edge of low water the beach with its reminders of the land seemed far away. The only sounds were those of the wind and the sea and the birds. There was one sound of wind moving over water, and another of water sliding over the sand and tumbling down the faces of its own wave forms. The flats were astir with birds, and the voice of the willet rang insistently. One of them stood at the edge of the water and gave its loud, urgent cry; an answer came from far up the beach and the two birds flew to join each other.

The flats took on a mysterious quality as dusk approached and the last evening light was reflected from the scattered pools and creeks. Then birds became only dark shadows, with no color discernible. Sanderlings scurried across the beach like little ghosts, and here and there the darker forms of the willets stood out. Often I could come very close to them before they would start up in alarm—the sanderlings running, the willets flying up, crying. Black skimmers flew along the ocean's edge silhouetted against the dull, metallic gleam, or they went flitting above the sand like large, dimly seen moths. Sometimes they "skimmed" the winding creeks of tidal water, where little spreading surface ripples marked the presence of small fish.

The shore at night is a different world, in which the very darkness that hides the distractions of daylight brings into sharper focus the elemental realities. Once, exploring the night beach, I surprised a small ghost crab in the searching beam of my torch. He was lying in a pit he had dug just above the surf, as though watching the sea and waiting. The blackness of the night possessed water, air, and beach. It was the darkness of an older world, before Man. There was no sound but the all-enveloping, primeval sounds of wind blowing over water and sand, and of waves crashing on the beach. There was no other visible life—just one small crab near the sea. I have seen hundreds of ghost crabs in other settings, but suddenly I was filled with the odd sensation that for the first time I knew the creature in its own world—that I understood, as never before, the essence of its being. In that moment time was suspended; the world to which I belonged did not exist and I might have been an onlooker from outer space. The little crab alone with the sea became a symbol that stood for life itself—for the delicate, destructible, yet incredibly vital force that somehow holds its place amid the harsh realities of the inorganic world.

The sense of creation comes with memories of a southern coast, where the sea and the mangroves, working together, are building a wilderness of thousands of small islands off the southwestern coast of Florida, separated from each other by a tortuous pattern of bays, lagoons, and narrow waterways. I remember a winter day when the sky was blue and drenched with sunlight; though there was no wind one was conscious of flowing air like cold clear crystal. I had landed on the surf-washed tip on one of those islands, and then worked my way around to the sheltered bay side. There I found the tide far out, exposing the broad mud flat of a cove bordered by the mangroves with their twisted branches, their glossy leaves, and their long prop roots reaching down, grasping and holding the mud, building the land out a little more, then again a little more.

The mud flats were strewn with the shells of that small, exquisitely colored mollusk, the rose tellin, looking like scattered petals of pink roses. There must have been a colony nearby, living buried just under the surface of the mud. At first the only creature visible was a small heron in gray and rusty plumage—a reddish egret that waded across the flat with the stealthy, hesitant movements of its kind. But other land creatures had been there, for a line of fresh tracks wound in and out among the mangrove roots, marking the path of a raccoon feeding on the oysters that gripped the supporting roots with projections from their shells. Soon I found the tracks of a shore bird, probably a sanderling, and followed them a little; then they turned toward the water and were lost, for the tide had erased them and made them as though they had never been.

Looking out over the cove I felt a strong sense of the interchangeability of land and sea in this marginal world of the shore, and of the links between the life of the two. There was also an awareness of the past and of the continuing flow of time, obliterating much that had gone before, as the sea had that morning washed away the tracks of the bird.

The sequence and meaning of the drift of time were quietly summarized in the existence of hundreds of small snails—the mangrove periwinkles—browsing on the branches and roots of the trees. Once their ancestors had been sea dwellers, bound to the salt waters by every tie of their life processes. Little by little over the thousands and millions of years the ties had been broken, the snails had adjusted themselves to life out of water, and now today they were living many feet above the tide to which they only occasionally returned. And perhaps, who could say how many ages hence, there would be in their descendants not even this gesture of remembrance for the sea.

The spiral shells of other snails—these quite minute—left winding tracks on the mud as they moved about in search of food. They were horn shells, and when I saw them I had a nostalgic moment when I wished I might see what Audubon saw, a century and more ago. For such little horn shells were the food of the flamingo, once so numerous on this coast, and when I half closed my eyes I could almost imagine a flock of these magnificent birds feeding in that cove, filling it with their color. It was a mere yesterday in the life of the earth that they were there; in nature, time and space are relative matters, perhaps most truly perceived subjectively in occasional flashes of insight, sparked by such a magical hour and place.

There is a common thread that links these scenes and memories —the spectacle of life in all its varied manisfestations as it has appeared, evolved, and sometimes died out. Underlying the beauty of the spectacle there is meaning and significance. It is the elusiveness of that meaning that haunts us, that sends us again and again into the natural world where the key to the riddle is hidden. It sends us back to the edge of the sea, where the drama of life played its first scene on earth and perhaps even its prelude; where the forces of evolution are at work today, as they have been since the appearance of what we know as life; and where the spectacle of living creatures faced by the cosmic realities of their world is crystal clear.

## Study suggestions

1.   Through what details does the author justify her words *strange, beautiful, dual*? What does she mean by "The difficult world of the shore"?

2.   Describe the effect on her of this "pool of beauty," "this magical zone," and the shore at night. How do we catch her moods?

3.   Study the last paragraph for her meaning of the "key to the riddle." How do you interpret the "meaning and significance"?

4.   Collect her words that describe the edge of the sea and make vivid her descriptions. Find sensory words. How does she make us feel the sense of remoteness?

5.    How observant is she in her *word* paintings of the edge of the sea?

6.    Using her first sentence, write a theme on your personal reflections inspired by the edge of the sea.

7.    Write a description of the different moods: the calm blue sea; the fog and mist; the driving storms—and the influence on you.

8.    Perhaps you, too, have studied some of the living things that are especially numerous at low tide. Describe these.

# NIGHT ON THE GREAT BEACH

*Henry Beston*

Our fantastic civilization has fallen out of touch with many aspects of nature, and with none more completely than the night. Primitive folk, gathered at a cave mouth round a fire, do not fear night; they fear, rather, the energies and creatures to whom night gives power; we of the age of machines, having delivered ourselves of nocturnal enemies, now have a dislike of night itself. With lights and ever more lights, we drive the holiness and beauty of night back to the forests and the sea; the little villages, the crossroads even, will have none of it. Are modern folk, perhaps, afraid of the night? Do they fear that vast serenity, the mystery of infinite space, the austerity of stars? Having made themselves at home in a civilization obsessed with power, which explains its whole world in terms of energy, do they fear at night for their dull acquiescence and the pattern of their beliefs? Be the answer what it will, to-day's civilization is full of people who have not the slightest notion of the character or the poetry of night, who have never even seen night. Yet to live thus, to know only artificial night, is as absurd and evil as to know only artificial day.

Night is very beautiful on this great beach. It is the true other half of the day's tremendous wheel; no lights without meaning stab or trouble it; it is beauty, it is fulfilment, it is rest. Thin clouds float in these heavens, islands of obscurity in a splendour of space and stars: the Milky Way bridges earth and ocean; the beach resolves itself into a unity of form, its summer lagoons, its slopes and uplands merging; against the western sky and the falling bow of sun rise the silent and superb undulations of the dunes.

My nights are at their darkest when a dense fog streams in from the sea under a black, unbroken floor of cloud. Such nights are rare, but are most to be expected when fog gathers off the coast in early summer; this last Wednesday night was the darkest I have ever known. Between ten o'clock and two in the morning three vessels stranded on the outer beach—a fisherman, a four-masted schooner, and a beam trawler. The fisherman and the schooner have been towed off, but the trawler, they say, is still ashore.

I went down to the beach that night just after ten o'clock. So utterly black, pitch dark it was, and so thick with moisture and trailing showers, that there was no sign whatever of the beam of Nauset; the sea was only a sound, and when I reached the edge of the surf the dunes themselves had disappeared behind. I stood as isolated in the immensity of rain and night as I might have stood in interplanetary space. The sea was troubled and noisy, and when I opened the darkness with an outlined cone of light from my electric torch I saw that the waves were washing up green coils of sea grass, all coldly wet and bright in the motionless and unnatural radiance. Far off a single ship was groaning its way along the shoals. The fog was compact of the finest moisture; passing by, it spun itself into my lens of light like a kind of strange, aerial, and liquid silk. Effin Chalke, the new coast guard, passed me going north, and told me that he had had news at the halfway house of the schooner at Cahoon's.

It was dark, pitch dark to my eye, yet complete darkness, I imagine, is exceedingly rare, perhaps unknown in outer nature. The nearest natural approximation to it is probably the gloom of forest country buried in night and cloud. Dark as the night was here, there was still light on the surface of the planet. Standing on the shelving beach, with the surf breaking at my feet, I could see the endless wild uprush, slide, and withdrawal of the sea's white rim of foam. The men at Nauset tell me that on such nights they follow along this vague crawl of whiteness, trusting to habit and a sixth sense to warn them of their approach to the halfway house.

Animals descend by starlight to the beach. North, beyond the dunes, muskrats forsake the cliff and nose about in the driftwood and weed, leaving intricate trails and figure eights to be obliterated by the day; the lesser folk—the mice, the occasional small sand-coloured toads, the burrowing moles—keep to the upper beach and leave their tiny footprints under the overhanging wall. In autumn skunks, beset by a shrinking larder, go beach combing early in the night. The animal is by preference a clean feeder and turns up his nose at rankness. I almost stepped on a big fellow one night as I was walking north to meet the first man south from Nauset. There was a scamper, and the creature ran up the beach from under my feet; alarmed he certainly was, yet was he contained and continent. Deer are frequently seen, especially north of the light. I find tracks upon the summer dunes.

Years ago, while camping on this beach north of Nauset, I went for a stroll along the top of the cliff at break of dawn. Though the path followed close enough along the edge, the beach below was often hidden, and I looked directly from the height to the flush of sunrise at sea. Presently the path, turning, approached the brink of the earth precipice, and on the beach below, in the cool, wet rosiness of dawn, I saw three deer playing. They frolicked, rose on their hind legs, scampered off, and returned again, and were merry. Just before sunrise they trotted off north together down the beach toward a hollow in the cliff and the path that climbs it.

Occasionally a sea creature visits the shore at night. Lone coast guardsmen, trudging the sand at some deserted hour, have been startled by seals. One man fell flat on a creature's back, and it drew away from under him, flippering toward the sea, with a sound "halfway between a squeal and a bark." I myself once had rather a start. It was long after sundown, the light dying and uncertain, and I was walking home on the top level of the beach and close along the slope descending to the ebbing tide. A little more than halfway to the Fo'castle a huge unexpected something suddenly writhed horribly in the darkness under my bare foot. I had stepped on a skate left stranded by some recent crest of surf, and my weight had momentarily annoyed it back to life.

Facing north, the beam of Nauset becomes part of the dune night. As I walk toward it, I see the lantern, now as a star of light which waxes and wanes three mathematical times, now as a lovely pale flare of light behind the rounded summits of the dunes. The changes in the atmosphere change the colour of the beam; it is now whitish, now flame golden, now golden red; it changes its form as well, from a star to a blare of light, from a blare of light to a cone of radiance sweeping a circumference of fog. To the west of Nauset I often see the apocalyptic flash of the great light at the Highland reflected on the clouds or even on the moisture in the starlit air, and, seeing it, I often think of the pleasant hours I have spent there when George and Mary Smith were at the light and I had the good fortune to visit as their guest. Instead of going to sleep in the room under the eaves, I would lie awake, looking out of a window to the great spokes of light revolving as solemnly as a part of the universe.

All night long the lights of coastwise vessels pass at sea, green lights going south, red lights moving north. Fishing schooners and flounder draggers anchor two or three miles out, and keep a bright riding light burning on the mast. I see them come to anchor at sundown, but I rarely see them go, for they are off at dawn. When busy at night, these fishermen illumine their decks with a scatter of oil flares. From shore, the ships might be thought afire. I have watched the scene through a night glass. I could see no smoke, only the waving flares, the reddish radiance on sail and rigging, an edge of reflection overside, and the enormous night and sea beyond.

One July night, as I returned at three o'clock from an expedition north, the whole night, in one strange burning instant, turned into a phantom day. I stopped and, questioning, stared about. An enormous meteor, the largest I have ever seen, was consuming itself in an effulgence of light west of the zenith. Beach and dune and ocean appeared out of nothing, shadowless and motionless, a

landscape whose every tremor and vibration were stilled, a landscape in a dream.

The beach at night has a voice all its own, a sound in fullest
harmony with its spirit and mood—with its little, dry noise of sand
forever moving, with its solemn, overspilling, rhythmic seas, with
its eternity of stars that sometimes seem to hang down like
lamps from the high heavens—and that sound the piping of a bird.
As I walk the beach in early summer my solitary coming disturbs
it on its nest, and it flies away, troubled, invisible, piping its sweet,
plaintive cry. The bird I write of is the piping plover, *Char drius
melodus,* sometimes called the beach plover or the mourning bird.
Its note is a whistled syllable, the loveliest musical note, I think,
sounded by any North Atlantic bird.

Now that summer is here I often cook myself a camp supper on
the beach. Beyond the crackling, salt-yellow driftwood flame, over
the pyramid of barrel staves, broken boards, and old sticks all
atwist with climbing fire, the unseen ocean thunders and booms, the
breaker sounding hollow as it falls. The wall of the sand cliff behind, with its rim of grass and withering roots, its sandy crumblings
and erosions, stands gilded with flame; the wind cries over it; a
covey of sandpipers pass between the ocean and the fire. There are
stars, and to the south Scorpio hangs curving down the sky
with ringed Saturn shining in the claw.

Learn to reverence night and to put away the vulgar fear of it,
with the banishment of night from the experience of man, there
vanishes as well a religious emotion, a poetic mood, which gives
depth to the adventure of humanity. By day, space is one with
the earth and with man—it is his sun that is shining, his clouds
that are floating past; at night space is his no more. When the
great earth, abandoning day, rolls up the deeps of the heavens and
the universe, a new door opens for the human spirit, and there are
few so clownish that some awareness of the mystery of being
does not touch them as they gaze. For a moment of night we have a
glimpse of ourselves and of our world islanded in its stream of
stars—pilgrims of mortality, voyaging between horizons across
eternal seas of space and time. Fugitive though the instant be,
the spirit of man is, during it, ennobled by a genuine moment of

emotional dignity, and poetry makes its own both the human
spirit and experience.

## Study suggestions

1.    How would you answer the author's questions in the first
paragraph? Explain what he means by people "who have never
seen night."

2.    In this solitary spot at night what gives life to the beach?

3.    What is the effect of the night and of the sea on him? What
does he reveal of himself?

4.    Compare Rachel Carson's and Beston's feeling for the sea
and the out-of-doors, for beauty, for solitude, and for style of
expressing these emotions. Study his use of the sensory words. To
what sense does he appeal most?

5.    Compare, also, the concluding paragraphs of each.

6.    Describe a night sky by the ocean, a sunset or a dawn, a fog
that drifts in and out. Use the sensory words and show the mood
that you feel and your reflections.

# PERSONAL ESSAYS

*To be able to fill leisure intelligently is the last product of civilization.*

BERTRAND RUSSELL

# HOBBIES

*Winston S. Churchill*

Many remedies are suggested for the avoidance of worry and mental overstrain by persons who, over prolonged periods, have to bear exceptional responsibilities and discharge duties upon a very large scale. Some advise exercise, and others, repose. Some counsel travel, and others, retreat. Some praise solitude, and others gaiety. No doubt all these play their part according to the individual temperament. But the element which is constant and common in all of them is Change.

Change is the master key. A man can wear out a particular part of his mind by continually using it and tiring it, just in the same way as he can wear out the elbows of his coat. There is, however, this difference between the living cells of the brain and inanimate articles: one cannot mend the frayed elbows of a coat by rubbing the sleeves or shoulders; but the tired parts of the mind can be rested and strengthened not merely by rest, but by using other parts. It is not enough merely to switch off the lights which play upon the main and ordinary field of interest; a new field of interest must be illuminated. It is no use saying to the tired 'mental muscles'— if one may coin such an expression—'I will give you a good rest,' 'I will go for a long walk,' or 'I will lie down and think of nothing.' The mind keeps busy just the same. If it has been weighing and measuring, it goes on weighing and measuring. If it had been worrying, it goes on worrying. It is only when new cells are called into activity, when new stars become the lords of the ascendant, that relief, repose, refreshment are afforded.

A gifted American psychologist has said, 'Worry is a spasm of the emotion; the mind catches hold of something and will not let it go.' It is useless to argue with the mind in this condition. The stronger the will, the more futile the task. One can only gently insinuate something else into its convulsive grasp. And if this something else is rightly chosen, if it is really attended by the illumination of another field of interest, gradually, and often quite swiftly, the old undue grip relaxes and the process of recuperation and repair begins.

The cultivation of a hobby and new form of interest is therefore a policy of first importance to a public man. But this is not a business that can be undertaken in a day or swiftly improvised by a mere command of the will. The growth of alternative mental interests is a long process. The seeds must be carefully chosen; they must fall on good ground; they must be sedulously tended, if the vivifying fruits are to be at hand when needed.

To be really happy and really safe, one ought to have at least two or three hobbies, and they must all be real. It is no use starting late in life to say: 'I will take an interest in this or that.' Such an attempt only aggravates the strain of mental effort. A man may acquire great knowledge of topics unconnected with his daily work, and yet hardly get any benefit or relief. It is no use doing what you like; you have got to like what you do. Broadly speaking, human beings may be divided into three classes; those who are are toiled to death, those who are worried to death, and those who are bored to death. It is no use offering the manual labourer, tired out with a hard week's sweat and effort, the chance of playing a game of football or baseball on Saturday afternoon. It is no use inviting the politician or the professional or businessman, who has been working or worrying about serious things for six days, to work or worry about trifling things at the week-end.

As for the unfortunate people who can command everything they want, who can gratify every caprice and lay their hands on almost every object of desire—for them a new pleasure, a new excitement is only an additional satiation. In vain they rush frantically round from place to place, trying to escape from avenging boredom by mere clatter and motion. For them discipline in one form or another is the most hopeful path.

It may also be said that rational, industrious, useful human beings are divided into two classes: first, those whose work is work and whose pleasure is pleasure; and secondly, those whose work and pleasure are one. Of these the former are the majority. They have their compensations. The long hours in the office or the factory bring with them as their reward, not only the means of sustenance, but a keen appetite for pleasure even in its simplest and most modest forms. But Fortune's favoured children belong to the second class. Their life is a natural harmony. For them the working hours are never long enough. Each day is a holiday, and ordinary holidays when they come are grudged as enforced interruptions in an absorbing vocation. Yet to both classes the need of an alternative outlook, of a change of atmosphere, of a diversion of effort, is essential. Indeed, it may well be that those whose work is their pleasure are those who most need the means of banishing it at intervals from their mind.

The most common form of diversion is reading. In that vast and varied field millions find their mental comfort. Nothing makes a man more reverent than a library. 'A few books,' which was Lord Morley's definition of anything under five thousand, may give a sense of comfort and even of complacency. But a day in a library, even of modest dimensions, quickly dispels these illusory sensations. As you browse about, taking down book after book from the shelves and contemplating the vast, infinitely-varied store of knowledge and wisdom which the human race has accumulated and preserved, pride, even in its most innocent forms, is chased from the heart by feelings of awe not untinged with sadness. As one surveys the mighty array of sages, saints, historians, scientists, poets and philosophers whose treasures one will never be able to admire—still less enjoy—the brief tenure of our existence here dominates mind and spirit.

Think of all the wonderful tales that have been told, and well told, which you will never know. Think of all the searching inquiries into matters of great consequence which you will never pursue. Think of all the delighting or disturbing ideas that you will never share. Think of the mighty labours which have been accomplished for your service, but of which you will never reap the harvest. But from this melancholy there also comes a calm. The bitter sweets of a pious despair melt into an agreeable sense of compulsory resignation from which we turn with renewed zest to the lighter vanities of life.

'What shall I do with all my books?' was the question; and the answer, 'Read them,' sobered the questioner. But if you cannot read

them, at any rate handle them and, as it were, fondle them. Peer
into them. Let them fall open where they will. Read on from the
first sentence that arrests the eye. Then turn to another. Make a
voyage of discovery, taking soundings of uncharted seas. Set them
back on their shelves with your own hands. Arrange them on your
own plan, so that if you do not know what is in them, you at
least know where they are. If they cannot be your friends, let them
at any rate be your acquaintances. If they cannot enter the circle
of your life, do not deny them at least a nod of recognition.

It is a mistake to read too many good books when quite young.
A man once told me that he had read all the books that mattered.
Cross-questioned, he appeared to have read a great many, but they
seemed to have made only a slight impression. How many had
he understood? How many had entered into his mental composition? How many had been hammered on the anvils of his mind
and afterwards ranged in an armoury of bright weapons ready
to hand?

It is a great pity to read a book too soon in life. The first impression is the one that counts; and if it is a slight one, it may be
all that can be hoped for. A later and second perusal may recoil
from a surface already hardened by premature contact. Young
people should be careful in their reading, as old people in eating
their food. They should not eat too much. They should chew it well.

Since change is an essential element in diversion of all kinds,
it is naturally more restful and refreshing to read in a different
language from that in which one's ordinary daily work is done. To
have a second language at your disposal, even if you only know it
enough to read it with pleasure, is a sensible advantage. Our edu-
cationists are too often anxious to teach children so many different languages that they never get far enough in any one to derive
any use or enjoyment from their study. The boy learns enough
Latin to detest it; enough Greek to pass an examination; enough
French to get from Calais to Paris; enough German to exhibit a di-
ploma; enough Spanish or Italian to tell which is which; but not
enough of any to secure the enormous boon of access to a second
literature.

Choose well, choose wisely, and choose one. Concentrate upon
that one. Do not be content until you find yourself reading in it

with real enjoyment. The process of reading for pleasure in another language rests the mental muscles; it enlivens the mind by a different sequence and emphasis of ideas. The mere form of speech excites the activity of separate brain-cells, relieving in the most effective manner the fatigue of those in hackneyed use. One may imagine that a man who blew the trumpet for his living would be glad to play the violin for his amusement. So it is with reading in another language than your own.

But reading and book-love in all their forms suffer from one serious defect: they are too nearly akin to the ordinary daily round of the brain-worker to give that element of change and contrast essential to real life. To restore psychic equilibrium we should call into use those parts of the mind which direct both eye and hand. Many men have found great advantage in practicing a handicraft for pleasure. Joinery, chemistry, book-binding, even brick-laying —if one were interested in them and skilful at them—would give a real relief to the over-tired brain. But, best of all and easiest to procure are sketching and painting in all their forms. I consider myself very lucky that late in life I have been able to develop this new taste and pastime. Painting came to my rescue in a most trying time, and I shall venture in a concluding chapter to express the gratitude I feel.

Painting is a companion with whom one may hope to walk a great part of life's journey,

> 'Age cannot wither her nor custom stale
> Her infinite variety.'

One by one the more vigorous sports and exacting games fall away. Exceptional exertions are purchased only by a more pronounced and more prolonged fatigue. Muscles may relax, and feet and hands slow down; the nerve of youth and manhood may become less trusty. But painting is a friend who makes no undue demands, excites to no exhausting pursuits, keeps faithful pace even with feeble steps, and holds her canvas as a screen between us and the envious eyes of Time or the surly advance of Decrepitude.

Happy are the painters, for they shall not be lonely. Light and colour, peace and hope, will keep them company to the end, or almost to the end, of the day.

## Study suggestions

1.    Discuss the reasons for the author's emphasis on *change*.

2.    An often much quoted sentence of his from this article has much truth: "It is no use doing what you like; you have got to like what you do." How is this possible?

3.    Note his broad classifications of people. What hobbies would you suggest for each of the three?

4.    Secondly, he divides the "rational, industrious, useful human beings" into two groups. Why does he feel the second group is more fortunate? Yet why does he think that both groups need diversion?

5.    Compare his attitude towards books and reading with your own feelings, especially not reading "a book too soon." Illustrate this from your own experiences.

6.    Do you agree with Churchill on the second language?

7.    How does he feel about painting? Read his small book *Painting as a Pastime.*

8.    Name at least five famous people who have hobbies quite different from their work or profession.

9.    Write fully about your own hobbies and interests. If reading is one, discuss some books or types of literature which have brought you "companionship."

# MICKEY

*Edward Weeks*

Overhead the oak leaves stir against the cloudless blue, and the shadow in which I am reading ripples like running water. At my feet on the borderline between the sunny and the cool grass lies Mickey dozing, gray muzzle pointed toward the driveway up which the family will return from their expedition. Periodically he rouses himself, shakes the catkins from his black curls, and moves closer to the sun. His movement renews the scolding of the mother robin in the bittersweet and interrupts my intake of print. I watch him, and through the forming impressions of the book in my lap, memory thrusts its feeling.

This is probably our last summer together. Mickey is sixteen and that is a great age for a cocker spaniel given to eating any old thing; indeed a great age for any dog. Implicit in every friendship is the trust that it will never break. Mick has no reason to doubt us, but we who note his fading hearing and his inability to spot us at any distance on the beach live with the warning to make these months good.

I remember William Morton Wheeler's remarking on the silent communication between dogs, and how, when he had taken one of his for a walk through the Arboretum, the others would gather about the traveler instantly on his return and by scent and emanation have all the news in a matter of seconds. On the Common with other dogs Mick is eager, quivering, and gregarious when I am along, and hair-on-end belligerent when accompanying his mistress. In canine years he is now well past the century mark, so it is small wonder that dogs in their prime have only a passing curiosity in what he has to say. They pause, there is the usual tail-wagging introduction. Then, while he is still standing on his dignity, they suddenly lope off. Mick will start after and then resign himself to his own grass, which he scratches up with a "What the hell." For ladies he has, I gather, the charm of an aging colonel. There is a honey-colored spaniel who, after the nosing, will describe mad circles about him as he stands immovable on the moonlit Common. But if she pushes him too roughly he loses his balance and shows his lip, and so they part.

At home his expressions are stressed for our benefit. His humor, as when with jaws open and tongue half a yard out he stands there grinning; his sneeze of expectation; his mutter—a kind of controlled yip—of annoyance; his jumping recognition of those most important words in a city dog's vocabulary, "Going out" and "Down country" (is it the special note that colors our voices as we say them?); his sharp demanding bark when his water dish is empty or when brownies, his passion, are cooking—these are a language no one could miss. So too his boredom when, after a decent interval in our friend's house, he fetches his leash and stands obdurate with it in his jaws.

And in his play, he loves to tease. Mickey came to us when he was three weeks old and in the pecking order he established himself as a contemporary of my daughter Sara and as a senior in every respect to young Ted. In his youth we spent the winters in an apartment on the Fenway, and here Mickey devised a series of games for his own and our amusement. There was one he liked to play with a Malaga grape. A grape would be given him and he would go through the motions of chewing it. Then he would lie down facing us, his head cocked on one side. With a sudden twist he would fling the grape, perfectly intact, over his shoulder and pounce upon it as it rolled along the rug or under the table. Again the mock seriousness of swallowing it, the fixed stare in our direction, and again, the quick projection. The wonder was that he could keep this up for such a long time without puncturing the thin-skinned grape.

He loved to tease Sara about her dollhouse. The open rooms

were just right for his inspection, and the inmates—known as Mr. and Mrs. Brewster—were much to his taste. He would stand gazing into the living room until he was sure Sara was watching him; then with a quick dart he would seize one of the little dolls and be off, up the hall, through the kitchen, through the dining room, across the living room, and into the hall again. It was a lovely circle, and Sara could seldom catch him without the help of May, the cook. Sara's revenge was unpremeditated. One evening she set Mr. and Mrs. Brewster at the dinner table and served each of them a chocolate-covered Ex-lax for their supper, and after she had gone to sleep Mickey ate both. On rising the next morning, I found that he used the bathroom in a hurry, and Sara, all unknowing, supplied the perfect caption at breakfast: "Now, Mother, I told you the dolls were alive. They ate their candy."

I remember those times when he seemed to speak my language, once for instance when in his puppyhood he was sick from a distemper injection. He began vomiting at midnight and at four I got the car and drove him to the vet's. He was so weak that he leaned limply against the corner of the seat and door, but in answer to my hand his eyes said, "I'm sorry to be such a mess. But I *am* sick." And again, years later, when he had to apologize for his hunting. It was summer and our little cottage adjoined the orchard and vegetable garden of our big neighbor. At sundown rabbits would make free with the tender lettuce and carrots, and their scent—when Mickey got it—drove him wild. One evening from our screened porch I spotted a cottontail in the green. Mick was asleep, but quietly opening the door I pointed him at the quarry and he got the idea. Rabbit and spaniel disappeared ever the horizon with yips marking every second bound. Two hours went by, and then in darkness there was Mick scratching at the screen. "No luck," he said, and in his mouth was the half-eaten carrot the rabbit had dropped in his haste. "No luck."

Mickey is by his nature a hunter and a retriever. But now, with his teeth gone, his retrieving is limited to fishermen's corks as they curve ahead of him on the beach, and to apples in the orchard. He fancied himself a hunter, and for years he nourished a grudge against squirrels. I used to tease him about this. Walking close to one of our oaks, I would peer up into the leaves and touch the bark significantly; whereupon Mick would leave the ground jumping and scrabbling as high as my arm.

The squirrels for their part, enjoyed the feud: they knew he could never catch them. I remember one summer day when Mickey was lying on the open porch soaking up the sun which radiated from the warm boards. Close to the house stood an old apple tree, one of whose branches reached over the porch. Along this bridge, as Mickey slept, stole one of his bushy-tailed enemies. With mathematical precision the squirrel nipped clean a hard green apple, which hit the porch with a thump an inch from Mickey's nose. It was as nice a piece of natural comedy as I have ever witnessed; and the aftermath was noisy.

That dogs remember, we know from their habits and from their twitching dreams when they are so palpably reliving some activity. But how far back does their memory reach, and do those little half-uttered cries indicate that, like man, they are long haunted by old fears? If so, then Mick may still feel the most painful terror of domesticated animals—the fear of desertion. The autumn of his second year, my wife and I had to answer a sudden call to New York. We closed the cottage, packed up the daughter, and to save time left the pup with the maid. She took him to her home in Watertown, and from it he naturally escaped in search of us. That was on Friday afternoon. They saw him for an instant at the garbage pail Saturday morning, and then he was gone for good.

By our return on Monday there wasn't a clue. We drove the unfamiliar street and we put our appeal in the newspapers and on the air. In twenty-four hours we had heard from seventeen spaniel owners, fifteen of whom had lost their own dogs. But one of them gave us a tip. In their search they had seen a small black dog in the vast reaches of the Watertown Arsenal. So, with the Governor's permission, we drove through the gates—this was long before the war—to explore the cement strips which led between the huge closed buildings. A sergeant's son gave us hope. "Sure," he said, "a little black dog. He's here all right, only you can't get close to him." "Don't scare him," I said. "Find him if you can." Whistling and calling, we went to point after point, and once on the knoll above a huge oil tank I thought I heard the short familiar bark, but nothing moved. Three hours later we came back to the same spot, and there was the boy lying full-length on the cement wall aiming an imaginary gun. "The buffalo is down here," he called. Ten yards farther, and I saw Mick's nest and his unmistakable head. "Mickey," I shouted. Then up the slope he came on the dead run, his ears brown pancakes of burr.

Is it the fear of our leaving him that so troubles him when he can now no longer hear us as we move about the house? The sight of an open suitcase makes him more doleful than does a thunderstorm. When we pack for the country there is no way to tell him that he will surely come too. In his heart of hearts Mick knows that he is dependent upon four people, and no comfort of maid or sitter can distract his vigil when we are gone for the evening. Our woods are his woods. The squirrels who used to scold him he no longer hears. He begins not to hear us. But we shall hear him long after he is gone.

## Study suggestions

1.    Through what means does the writer make Mickey seem almost human? What qualities does he have?

2.    How does Mr. Weeks show his own affection and understanding of Mickey as well as that of the family?

3.    What do the incidents add to the portrait of Mickey?

4.    Write a characterization of some animal or pets you have enjoyed.

5.    Read *The Incredible Journey,* by Sheila Burnford, for the personality of three animals, loyal and devoted.

# FIRST NIGHT JITTERS

*Cornelia Otis Skinner*

A good long while ago, when I was first facing the horrors of an opening night in a leading role, I sought out my father for advice and reassurance, of which he gave me what he could. When, however, I asked him piteously how long one had to be in the theatre before outgrowing stage fright, he looked at me with quizzical compassion and said, "Kiddie (a term of endearment he used even after I was well on into maturity), I have been in the theatre for fifty years and I've *never* outgrown it. Any actor who claims he is immune to stage fright is either lying or else he's no actor." And he added further glad tidings: "What's more," he said, "the longer you stay in the theatre, the worse it becomes, because you learn more and you know all the mistakes you can make."

The realization that one's betters have gone through similar anguish is consoling, even if such realization doesn't in the least mitigate the anguish. No less triumphant an artist than Sarah Bernhardt, on overhearing a pert little ingénue boasting of not knowing what *le trac* (stage fright) was even like, is said to have snorted, "Wait until you become a good performer, my girl, and you'll find out." And another French actress, the delicious comedienne Marie Bell, suffered such ghastly and chronic stage fright, she had, literally and physically, to be shoved out from the wings for every first entrance by a sharp clip on her round little rear.

Such occupational panic is not the sole prerogative of people in the theatre. Singers, musicians, all public performers have known stage fright. Lily Pons once told me that every day of every concert or opera appearance she has ever given (and happily for the world, she has given quite a few), she has spent the preceding hours being actively sick at her stomach. Well, at any rate, that's one way of maintaining a trim and lovely figure.

One takes a certain chill comfort in assuming that persons of other professions have their corresponding heebie-jeebies—the lawyer about to plead a difficult case; the politician faced with a critical speech; even the clergyman, who, albeit he has the advantage of divine sponsorship, must feel an occasional quake of a knee as he mounts the steps of the pulpit. But not one of these worthies is as vulnerable as the wretched actor who has to walk out before an audience and be judged, in the long run, less by his technical skill than by his over-all personality—and then next day must read the verdict.

It's as though some poor devil were to set out for a large dinner party with the knowledge that the following morning he would be hearing exactly what each of the other guests thought about him. Only it's considerably worse when not just the victim but several million readers of newspapers are going to be reading the verdict. For there is no denying critics—except by the Shuberts, who for a time denied press tickets in any of their houses to a certain eminently vitriolic one. (He, however, purchased his own and continued to write his reviews, which were in no wise softened by the reprimand.) Toward the end of the seventeenth century, Wycherly, while going through the birth pangs of a new play, referred to critics as "those vermin of Parnassus," and, in case any critics should chance to be glancing over this piece, let me hasten to point out that such was William Wycherly's opinion and not necessarily mine.

Essential as it may be, the presence of these gentlemen of the press (to say nothing of that lady of same out in Chicago) is a definitely contributing factor to stage fright. There are a few actors who claim that they give a better performance under the challenge of knowing that critics are out in front. Well, that's what they claim and far be it from me to question the veracity of a fellow player. I can only record the fact (again an example of misery seeking out comfort) that Sir Henry Irving felt his style to be so cramped by the presence of reviewers that he set down a firm and fast rule that none should attend any opening night of his, but granted permission for them to filter in for subsequent performances, provided that he himself was never informed when they were there. Nice rule if you can make it, but who today commands Sir Henry's power?

The critics, awesome as they are, are only a portion of that other fright-provoking arbiter, that beloved monster, the Audience. Again, there are actors who will tell you not to think about the audience, to ignore it with the lofty attitude that there is not one in it who could step onto the stage and get away with your part. This advice not only does the quaking actor no damn bit of good, it is highly erroneous reasoning. To pay no attention to an audience would, in my opinion, be to violate one of the principal tenets of acting. For a good performance requires a constant give and take between player and public. It is a sort of ceaseless love affair with all of a love affair's breathless uncertainty, tip-toe sensitivity and eventual delight—or despair, as the case may prove.

In reality, the basic factor of stage fright is not so much fear of the audience, not even of the critics, but fear of one's self: fear that you won't be able to put on any halfway adequate sort of a show; fear that you'll go completely blank and forget all your lines, or that you'll develop an uncontrollable speech impediment. And there are grotesque fears, the sort Oscar Wilde attributed to an "imp of incongruity," like thinking you might suddenly go mad and goose the leading man, or walk calmly up to the footlights and stick out your tongue at Brooks Atkinson. And, of a thousand other goblins, not the least is the one identified by Mr. Roosevelt, the fear of fear itself.

With me, first-night jitters start long before the zero hour of the rising curtain. Like most players, I decide to take on a new role only if I am enthusiastically keen to play it, and, for the first weeks after making the decision, I'm all confidence and starry-eyed anticipation. Then, some 3 A.M., when I'm sleeping with the sweet innocence of those night-before-Christmas infants, instead of visions of sugar-plums dancing in my head, plonk! comes the old shaky-elevator dream.

In this, I am standing on a rickety platform without walls or railing, which, as it rises up a dingy shaft, wobbles and shudders, until at last I stare in horror down a yawning gap across which, the operator informs me, I must step or else plunge some twenty stories to my doom.

This fantasy, to the Freudian, will doubtless be fraught with significance indicative of unspeakable aspects of my nature and, if it is, I trust no one will enlighten me. I recognize it only as the first of a series of pre-opening dreams. They are indication of the doubts and misgivings which have plagued me ever since, at the age of 19, I waved a fan in the second act of *Blood and Sand* and said, "The bull can't help being a bull, can he?" (my part in its entirety) and they will doubtless continue to do so until I have been admitted to the Actors' Home. Even in those thespian Elysian Fields, if I am obliged to take part in any local theatricals, I am sure the same dear old doubts and misgivings will come flocking in.

Besides the shaky elevator incubus there are those standard nightmares known, I dare say, for centuries to anyone connected with show business. There is a hackneyed one about finding yourself in a strange dressing room, frantically slathering on someone else's make-up, while an irate stage manager tells you to hurry, you're late, and you ask, "What's my part?" To which he answers, "I don't know. Just get on the stage." So you ask, "What's the play?" But he doesn't know that either. At which point you wake trying desperately to say over the lines you memorized the day before—and, of course, you can't remember a single word.

There is the other routine dream about trying to get onto the stage and being hindered by innumerable huge obstacles, and the one about finally reaching it but finding yourself in a semi-paralyzed state in which you either are unable to move or do so with the slow-motion laboriousness of a giant sloth with lead weights on its feet. And there is the lockjaw chimera—you start to say your lines but can't utter a word because your jaws are clenched in a grinding vise which, on waking, you think may have damaged your front-tooth jackets. I used to have a recurrence of that other stand-by, the whimsy in which, amid a formally attired cast, I walked on stark naked—but that was when I was younger and more modest. Now that I am older and more shameless I don't dream it any more.

As the starting date for rehearsals approaches, the nightmares repeat themselves with increasing frequency until the eve of the initial reading when you dream not at all, because, as a rule, you sleep not at all. This means that next morning, with raddled face and halting gait, you slink onto the bare stage of an empty theatre to confront for the first time a brand-new cast, crew and director in the white, unshaded glare of the work lights. This is an illumination as relentless as that of the morning line-up at police headquarters; it would reduce the appearance of the prettiest starlet to that of an elderly character woman.

You try to assume a charming manner, bare your teeth at everyone in what you hope is a dazzling smile and settle with as much willowy grace as is possible onto a rehearsal chair, which is the wooden kitchen variety and often as not has lost its back. You feel that the other members of the company are wondering why the management dug up this old hag for a leading part and you note the speculative eye of your understudy.

The reading starts and you have the further feeling that you've completely forgotten how to act—if not, indeed, how to read. But then, here and there, among the circle of readers, you catch a fleeting expression of anguished uncertainty, the nervous clearing of a throat, the rapid trembling of a script, and are comforted.

During the week of rehearsal, stage fright lets up thanks to hard work and fatigue. And it's not too bad in the interim of road tryouts because of cuts, rewrites, new staging and similar pandemonium. But eventually, there looms the prospect of the Broadway opening.

At the end of a hideous day, there comes the walk to the scaffold in the form of a taxi ride to the theatre. In transit, I keep praying that we'll have a nice, easy accident, the sort that will incapacitate but not hurt, or that New York will be visited by a space ship from Mars and Mayor Wagner will order the closing of all theatres.

In my dressing room, where I arrive long before it's necessary, I go through the mechanics of making up, an especially complicated process for me because I suffer from shaky hands, which, under stress, become practically uncontrollable. All the while, of course, I continue my prayers for an honorable way out. Maybe with luck, just after my entrance, I'll be struck down by a falling sandbag, or perhaps I'll be fortunate enough to expire in some less ludicrous fashion, a highly becoming heart attack, for instance. But no such reprieve ever takes place and somehow we live through an opening night as we live through ensuing ordeals.

For the nasty thing about stage fright is that its attacks are not limited to opening nights. There are times when, for no good reason, it will strike and there is no anticipating them. You may be appearing in a long-run success, assured and cool as a cucumber, when all at once you hear another actor saying his lines and it's as though you were hearing them for the first time and you think, "What do I say when he finishes talking? What the hell is my next speech?" and you may go into a frozen paralysis from which prompter or fellow player rescues you by throwing you a cue, although, mercifully, more often habit or the subconscious produces the elusive words, which come forth automatically and often in such hollow tones you have an illusion that a complete stranger is saying them.

This Gehenna of anticipating lines can become epidemic and run through an entire company. One season, in *Major Barbara*, it was solacing to find out that a seasoned veteran like Charles Laughton came successfully through an attack; and when, one evening, Eli Wallach went up in a line he knew backwards (and backwards was about the way he said it, too) I felt better about the moment when I looked with a wild surmise at Glynis Johns, who played my daughter, and couldn't for the life of me think of her name.

I, who behind the exterior appearance of a lady am at heart the Wife of Bath, occasionally become the victim of another long-run neurosis, namely the dirty-word complex, in which one realizes that by the mere changing of a letter or two, or the shifting of a simple noun or mild adjective, the most innocent of speeches might be deformed into something censorable in the extreme.

The classic example (and just about the only one which can be printed on these pages) took place on the opening night of the revival of Maugham's *The Circle*. An actor whose line, in reference to Lily Langtry, was, "Her beauty was such that it took your breath away," declaimed clearly, "Her breath was such that it took your beauty away."

I have yet to play a part in which there is not the possibility of one of these verbal pitfalls. The terror of falling into one can become an obsession. As the sentence involving it approaches, I have found myself breaking into a clammy sweat. Am I going to say it? Please God, don't let me say it! And, even after the line has been delivered, I'll sometimes think, did I say it? Are people getting up from their seats and demanding their money back at the box office? But it is too painful to enumerate more of the actor's troubles.

What masochistic impulse drives us into this painful profession? What makes any woman become an actress? What, for that matter, makes her think she *is* an actress? Such doleful speculation is for psychiatrists and it seems to me I've already given them plenty to speculate about. The question arises, is it worth it? Is a theatrical career worth all the *Sturm und Drang?* And the answer —again a possible indication of mental unbalance—is yes.

If a show is a hit, the question never, obviously, arises. Rave reviews and a line-up at the box office can obliterate the memory of pain and apprehension as sweetly as the sight of her new-born can obliterate a woman's memories of labor pains. And if you're in a flop? It's hell, miserable, wretched hell.

But the very disappointment and misery seem eventually to rouse a doggedness, a determination to go on and try to make a go of it the next time. I guess what it comes down to is a simple and honest love of one's trade—for better for worse, for richer for poorer, in sickness and in health and even, for some, till death do them part.

## Study suggestions

1.   How comforting are the first paragraphs to all of us? Would athletes, aviators, acrobats—and others—join the ranks also? List the words that show her emotions.

2.   Explain all the factors of fear and stage fright. According to the author which are the worst? How does she regard her audience?

3.   Note her focus on fear and stage fright through repetition. Does this weaken the impression or convince the reader?

4.   How does she show her love for her profession in spite of all her forebodings? Also her humor and personality?

5.   Relate some experiences you have had in performing in some field of activity that involves public appearance—make vivid your emotions and fears of being ridiculous.

6.   Write an empathy theme in which you are the *leading* character. Start the theme with the word "Suddenly. . . ."

> The curtain went up (singer, speaker, actor)
> The man at the bat (critical period of a game)
> The door opened . . .

7.   Write on Dreams That Haunt Me.

# THE IMPORTANCE OF LOAFING:
## The Chinese Theory of Leisure

*Lin Yutang*

The American is known as a great hustler, as the Chinese is known as a great loafer. And as all opposites admire each other, I suspect that the American hustler admires the Chinese loafer as much as the Chinese loafer admires the American hustler. Such things are called the charms of national traits. I do not know if eventually the West and the East will meet; the plain fact is that they are meeting now, and are going to meet more and more closely as modern civilization spreads, with the increase of communication facilities. At least, in China, we are not going to defy this machine civilization, and there the problem will have to be worked out as to how we are going to merge these two cultures, the ancient Chinese philosophy of life and the modern technological civilization, and integrate them into a sort of working way of life. The question is more problematical as to Occidental life ever being invaded by Oriental philosophy, although no one would dare to prophesy.

After all, the machine culture is rapidly bringing us nearer to the age of leisure, and man will be compelled to play more and work less. It is all a matter of environment, and when man finds leisure hanging on his hands, he will be forced to think more about the ways and means of wisely enjoying his leisure, conferred upon him, against his will, by rapidly improving methods of quick production. After all, no one can predict anything about the next century. He would be a brave man who dared even to predict about life thirty years from now. The constant rush for progress must certainly one day reach a point when man will be pretty tired of it all, and will begin to take stock of his conquests in the material world. I cannot believe that, with the coming of better material conditions of life, when diseases are eliminated, poverty is decreased and man's expectation of life is prolonged and food is plentiful, man will care to be as busy as he is today. I'm not so sure that a more lazy temperament will not arise as a result of this new environment.

Apart from all this, the subjective factor is always as important as the objective. Philosophy comes in as a way of changing man's outlook and also changing his character. How man is going to react toward this machine civilization depends on what kind of a man he is. In the realm of biology, there are such things as sensibility to stimulus, slowness or quickness of reaction, and different behaviors of different animals in the same medium or environment. Some animals react more slowly than others. Even in this machine civilization, which I understand includes the United States, England, France, Germany, Italy, and Russia, we see that different reactions toward the mechanical age arise from different racial temperaments. The chances of peculiar individual reactions to the same environment are not eliminated. For China, I feel the type of life resulting from it will be very much like that in modern France, because the Chinese and the French temperaments are so akin.

America today is most advanced in machine civilization, and it has always been assumed that the future of a world dominated by the machine will tend toward the present American type and pattern of life. I feel inclined to dispute this thesis, because no one knows yet what the American temperament is going to be. At best we can only describe it as a changing temperament. I do not think it at all impossible that there may be a revival of that period of New England culture so well described in Van Wyck Brooks' new book. No one can say that that flowering of New England culture was not typically American culture, and certainly no one can say that that ideal Walt Whitman envisaged in his *Democratic Vistas*, pointing to the development of free men and perfect mothers, is not the ideal of democratic progress. America needs only to be given a little respite, and there may be—I am quite sure there will be—new Whitmans, new Thoreaus and new Lowells, when that old American culture, cut short literally and figuratively by the gold rush, may blossom forth again. Will not, then, American temperament be something quite different from that of the present day, and very near to the temperament of Emerson and Thoreau?

Culture, as I understand it, is essentially a product of leisure. The art of culture is therefore essentially the art of loafing. From the Chinese point of view, the man who is wisely idle is the most cultured man. For there seems to be a philosophic contradiction between being busy and being wise. Those who are wise won't be busy, and those who are too busy can't be wise. The wisest man is therefore he who loafs most gracefully. Here I shall try to explain, not the technique and varieties of loafing as practiced in China, but rather the philosophy which nourishes this divine desire for loafing in China and gives rise to that carefree, idle, happy-go-lucky—and often poetic—temperament in the Chinese scholars, and to a lesser extent, in the Chinese people in general. How did that Chinese temperament—that distrust of achievement and success and that intense love of living as such—arise?

In the first place, the Chinese theory of leisure, as expressed by a comparatively unknown author of the eighteenth century, Shu Paihsiang, who happily achieved oblivion, is as follows: time is useful because it is not being used. "Leisure in time is like unoccupied floor space in a room." Every working girl who rents a small room where every inch of space is fully utilized feels highly uncomfortable because she has no room to move about, and the moment she gets a raise in salary, she moves into a bigger room where there is a little more unused floor space, besides those strictly useful spaces occupied by her single bed, her dressing table and her two-burner gas range. It is that unoccupied space which makes a room habitable, as it is our leisure hours which make life endurable. I understand there is a rich woman living on Park Avenue, who bought up a neighboring lot to prevent anybody from erecting a skyscraper next to her house. She is paying a big sum of money in order to have space fully and perfectly made useless, and it seems to me she never spent her money more wisely.

In this connection, I might mention a personal experience. I could never see the beauty of skyscrapers in New York. And it was not until I went to Chicago that I realized that a skyscraper could be very imposing and very beautiful to look at, if it had a good frontage and at least half a mile of unused space around it. Chicago is fortunate in this respect, because it has more space than Manhattan. The tall buildings are better spaced, and there is the possibility of obtaining an unobstructed view of them from a long distance. Figuratively speaking, we, too, are so cramped in our life that we cannot enjoy a free perspective of the beauties of our spiritual life. We lack spiritual frontage.

## Study suggestions

1.   Explain what the problem would be in integrating the "ancient Chinese philosophy of life and the modern technological civilization."

2.   Discuss the problems of leisure time. Why is culture a "product of leisure"? Why does the writer call loafing an art?

3.   Explain: "Philosophy comes in as a way of changing man's outlook and also changing his character."

4.   Write your reaction to his thinking in which you show, too, your opinion of Americans' use of leisure. Are we too tense and restless?

# ROBERT FROST: A NEIGHBOR OF MINE

*Dorothy Canfield Fisher*

A much-experienced cosmopolitan visitor to our region sat chatting the other day on the bench overlooking our garden. The talk chanced to turn to books, and after a moment's silence, he said to me abruptly, "Maybe you can give me the answer. You must know authors through and through. WHAT'S THE MATTER WITH THEM?"

I knew perfectly well what he meant, but I was nettled, and pretended not to. "Matter?" I asked.

"Well, why is it that after you meet a famous writer, you usually decide his books can't be as good as you thought? Why are authors harder to talk to than a professional beauty? In my line of business I've met dozens of them," and he rattled off a list of glittering names. "They're simply impossible, all of them. Clammy as dead fish on any subject you can bring up if it's not going to get them more publicity. They don't seem to have any *natural* interests, as other human beings do, that take them out of themselves. And every word they say sounds like a move in a game, not an expression of what they think. What can there be about writing that turns a man into a posing self-conscious—I tell you, every time I've had to talk to one I go off and hunt me up a nice garage hand—"

I thought he had said about enough and interrupted him, "It's not writing. There's no more occupational risk in authorship than in farming or plumbing. The trouble is this lionizing business. Put your farmers or your plumbers or your nice, natural, unself-conscious garage hands into the damp hotness that lionizers create around authors—around any famous people—they'd spindle up the same sickly way, and put out shoots in the one direction that flattery comes from. But it's absurd to lump authors all together. You just notice any author who lives in ordinary, honest, human relationships with other people and with the earth—"

"I'd like fine to notice such an author!" broke in my interlocutor dryly.

A Chevrolet car began to climb the road up our hill. "I beg your pardon," I said. "Those are some neighbors of mine, and they're coming here to get some roots out of our garden. They've moved lately, from the farm where they lived to another one, and are starting a new perennial garden. I offered them some of the overflow from ours. You know how phlox and iris multiply."

The small car stopped. A middle-aged man and woman and a little boy got out from it. "Oh, they've brought along one of their grandchildren," I said. "That's fine. They have such lovely grandchildren. Come on, won't you, and help us dig roots?"

We were soon at it, spades and trowels in hand, the fair-haired five-year-old tagging tirelessly beside his grandfather, half listening to the talk, half dreamily soaking up the spring sunshine. There was plenty of talk to listen to, as, Yankee-fashion, it ranged from local gossip, zestfully passed along, to pungent comments on world news. My city visitor was evidently greatly taken with my Vermont neighbors, laughed out several times at a shrewd comical fancy of the husband, and after a brief, wise comment on life from the wife, looked with a quick pleasure of appreciation into her serene face and quiet eyes.

We finished, brushed the drying earth from our fingers, knocked off most of the mud from our shoes, and walked back to the bench for a rest. The little boy came to lean against his grandfather's knee. "You two are great friends, I see," said the city man.

My neighbor bent his graying head to look down at his grandson, who responded by nestling a little closer. "We get along together all right," said the grandfather.

The talk ran from one subject to another, baseball, Mussolini, politics, India, and fell on forestry—always a subject of interest to Vermonters. My neighbor knew all about white-pine plantations, and on being questioned by the man from the city, gave a disquisition on how to plant them and what they do for poor land, which made his listener reach for a notebook and jot down some pointers. It was his turn later to talk at length, when, someone happening to mention Ireland, it came out that he had just returned from a summer there. My country neighbor began at once to ask searching questions about the situation under the Free-State regime. At first the city man answered with caution, the cynical caution of experience which has found out that nobody ever really wants to hear about another person's travels. But he was soon enthusiastically recounting what he had seen, having found, apparently, the exception to his cynical rule in the countryman who sat next him, his shirt open at the throat, his gray hair ruffled by the breeze, his hands stained with earth hanging relaxed between his knees. He fixed intent blue eyes on the speaker, and with question and creative attention drew out the best of what the other had to give. I learned a great deal about Ireland in the five minutes that followed.

Just then another neighbor came across through the pine plantation back of us, looking for a strayed cow, and asked if we had seen her. After we said we hadn't, he stood there in his overalls, for a chat. "Have folks down your way got their oats in yet?" he asked the farmer from down the road, and they were off on farm talk, swapping stories about lost cows, laughing, comparing notes about firewood. He nodded, finally, and went his way, and so did the three who had come in the Chevrolet, which departed loaded to the gunwales with roots and seedlings.

"There," said my city visitor, "that's a good example of what I was talking about. Why can't authors be like that farmer? Did you notice how *natural* he was? Nothing said for effect, not a word. And open to the world outside himself. Do you know why his questions about Ireland were so intelligent, went to the heart of the matter? I'll tell you why. It was because he was thinking about Ireland, and not about himself. Because he really wanted to find out something about it—he wasn't just making me talk as one way of soft-soaping me. The way he listened! Just show me an author who's as fine a human being as that gray-haired farmer— who's moved out of himself into a bigger place as that countryman has, who can talk on equal terms with another farmer and with

a transatlantic traveler, who's grown to be one with a fine wife as a
man can only after years of deep living, who has time to live with
his grandchildren, and who never once in a long conversation
brings the talk around to himself. Why, just the way that man looks
at a person, sees that he's there, as much a human being as he is!
No author—" He stopped, staring at me. I imagine I was looking
rather odd.

"You didn't, I take it," I said, "catch his name, when I introduced you."

"No, I don't believe I did."

"His name," I said, "is Robert Frost."

### Study suggestions

1.   How common is this concept of a writer as a poseur? How
did Dorothy Canfield Fisher react to the visitor's criticisms?

2.   What facets of the *neighbor* were revealed in the conversation?

3.   Analyze the city visitor's reaction to the neighbor.

4.   Note the climactic ending, not spoiled by further comment.

5.   Although some years have elapsed since this vignette was
written, how does this sketch tally with the interest and alertness
of Robert Frost today?

6.   Read *Robert Frost: The Trial by Existence,* by Elizabeth
Shepley Sergeant, for a more recent review.

# LITTLE PEOPLE AND BIG WORDS

*Sherwood Anderson*

On my farm in Virginia is a man who has been there, as farmer, for twelve years. He works hard, trying to make the farm pay its own way. I live there in the summers and wander around America in the winters. I meet a good many people of the so-called artist class —authors, musicians, poets, painters. Mostly, I have found, they are very sour on life.

They think that civilization is going to pieces. Things are not right with our country or with the world. I gather that of course none of this is their own fault. It is the fault of the people, they say; the people, who are too dumb.

I think all this would be of no importance except that from these men and women come the books and articles that people read. So they influence the thinking of others.

These writers and poets and painters seem to be in a terrible hurry. I find that they do not have much time to make acquaintances outside their own circle. So they can never understand the people of whom they complain. The people are "the masses." They dismiss them with a word.

Not long ago I was walking with a friend along crowded city streets. For an hour he talked of himself, of what a terrible problem life was to him. Civilization, he said, was falling into chaos. Why? He used vague words. "People are too stupid." He spoke of "the people," but he did not mean the hundreds of individuals who passed us as we walked, for he was not aware of them. His ears were filled only with the sound of his own complaint.

We passed a boy and girl and I heard her saying: "You don't want to worry. There've been things worse than this before. We're going to come out all right. Why, if things were all right all the time, we'd never appreciate it!" I saw her smiling at him. The boy's frown changed and I saw him smiling back at her.

"These dumb masses," my friend said, making a sweeping gesture. He had seen nothing but what he had been thinking in his head. "Like cattle! How can you make them understand?"

Another friend of mine is a young poet. I took him with me once to spend an evening with a certain family. They are what is called "middle class." They had heard that my friend was a poet, and so they were a little overawed. For a while conversation did not go easily.

A boy of perhaps twenty came by to visit one of the daughters. He stood waiting for her and he seemed embarrassed, talking too loudly and saying things he did not mean. After he and the girl had gone out together, I was told that they had been sweethearts from childhood, but that lately the girl had been attracted to an older man with a successful business. The mother favored the older man, but the father liked the boy. The girl's sister favored the boy, too. "She wouldn't be happy with Tommy," the mother said. "I don't want to see any more unhappiness."

The girl's sister got up and excused herself; she was smiling, but I saw that her face was strained. "I shouldn't have said that," the mother said. Then I learned that the man this other daughter had been going to marry had suddenly gone insane. She was herself nearly half insane with grief. But she had been sitting there with us, covering up her grief, smiling, talking, trying to come back to normal.

"She'll get over it," the father said. "It's hard for her now, but she won't let it beat her."

When we left, my friend the poet asked me what I saw "in dull middle-class people like that."

These are the words we hear—"the masses," "the middle class," "the capitalists." Thousands of men working in the great facto-ries; one word, "the masses," makes them all the same, pigeonholed and dismissed. The people who use the word do not see the lines on their faces; they are not aware of the ideas, the problems, the emotions that make these thousands of faces, these thousands of lives, each one different from the other, each with its own strivings and ambitions, its sorrows and joys.

"The people are stupid." But there is no such thing as "the people." There is instead the individual. He can be put into this "class" or that "class," but he does not know it. He remains himself, a man or woman shaping his life, living an adventure, striving for happiness, for decency. He knows what he is striving for. He knows so well that he will die for it, if need be. The good fights have never been fought and won by those who use the big empty words and find "the people" dull.

I used to talk with a woman who worked at a machine in a factory. Her husband was dead; there were two children at home to support. She was not a machine that guided another machine. Her children were going to school; she read their schoolbooks and taught herself through her children's minds. She talked of the machine she worked at. "It is a wonderful thing," she said. "My boy knows how it is made, and he taught me. Some day he is going to make a better machine. I think that is the idea of America. It says, 'Here! There are things to do, things to make better. No one is holding you back. You go out, all you young ones, and learn, and work, and make things better.' "

She was a part of "the masses." Her life was not dull. Her life was joy and adventure.

I spoke of the farmer on my place. He has been struggling for years to improve the half-worn out-soil of my farm. He gains a little, year by year. That poor soil is a living thing to him, a sick thing that he is nourishing and helping back to health. He is a man of few words, but occasionally he talks of what he thinks about.

Once in a while when I have been listening for too long to the big thinkers, I go out to the barn where he is perhaps milking a cow. I talk with him and my mind clears of the big words I have heard, all the complaints and questionings. "This is 'the people,' " I think as I listen to him. "This is what is so ordinary and commonplace." And I wish that I had my friends v ith me, to listen too.

The farmer is talking to me of his life, of the soil he nourishes, of an idea that came to him out in the fields the other day. Then he talks of the people of the neighborhood. The son of the family down the road has come back from an agricultural college, and he has a lot of new ideas. His father pretends to be dubious, and they argue, but behind his son's back he says to the other farmers, "You ought to come and listen to my boy." And a young man near by, who married the girl no one thought much of, the girl he found in the city—well, it seems he broke his leg and couldn't work, and this girl got out and did the work, and took care of him too. It seems she is a fine girl, after all.

The farmer tells me all this. He makes me aware, if I had never been aware before, that each individual's life is a world of its own. It may be a very little world, compounded of things that would be of no importance elsewhere; but it is separate, it is individual, it has its own color and adventure.

That is the answer to those who say "the masses," "the classes," who use the words that mean nothing. They do not see beneath the big empty words to what is right next to them, to what is all around them, to the individuals who are "the people," to the adventure of their days, the ever-varied texture of their lives, the dreams and hopes that, slowly, they work to make into reality. The words are dead, empty and bitter; "the people" are unaware of them, for the people are alive.


## Study suggestions

1.   According to the writer, the people of the "so-called artist class" are "sour on life" and are snobbish concerning other people, yet influence the thinking of others. Is this too much of a generalization? Discuss the tendency to pigeonhole people.

2.   "There is no such thing as *the people*. There is instead the individual." How does the author feel about people and about clichés?

3.   How does Sherwood Anderson prove "that each individual's life is a world of his own"? Analyze his conclusion.

4.   Compare this with that of the city visitor in the previous essay.

5.   Theme suggestions:
People in My Life
As I See People
Snobs and Critics
A Character I Admire

# HUMOR AND SATIRE

*No mind is thoroughly well organized that is deficient in a sense of humor.*

SAMUEL T. COLERIDGE

*He who laughs lasts.*
WILSERD PETERSON

# UNIVERSITY DAYS

*James Thurber*

I passed all the other courses that I took at my University, but I could never pass botany. This was because all botany students had to spend several hours a week in a laboratory looking through a microscope at plant cells, and I could never see through a microscope. I never once saw a cell through a microscope. This used to enrage my instructor. He would wander around the laboratory pleased with the progress all the students were making in drawing the involved and, so I am told, interesting structure of flower cells, until he came to me. I would just be standing there. "I can't see anything," I would say. He would begin patiently enough, explaining how anybody can see through a microscope, but he would always end up in a fury, claiming that I could *too* see through a microscope but just pretended that I couldn't. "It takes away from the beauty of flowers anyway," I used to tell him. "We are not concerned with beauty in this course," he would say. "We are concerned solely with what I may call the *mechanics* of flars." "Well," I'd say, "I can't see anything." "Try it just once again," he'd say, and I would put my eye to the microscope and see nothing at all, except now and again a nebulous milky substance—a phenomenon of maladjustment. You were supposed to see a vivid, restless clockwork of sharply defined plant cells. "I see what looks like a lot of milk," I would tell him. This, he claimed, was the result of my not having adjusted the microscope properly, so he would readjust it for me, or rather, for himself. And I would look again and see milk.

I finally took a deferred pass, as they called it, and waited a year and tried again. (You had to pass one of the biological sciences or you couldn't graduate.) The professor had come back from vacation brown as a berry, bright-eyed, and eager to explain cell-structure again to his classes. "Well," he said to me, cheerily, when we met in the first laboratory hour of the semester, "we're going to see cells this time, aren't we?" "Yes, sir," I said. Students to right of me and to left of me and in front of me were seeing cells; what's more, they were quietly drawing pictures of them in their notebooks. Of course, I didn't see anything.

"We'll try it," the professor said to me, grimly, "with every adjustment of the microscope known to man. As God is my witness, I'll arrange this glass so that you see cells through it or I'll give up teaching. In twenty-two years of botany, I—" He cut off abruptly for he was beginning to quiver all over, like Lionel Barrymore, and he genuinely wished to hold onto his temper; his scenes with me had taken a great deal out of him.

So we tried it with every adjustment of the microscope known to man. With only one of them did I see anything but blackness or the familiar lacteal opacity, and that time I saw, to my pleasure and amazement, a variegated constellation of flecks, specks, and dots. These I hastily drew. The instructor, noting my activity, came back from an adjoining desk, a smile on his lips and his eyebrows high in hope. He looked at my cell drawing. "What's that?" he demanded, with a hint of a squeal in his voice. "That's what I saw," I said. "You didn't, you didn't, you *did*n't!" he screamed, losing control of his temper instantly, and he bent over and squinted into the microscope. His head snapped up. "That's your eye!" he shouted. "You've fixed the lens so that it reflects! You've drawn your eye!"

Another course that I didn't like, but somehow managed to pass, was economics. I went to that class straight from the botany class, which didn't help me any in understanding either subject. I used to get them mixed up. But not as mixed up as another student in my economics class who came there direct from a physics laboratory. He was a tackle on the football team, named Bolenciecwcz. At that time Ohio State University had one of the best football teams in the country, and Bolenciecwcz was one of its outstanding stars. In order to be eligible to play it was necessary for him to keep up in his studies, a very difficult matter, for while he was not dumber than an ox he was not any smarter. Most of his professors were lenient and helped him along. None gave him more hints, in answering questions, or asked him simpler ones than the economics professor, a thin, timid man named Bassum. One day when we were on the subject of transportation and distribution, it came Bolenciecwcz's turn to answer a question. "Name one means of transportation," the professor said to him. No light came into the big tackle's eyes. "Just any means of transportation," said the professor. Bolenciecwcz sat staring at him. "That is," pursued the professor, "any medium, agency, or method of going from one place to another." Bolenciecwcz had the look of a man who is being led into a trap. "You may choose among steam, horse-drawn, or electrically propelled vehicles," said the instructor. "I might suggest the one which we commonly take in making long journeys across land." There was a profound silence in which everybody stirred uneasily, including Bolenciecwcz and Mr. Bassum. Mr. Bassum abruptly broke this silence in an amazing manner. "Choo-choo-choo," he said, in a low voice, and turned instantly scarlet. He glanced appealingly around the room. All of us, of course, shared Mr. Bassum's desire that Bolenciecwcz should stay abreast of the class in economics, for the Illinois game, one of the hardest and most important of the season, was only a week off. "Toot, too, too-tooooot!" some student with a deep voice moaned, and we all looked encouragingly at Bolenciecwcz. Somebody else gave a fine imitation of a locomotive letting off steam. Mr. Bassum himself rounded off the little show. "Ding, dong, ding, dong," he said, hopefully. Bolenciecwcz was staring at the floor now, trying to think, his great brow furrowed, his huge hands rubbing together, his face red.

"How did you come to college this year, Mr. Bolenciecwcz?" asked the professor. *"Chuff*a chuffa, *chuff*a chuffa."

"M'father sent me," said the football player.

"What on?" asked Bassum.

"I git an 'lowance," said the tackle, in a low, husky voice, obviously embarrassed.

"No, no," said Bassum. "Name a means of transportation. What did you *ride* here on?"

"Train," said Bolenciecwcz.

"Quite right," said the professor. "Now, Mr. Nugent, will you tell us—"

If I went through anguish in botany and economics—for different reasons—gymnasium work was even worse. I don't even like to think about it. They wouldn't let you play games or join in the exercises with your glasses on and I couldn't see with mine off. I bumped into professors, horizontal bars, agricultural students, and swinging iron rings. Not being able to see, I could take it but I couldn't dish it out. Also, in order to pass gymnasium (and you had to pass it to graduate) you had to learn to swim if you didn't know how. I didn't like the swimming pool, I didn't like swimming, and I didn't like the swimming instructor, and after all these years I still don't. I never swam but I passed my gym work anyway, by having another student give my gymnasium number (978) and swim across the pool in my place. He was a quiet, amiable blond youth, number 473, and he would have seen through a microscope for me if we could have got away with it, but we couldn't get away with it. Another thing I didn't like about gymnasium work was that they made you strip the day you registered. It is impossible for me to be happy when I am stripped and being asked a lot of questions. Still, I did better than a lanky agricultural student who was cross-examined just before I was. They asked each student what college he was in—that is, whether Arts, Engineering, Commerce, or Agriculture. "What college are you in?" the instructor snapped at the youth in front of me. "Ohio State University," he said promptly.

It wasn't that agricultural student but it was another a whole lot like him who decided to take up journalism, possibly on the ground that when farming went to hell he could fall back on newspaper work. He didn't realize, of course, that that would be very much like falling back full-length on a kit of carpenter's tools. Haskins didn't seem cut out for journalism, being too embarrassed to talk to anybody and unable to use a typewriter, but the editor of the college paper assigned him to the cow barns, the sheep house, the horse pavilion, and the animal husbandry department generally. This was a genuinely big "beat," for it took up five times as much ground and got ten times as great a legislative appropriation as the College of Liberal Arts. The agricultural student knew animals, but nevertheless his stories were dull and colorlessly written. He took all afternoon on each of them, on account of having to hunt for each letter on the typewriter. Once in a while he had to ask somebody to help him hunt. "C" and "L," in particular, were hard letters for him to find. His editor finally got pretty much annoyed at the farmer-journalist because his pieces were so uninteresting. "See here, Haskins," he snapped at him one day, "why is it we never have anything hot from you on the horse pavilion? Here we have two hundred head of horses on this campus—more than any other university in the Western Conference except Purdue—and yet you never get any real lowdown on them. Now shoot over to the horse barns and dig up something lively." Haskins shambled out and came back in about an hour; he said he had something. "Well, start it off snappily," said the editor. "Something people will read." Haskins set to work and in a couple of hours brought a sheet of typewritten paper to the desk; it was a two-hundred-word story about some disease that had broken out among the horses. Its opening sentence was simple but arresting. It read: "Who has noticed the sores on the tops of the horses in the animal husbandry building?"

Ohio State was a land grant university and therefore two years of military drill was compulsory. We drilled with old Springfield rifles and studied the tactics of the Civil War even though the World War was going on at the time. At 11 o'clock each morning thousands of freshmen and sophomores used to deploy over the campus, moodily creeping up on the old chemistry building. It was good training for the kind of warfare that was waged at Shiloh but it had no connection with what was going on in Europe. Some people used to think there was German money behind it, but they didn't dare say so or they would have been thrown in jail as German spies. It was a period of muddy thought and marked, I believe, the decline of higher education in the Middle West.

As a soldier I was never any good at all. Most of the cadets were glumly indifferent soldiers, but I was no good at all. Once General Littlefield, who was commandant of the cadet corps, popped up in front of me during regimental drill and snapped, "You are the main trouble with this university!" I think he meant that my type was the main trouble with the university but he may have meant me individually. I was mediocre at drill, certainly—that is, until my senior year. By that time I had drilled longer than anybody else in the Western Conference, having failed at military at the end of each preceding year so that I had to do it all over again. I was the only senior still in uniform. The uniform which, when new, had made me look like an interurban railway conductor, now that it had become faded and too tight made me look like Bert Williams in his bellboy act. This had a definitely bad effect on my morale. Even so, I had become by sheer practice little short of wonderful at squad manoeuvres.

One day General Littlefield picked our company out of the whole regiment and tried to get it mixed up by putting it through one movement after another as fast as we could execute them: squads right, squads left, squads on right into line, squads right about, squads left front into line, etc. In about three minutes one hundred and nine men were marching in one direction and I was marching away from them at an angle of forty degrees, all alone. "Company, halt!" shouted General Littlefield, "That man is the only man who has it right!" I was made a corporal for my achievement.

The next day General Littlefield summoned me to his office. He was swatting flies when I went in. I was silent and he was silent too, for a long time. I don't think he remembered me or why he had sent for me, but he didn't want to admit it. He swatted some more flies, keeping his eyes on them narrowly before he let go with the swatter. "Button up your coat!" he snapped. Looking back on it now I can see that he meant me although he was looking at a fly, but I just stood there. Another fly came to rest on a paper in front of the general and began rubbing its hind legs together. The general lifted the swatter cautiously. I moved restlessly and the fly flew away. "You startled him!" barked General Littlefield, looking at me severely. I said I was sorry. "That won't help the situation!" snapped the general, with cold military logic. I didn't see what I could do except offer to chase some more flies toward his desk, but I didn't say anything. He stared out the window at the faraway figures of co-eds crossing the campus toward the library. Finally, he told me I could go. So I went. He either didn't know which cadet I was or else he forgot what he wanted to see me about. It may have been that he wished to apologize for having called me the main trouble with the university; or maybe he had decided to compliment me on my brilliant drilling of the day before and then at the last minute decided not to. I don't know. I don't think about it much any more.

## Study suggestions

Humor often depends on the overstatement or exaggeration, understatement, saying the opposite, or caricature, but the particular brand of James Thurber's humor is difficult to explain or evaluate as it is funny in a "unique and inimitable" way. There is whimsy and exaggeration, irony and satire, but with a pathos behind it. T. S. Eliot remarks that "There is a criticism of life at the bottom of it."

His own artistic credo has been quoted as follows: "Humor is a kind of emotional chaos told about calmly and quietly in retrospect."

1. Why is his humor called whimsical and comically autobiographical? In this essay on what does his humor depend? How does it tally with his credo?

2. Write with some exaggeration an account of some embarrassing moments in your life.

# MY FISHING POND

*Stephen Leacock*

It lies embowered in a little cup of the hills, my fishing pond. I made a last trip to it just as the season ended, when the autumn leaves of its great trees were turning color and rustling down to rest upon the still black water. So steep are the banks, so old and high the trees, that scarcely a puff of wind ever ruffles the surface of the pond. All around, it is as if the world were stilled into silence, and time blended into eternity.

I realized again as I looked at the pond what a beautiful, secluded spot it was, how natural its appeal to the heart of the angler. You turn off a country road, go sideways across a meadow and over a hill, and there it lies—a sheet of still water, with high, high banks, grown with great trees. Long years ago someone built a sawmill, all gone now, at the foot of the valley and threw back the water to make a pond, perhaps a quarter of a mile long. At the widest it must be nearly two hundred feet—the most skillful fisherman may make a full cast both ways. At the top end, where it runs narrow among stumps and rushes, there is no room to cast except with direction and great skill.

Let me say at once, so as to keep no mystery about it, that there are no fish in my pond. So far as I know there never have been. But I have never found that to make any difference. Certainly none to the men I bring there—my chance visitors from the outside world—for an afternoon of casting.

If there are no fish in the pond, at least they never know it. They never doubt it; they never ask, and I let it go at that.

It is well known hereabouts that I do not take anybody and everybody out to my fishpond. I only care to invite people who can really fish, who can cast a line—experts, and especially people from a distance to whom the whole neighborhood is new and attractive, the pond seen for the first time. If I took out ordinary men, especially men near home, they would very likely notice that they got no fish. The expert doesn't. He knows trout fishing too well. He knows that even in a really fine pond, such as he sees mine is, there are days when not a trout will rise. He'll explain it to you himself; and, having explained it, he is all the better pleased if he turns out to be right and they don't rise.

Trout, as everyone knows who is an angler, never rise after a rain, nor before one; it is impossible to get them to rise in the heat; and any chill in the air keeps them down. The absolutely right day is a still, cloudy day, but even then there are certain kinds of clouds that prevent a rising of the trout. Indeed, I have only to say to one of my expert friends, "Queer, they didn't bite!" and he's off to a good start with an explanation. There is such a tremendous lot to know about trout fishing that men who are keen on it can discuss theories of fishing by the hour.

Such theories we generally talk over—my guest of the occasion and I—as we make our preparations at the pond. You see, I keep there all the apparatus that goes with fishing—a punt, with lockers in the sides of it, a neat little dock built out of cedar (cedar attracts the trout), and, best of all, a little shelter house, a quaint little place like a pagoda, close beside the water and yet under the trees. Inside is tackle, all sorts of tackle, hanging round the walls in a mixture of carelessness and order.

"Look, old man," I say, "if you like to try a running paternoster, take this one," or, "Have you ever seen these Japanese leads? No, they're not a gut; they're a sort of floss."

"I doubt if I can land one with that," he says.

"Perhaps not," I answer. In fact, I'm sure he couldn't; there isn't any to land.

On pegs in the pagoda hangs a waterproof mackintosh or two, for you never know—you may be caught in a shower just when the trout are starting to rise. Then of course, a sort of cellarette cupboard with decanters and bottles, and gingersnaps, and perhaps an odd pot of anchovy paste—no one wants to quit good fishing for mere hunger. Nor does any real angler care to begin fishing without taking just a drop (Just a touch—be careful! Whoa! Whoa!) of something to keep out the cold, or to wish good luck for the chances of the day.

I always find, when I bring out one of my friends, that these mere preparatives or preparations, these preliminaries of angling, are the best part of it. Often they take half an hour. There is so much to discuss—the question of weights of tackle, the color of the fly to use, and broad general questions of theory, such as whether it matters what kind of hat a man wears. It seems that trout will rise for some hats, and for others not. One of my best guests, who has written a whole book on fly fishing, is particularly strong on hats and color. "I don't think I'd wear that hat, old man," he says, "much too dark for a day like this." "I wore it all last month," I said. "So you might, but that was August. I wouldn't wear a dark hat in September; and that tie is too dark a blue, old man."

So I knew that that made it all right. I kept the hat on. We had a grand afternoon; we got no fish.

I admit that the lack of fish in my pond requires sometimes a little tact in management. The guest gets a little restless. So I say to him, "You certainly have the knack of casting!"—and he gets so absorbed in casting farther and farther that he forgets the fish. Or I take him toward the upper end and he gets his line caught on bulrush—that might be a bite. Or, if he still keeps restless, I say suddenly, "Hush! Was that a fish jumped?" That will silence any true angler instantly. "You stand in the bow," I whisper, "and I'll paddle gently in that direction." It's the *whispering* that does it. We are still a hundred yards away from any trout that could hear us even if a trout were there. But that makes no difference. Some of the men I take out begin to whisper a mile away from the pond and come home whispering.

You see, after all, what with frogs jumping, and catching the line in bulrushes, or pulling up a water-logged chip nearly to the top, they don't really know—my guests don't—whether they have hooked something or not. Indeed, after a little lapse of time, they think they did: they talk of the "big one they lost"—a thing over which any angler gets sentimental in retrospect. "Do you remember," they say to me months later at our club in the city, "that big trout I lost up on your fishpond last summer?" "Indeed I do," I say. "Did you ever get him later on?" "No, never," I answer. (Neither him nor any other.)

Yet the illusion holds good. And besides, you never can tell: there *might* be trout in the pond. Why not? After all, why shouldn't there be a trout in the pond? You take a pond like that and there ought to be trout in it!

Whenever the sight of the pond bursts on the eyes of a new guest he stands entranced. "What a wonderful place for trout!" he exclaims. "Isn't it?" I answer. "No wonder you'd get trout in a pond like that." "No wonder at all." "You don't need to stock it at all, I suppose?" "Stock it!" I laughed at the idea. Stock a pond like that! Well, I guess not!

Perhaps one of the best and most alluring touches is fishing out of season—just a day or two after the season has closed. Any fisherman knows how keen is the regret at each expiring season—

swallowed up and lost in the glory of the fading autumn. So if a guest turns up just then I say, "I know it's out of season, but I thought you might care to take a run out to the pond anyway and have a look at it." He can't resist. By the time he's in the pagoda and has a couple of small drinks (Careful, not too much! Whoa! Whoa!) he decides there can be no harm in making a cast or two. "I suppose," he says, "you never have any trouble with the inspectors?" "Oh, no," I answer; "they never think of troubling me." And with that we settle down to an afternoon of it. "I'm glad," says the guest at the end, "that they weren't rising. After all, we had just the same fun as if they were."

That's it: illusion! How much of life is like that! It's the idea of the thing that counts, not the reality. You don't need fish for fishing, any more than you need partridge for partridge shooting, or gold for gold mining. Just the illusion or expectation.

So I am going back now to the city and to my club, where we shall fish all winter, hooking up big ones, but losing the ones bigger still, hooking two trout at one throw,—three at a throw!—and for me, behind it all, the memory of my fishing pond darkening under the falling leaves . . . At least it has made my friends happy.

## Study suggestions

1. From the title and the first two paragraphs what are you led to expect?

2. Why does he limit his invitations to fish in his pond to the expert and to non-local people?

3. How does he keep up the *illusion* and explain it? Does he really lie about the fish?

4. What glimpses of the guests and fishermen does the reader get?

5. Explain the meaning in the next to last paragraph.

6. Compare his humor with that of Thurber.

# ON WEEKEND GUESTS

*Russell Lynes*

What makes a good guest is a subtle complex of personality, manners, and delicacy of feeling, coupled with one's own state of forbearance at the moment when the guest appears. There are friends one can always depend on, but they are likely to be old friends for whom no amount of trouble is a burden and whose awareness of one's shortcomings is equaled by their readiness to accept them.

But not all guests can be old friends; they are merely the certain islands of calm and delight in a summer filled with potential catastrophe. Let us consider those other guests, most of whom we have invited in overexpansive moments to share our hospitality.

The standard weekend guests are a couple, but there the standard stops and the variations set in. We cannot discuss all of the variations, but let us take a few common ones and face up to this problem now that summer is well under way and it is too late to do anything about it.

Age makes less difference in guests than you would think; it is "habit patterns" (as the psychologists call the ruts of behavior) that are important to consider in dealing with guests. If, for example, you have invited what seemed to you on urban acquaintance a lively, active couple, you may as well resign yourself to their spending most of the weekend asleep. Being lively in the city is an extremely enervating business, and your couple will make up for it over the weekend. There is no use leaving the lawnmower conspicuously displayed; these are not the kind of people who are going to volunteer to push it. The chances are that they will arrive late for dinner on Friday, completely equipped for tennis, golf, and swimming, and it will take the whole family to stow them and their tack in the guest room. By nine o'clock one of them will say: "Oh, this country air. I can hardly keep my eyes open." And by nine-thirty they'll both be asleep upstairs.

On Saturday morning it becomes obvious that these active urban types are country sluggards. They emerge dressed like manikins from a resort shop—the man in slacks and loafers and plaid shirt and his wife in shorts and sandals and halter—in the clothes, in other words, that people who spend much time in the country haven't time for—and they wear dark glasses. If you are sensible, you have been up for a good while yourself and got the lawn mowed (your guests love to lie in bed and listen to the reassuring whir of a lawnmower) and had your breakfast. You have made a list of the things you want to do without regard to what your friends want to do. If they feel like it they'll patter along when you go to town to shop; if they don't, they are perfectly happy sitting in reclining chairs, their faces lifted like platters to the sun.

You need not worry about all the sports equipment they brought with them. That was a gesture. They won't begin to bustle until late afternoon when it is cocktail time. Then they will replace their shorts with something longer, and emerge after they have used up all the hot water, ready to use up all the gin.

The chances of what may then happen are about equally divided; they may drink so fast and furiously (they feel so full of health from a day in the sun) that they will again be ready for bed by nine-thirty. If this happens, Sunday's performance will echo Saturday's. If, however, they decide to make an evening of it, they won't appear until just before lunch on Sunday, by which time you can have had at least a half a day to yourself. The rest of the day you may as well throw away.

By contrast, let us look at a quite different sort of couple from the city. It would be risking too much to say that the opposite type, the kind of couple who reflect the cares and the harrying tempo of urban life and have a peaked air about them, are invariably the active ones over a weekend in the country, but there is some truth in it. They are likely to arrive somewhat bedraggled, usually by train, with the hot sooty look of people emerging from a couple of hours on a local in which the air conditioning has broken down. The first breath of clear country air brightens their gray faces; they stand on the platform and look around them as though refreshing their memories of what a tree looks like. They have a small suitcase each and carry no athletic equipment. If everything about the landscape enchants them as you drive them home, you should be warned that you are in for an active two days.

This sort of couple has a good deal in common with puppies. You throw out any kind of suggestion, and they scamper after it and bring it back and drop it at your feet. Everything is grist for their mill, but they have forgotten to bring the mill. If you suggest tennis, they'd just love tennis, but, of course, they have no rackets and no sneakers, and after you have ransacked the house and tried your own, your wife's, and your children's sneakers on them and have concluded that you are in for a game of patball, they settle down to beat the pants off you with rackets that you have long since given up as warped and worthless.

You can save up the lawn for this type. One will surely cut it for you while the other weeds the flowers, or they may work in shifts. You will have difficulty keeping them out of the kitchen, if you are the sort who thinks of the kitchen as your private sanctum, because they will insist on helping with the dishes. The only real trouble you will encounter arises if you are so misguided as to leave them to their own devices to entertain themselves. Their puppy eyes will look at you as though you ought to be throwing a ball for them. You even have to suggest to them that it is time to go to bed. When you put them on the train on Sunday evening, you will notice that for all the healthful paces through which they have put you and themselves, they will have that same gray and harried look they had when they arrived.

These two kinds of couples are, of course, merely composites of many other species. But what of the couples who do not seem to make pairs and who go their separate ways? And what of those couples of which you like one member and can't abide the other? For our purposes they have to be considered as individuals. There are those who think that the state of being a guest relieves them of all responsibility and those who consider guesthood a perpetual challenge. In either case the extremes are difficult to cope with.

The range of individual guests is, of course, endless, and perforce we must confine ourselves to those whose eccentricities have some chance of seeming to be part of larger and more universally recognized patterns. You can make your own synthesis (nobody is anybody these days who doesn't at least try to make a synthesis) and match them as you please.

Some guests want to be left alone, and some say they want to ("Don't bother about me. Just go about your business. I'll find plenty to do.") and are miserable if they are.

The first of these lone wolves can be the pleasantest of all guests if they are resourceful, can take care of themselves happily, and at the same time pervade your household with the warm feeling that they enjoy just being in it. At their best they don't mind being interrupted in their own pursuits if there is some activity in which you want them to join. At their worst they make you feel that all they want out of you is a bed and three meals a day and a chance to ignore you. These are the men and women who come for the weekend to get away from people (including you) and to have a little quiet. They think they have discharged all of their responsibilities if they bring a box of chocolates that they have bought in the railroad station. They are so well able to take care of themselves that they make you feel as though you were in their employ.

A guest of the second type (who really does not want to be left alone but protests that he does) offers an acute problem of tact. He appears at breakfast with a small stack of books, a magazine, and some writing paper, bright-eyed and presumably equipped for the day. He quickly sets the books aside and takes your morning paper. (The sort of person who has a number of books from which to choose is rarely a reader. He is always looking for a chance to find time to sit down with a good book, but curiously he never seems to find it. He won't find it over the weekend either.) After his third cup of coffee, you may get back the paper, and your friend will wander off to find a place to read one of the books. In half an hour or less he'll be hovering around again. "Too nice a day to sit and read," he'll say, and that is your signal to quit whatever you are doing and invent something to keep him busy. His resources and imagination were exhausted by picking out which books in your library he would fondle.

If this type stretches your tact, then you should be especially warned of the guest who makes an elaborate show of being tactful about you. He acts as though he knows that he is too much trouble and that everything you do for him is a great nuisance. He is constantly leaping out of his chair to perform some little service for you or for your wife, to get out the ice, to find the children's ball in the bushes, or to fetch the wood for the fireplace, all of which would be ingratiating if it weren't done half-apologetically. You soon find yourself wanting to tell him to sit down and relax, but instead you respond with an elaborate display of tact on your part. He is wearisome because he is so hard to live up to.

Even so he is preferable to the intentionally tactless guest who thinks that to make light of your shortcomings as a host is a demonstration of easy fellowship and poise. He laughs at the way you lay a fire, and insists on taking your effort apart and stacking the kindling in his way. He reminds you that the leaky faucet in the bathroom could be fixed with a five-cent washer and fifteen minutes' work, and that you have put the wrong kind of composition shingles on your house; he could have got a much better brand for you wholesale at half the price you paid. He follows you wherever you go all weekend long; he stands in the kitchen door while you are getting drinks or a meal. If you play golf with him he tells you how to correct your slice, and if he sees you chopping wood he will observe that you are lucky you haven't cut your leg off long since, handling an axe the way you do. When he is not telling you how you ought to live, his conversation is almost entirely about the remarkable place at which he spent last weekend, with friends who did everything in such style. He is unaware that the walls of most country places are excellent conductors of sound, and you have no respite from him for some time after he had presumably gone to bed. If he is married, you can listen to him telling his wife that you would have a nice little place if you only knew how to take care of it.

Even the careless guest is preferable to the tactless type, though he too offers some minor aggravations. He strews the place with his belongings, he breaks a blade of the lawnmower on a rock anyone ought to be able to see, and he invariably is inspired to take a dip in the lake or river or ocean just as you are about to produce lunch or supper. When he does ultimately appear to be fed he will have deposited his wet bathing suit over the back of a piece of upholstered furniture. There is no malice in his soul, though, and it is possible to love him.

It is impossible, on the other hand, to love the belligerently indolent guest who frustrates all attempts to make his visit pleasant or interesting. That is not to say that a host should force entertainment on anyone who doesn't want it, for a good host knows when to put enticements in his guest's way and when not to. But the belligerently indolent guest has a gift for making it quite obvious to his host that he expects to be entertained, yet displays a distinct distaste for any diversion that may be suggested to him. This is a common characteristic in children, and in adults it is, I believe, an indication of retarded maturity. I have often seen adults behave like a child I know who continually asks, "What'll I do now?" When a suggestion is made to him he has a pat reply. "Would you like to go swimming?" you ask him, and the reply is invariably, "Not particularly." "Well then," you say, trying again, "how would you like to play catch?" "Not particularly," he says, and so it goes. When such guests, children or adults, do finally submit themselves to some plan you have suggested, they give you the uncomfortable sensation that they wish you had been bright enough to invent something really entertaining.

If this kind of guest is tiring because he is a constant challenge to your ingenuity, the opposite type, the ebullient guest, who sets out to give his host and hostess a rousing good time, takes the least planning and is the most exhausting. He arrives full of ideas, of projects for excursions, of resolve to get you out and give you some real exercise, and unless you want to be rude to him (which is necessary in extreme cases) it is best just to put yourself in his hands.

There are a number of common manifestations of the ebullient guest, each requiring a special defensive operation and its own system of logistics. I happen to have a house in the Berkshires. These gentle hills were at one time (especially in the environs of Stockbridge and Lenox) remarkable for the size and extravagance of the summer estates which graced their slopes. There is a legend in the Berkshires that a young man who was at Yale just before the turn of the century sent his mother a telegram in which he said, "Bringing some '97 friends for weekend," and his mother wired back, "Terribly sorry have room for only seventy-six." Most of the big estates are now hotels, or schools, or church institutions, and the Berkshires have become a hotbed of summer culture. We have music festivals at Tanglewood that rival Salzburg and Glyndebourne in fame. We have dance festivals at a place called Jacob's Pillow, and we have enough summer theaters to give several platoons of Broadway stars their annual breath of fresh air. We used to frequent these places; in fact months before the music festival our friends could be seen conspicuously angling for invitations. We finally grew tired of running a lodging house for our music- and dance-minded acquaintances, and we ourselves took to angling for invitations elsewhere during that part of the summer. It was the ebullient guests who wanted to be sure that we got our dosage of culture who finally drove us to take umbrage.

Umbrage is one way to cope with the ebullient. Another way is to lend your guest the family car, and if necessary your wife, and let them go on an excursion of their own making. A third method is to buy two tickets to the festival or the dance or the theater and say that they are all you could get (which could easily be true) and insist that the guests use them. This is both a generous gesture and assurance of a few hours' respite.

There is one kind of ebullience, however, which I have frequently encountered and have never been able to discover an answer to. It is found in a single guest or in a couple who seem to know a great many more people in the vicinity to which you have invited them than you do. The minute they get in the house they start calling up friends. By the end of fifteen minutes they have invited themselves and you to one house for lunch, another for drinks, and have possibly even got you committed to appear at the Saturday night country club dance. You may, on the other hand, find yourself giving a cocktail party for a lot of people you scarcely know and have been successfully avoiding for years. Short of cutting the telephone wires before your guests arrive, I know of no way to keep their socially manic behavior in control.

1. Explain the author's use of "habit patterns."
2. Note his plan in describing the various types. Outline informally. Can you identify any of these from your own experiences or are they too much overdrawn? What proportion of these irritate the host?
3. Turn this around and write "On Weekend Hosts."
4. Describe one of the following:
   A Miserable Weekend
   A Fussy Eater
   My Idea of the Perfect Guest
   A Cook-out Party

# COMPULSIVE SUBURBIA

*John Keats*

Nick and Fran Baxter live, so to speak, with their three children in one of the five hundred three-bedroom houses of a real-estate nightmare we shall call Apple Drive. Neat, clean, wholesome, slightly vacuous, the Baxters look like one of those idealized suburban families you see in the full-color advertisements of the women's magazines. They bought their house because a) they were told that a family should own one, and b) they imagined it would be cheaper to buy a house in the suburbs than to rent in the city. This was thoughtless of them, and they are now beginning to discover the hidden prices: the years wasted in commuting, the rising assessments. Together with all others trapped in this development miles from nowhere, the Baxters are the prey of pressures less readily apparent to them, but which conspire to make suburban life somewhat disappointing. For one thing, Apple Drive, like most developments, is a jail of the soul, a wasteland of look-alike boxes stuffed with look-alike neighbors.

Here are no facilities for human life, other than bedrooms and bathrooms. Here is a place that lacks the advantages of both city and country but retains the disadvantages of each. Each suburban family is somehow a broken home, consisting of a father who appears as an overnight guest, a put-upon housewife with too much to do, and children necessarily brought up in a kind of communism. For Apple Drive children, life is play school at age three, preschool at age four, kindergarten at age five. Thus do suburban mothers force their primary responsibilities upon someone else as soon as they can, in order to cope with the lesser but insistent needs to drive to the supermarket, clean the house, gabble on the telephone, and attend the *Kaffeeklatsch*. So, suburban children learn the dreary steaminess of group life as soon as they can walk, and after school they are plunked down before the television set to watch the slaughter in the late afternoon while mom thaws supper. In the evening the baby sitters arrive.

In addition, the families who live in our nation's Apple Drives are divided by the rifts in interest between mothers and fathers; they encounter the schizoid experience of the boring workday and the glittery weekend, the problems of shopping in person by automobile at the low-quality stores of the anonymous shopping centers, the eternal chauffeuring of the children, the pressure of having to be friends with the folks next door simply because they live next door. Then they try to reconcile the fact that this is a man's world with the obvious fact that suburbia is a world of women without men, a matriarchy by default. Uneasily, some suburbanites suspect —along with many psychiatrists—that a matriarchy is no fit place to raise a child.

Moreover, suburban developments are stratified societies—stratified by difference in price. All families in the $14,000 ranch houses are very much like each other but are different from the families in the $7500 Cape Cods and different again from the people in the $17,000 split levels. Specific effects of this stratification will be seen in a moment, but meanwhile it should be remarked that nearly everyone in suburbia is in transit between one and another of America's social classes. The residents believe they are either on their way up or that they have taken a step down. For instance, there is a current argument over the local school that serves one sprawling Pennsylvania development area. No racial question is involved. The problem is that some of the people in the $17,000 houses do not want their children to attend the same school that children from the $14,000 houses attend.

Here is certainly a milieu that shrieks for mitigation. It is absolutely different from any other society that America has ever produced, and it is new since the last world war. Its pressures are great, but rather than attempting to deal with these uncomfortable realities in any constructive way, most suburbanites, like the Baxters, try to drift away from them. The most prevalent form of escape can be called compulsive buying, and Nick is a practitioner and victim of it.

Easygoing and affable, Nick wears a grin and is generally regarded as a good guy. Of course, he pads his expense account, an act which makes him a liar and a thief, but Nick sees nothing wrong with doing what everybody else does. At the end of his working day, Nick drives home in his new, unpaid-for car. He mows the lawn with his encumbered power mower, then relaxes in his mortgaged house to watch a program on his not-entirely-paid-for television set. Last summer he hitched his still-unpaid-for outboard cruiser behind the old car that he has not yet finished buying and, using his gasoline credit card at filling stations and his hotel credit card at restaurants and motels, enjoyed three weeks of family fun in America's Northwest. He allows Fran charge accounts at the shopping center's clothing and furniture shops and is thinking about a fly-now pay-later vacation in the Caribbean next Christmas. His $8200 a year just meets all the monthly payments.

What is wrong with this? And how does this make Nick immoral? Frankly, Nick doesn't see a thing in the world wrong with it; as he says, "I'm feeling no pain."

The answer is that Nick is immoral because he has no sense of obligation. Morality pertains to action with reference to right and wrong, with reference to duty. Credit, after all, is a promise. The too-easy acceptance of too-easy credit is clearly immoral, for there is nothing behind such promises except naked, hopeful greed on the part of both debtor and creditor. Morality, by definition, implies hard thought and conscious choice, but Nick neither thinks nor chooses.

Nick and Fran Baxter never ask each other, "Do we really need this or do we just want it?" Nor do the sellers, who batten on customers like the Baxters, nor do the credit agencies, who batten even more, ask themselves, "Should I sell to *this* guy or do I just want to make a sale?" Instead, the Baxters simply wonder, "What will the payments be?" and the merchants tell them.

Neither Nick nor Fran ever wonders what would happen if, for any reason, that $8200 stopped coming in. Their basic immorality is that they not only have mortgaged their own future but, worse, are also trifling with their children's future. They have mortgaged that, too, when it is their clear responsibility to do exactly otherwise. If it is immoral to shirk responsibility, surely it is even less moral to accept implied responsibility without being able to distinguish between a sound value and a passing fad.

It is precisely here that suburbia's basic immorality begins. It is not lurid but rather a kind of garden, or crab grass, immorality, and the occasional drunks and adulterers of suburbia may be regarded as the logical end products of a consistent failure to act thoughtfully and choose wisely in homely things.

Living on credit and buying compulsively are by no means limited to suburbia; indeed, this sort of drift is a national failure. In suburbia, however, the drift is seen at its flaccid worst, because nowhere else in America do people drift together in such huge, homogeneous clots, so moored to nothing. This homogeneous grouping, together with the physical deficiency of cluttered isolation, is what makes suburbia such a special place, so inviting to the anthropologist. Both the homogeneity and the isolation occur because housing developments do not grow out of life's conditions and needs, as a city or a country village grows. Developments are simply collections of cubicles that rise out of a bulldozed plain at a real-estate promoter's desire; they are connected with no reality but a bank and have no roots but mortgages that are valuable solely to the builder. Because America still tends to stratify itself by income, the difference in the prices of development homes works to create populations that share the same basic tastes and ideas; within each development people hold the same kinds of jobs, enjoy the same incomes, meet the same problems, have the same number of children, and, possibly, have a common blood type.

Proof of suburban homogeneity is pathetically obvious. In one housing development, for example, nearly every house has a peculiar lamp, with an enormous shade, in the exact center of each picture window. In another, a couple of miles away, nearly everyone has built little shelves across his picture window and has filled these shelves with small glass animals. In enterprising Apple Drive, nearly everyone has thrown out the old sling chairs and has gone in for French Provincial. In these barrack communes, where nearly everyone is alike to begin with and where all are subjected to the same advertisements and limited to the same shopping centers, compulsive thing-purchase becomes an attempt to escape in lock step. Fran didn't buy new chairs because the old chairs wore out; she bought them because they were the new thing. Her chandelier does not light her life but represents her joining in the new fad for chandeliers.

When any activity reaches fad proportions, sociologists remark that it is evidence of public boredom and an attempt to escape from boredom. But the sociologists add that, because a fad is by its own nature boring, it is quickly exhausted; the boredom returns increased, and the stage is set for the new fad. Thus it is that the French Provincial and the chandeliers will be gone tomorrow from Fran's life.

Being segregated populations, suburbanites may have a natural tendency to conformity, but, more than any other group of people, they tend to look anxiously around to see what their neighbors are doing and buying. In a sense, this is a rather pathetic clutching at a mutual straw; at any rate, suburbanites seem to think they must have whatever anyone else has, not because they need it but because other people have it, and they seem to want very much to be part of the group. It is not altogether clear just why suburbanites want to be groupy. Perhaps, being largely the generation now in its late thirties and early forties, they inherit a legacy of groupiness from the Depression days, or from the New Deal, or from the experience of the war, or, more prosaically, it may be because they share a feeling of inadequacy. Whatever the reason, there is no doubt that suburbia's watchword is "Get with it." Heresy is the worst suburban sin, ostracism the worst fate, adjustment to the group is held to be the highest good; and suburbia's factorylike new schools are generally temples to this creed.

Getting along with the group is a good thing only if it can be generally established that what everyone is doing is good. Suburbia is immoral in that it applies no such test. Nick Baxter, as noted, pads his expense account because this is a general practice. Since everybody else does it, he says, he would be silly not to.

One by one, an increasing number of suburbanites are beginning to wonder whether their communal life is good. Fran's neighbor Sarah Howard, for instance, questions the second most prevalent form of suburban escape, the weekend cocktail party. Her objection is important, for it goes past a simple loathing for the games played on these occasions and strikes at the basic reason for the parties. "The trouble with us," she said, "is that we drink too much."

Sarah made her discovery after nursing a single Martini through a Saturday night. It was purely an experiment. Cold sober, she saw the emptiness of her life for the first time, or, rather, she discovered that nobody had anything to say to anybody else.

"Everybody was standing around yakking and laughing," she said. "It was all gabble, gabble, gabble. People would say the same things over and over again, never finishing sentences. Nobody really listened to anybody. Everybody stood around dumb and happy with a big, fat smile, talking louder and louder about nothing at all. A big, fat nothing is what it was.

"I tell you," Sarah said, "next time I'm going to drink. At least you think you're having a good time when you're half crocked."

She said this quite simply, as though it made perfectly good sense. She saw nothing fantastic in the idea that a group of young American parents, like herself and her husband and the Baxters, could find only the illusion of happiness when they gathered together, and then only when half stoned. At the same time she realized a) that everyone drank too much, and b) that no one had anything to say. Asked why she intended to go to another such affair, Sarah explained, "We have to live with these people." Only to an outsider would this suburban proposition seem open to question.

What hope for suburbia there is lies in such twinges of healthful doubt as are now beginning to assail Fran and Sarah. Nothing can be done to cut the commuting time that produces the daily divorce. A little, but not much, can be done to relieve the physical monotony; something can be done now and again to make the development more than a collection of bedrooms. For instance, one group of suburbanites bought one house when it came on the market and converted it into a library. In the main, however, a development is an environment that cannot be altered for the better by any means short of dynamite and bulldozing; if anything is to be salvaged out of suburbia, it must be the people who live there.

Since salvation is always acutely personal, dependent upon self-examination and self-imposed tasks, you will find no detailed formulas here under the heading "How To Be Yourself." On the other hand, we can make a general observation: It is fairly obvious that suburbanites will have to dispense with their drive toward groupiness if they are to be saved, that each must conclude for himself that group activity is generally so much back-scratching, that any group is most often merely the infinite reflection you see in the distorting mirrors of the glass house at the amusement park.

The chances are nil that suburbia will come to any such conclusions in the immediate future, however, because most suburbanites are apt to join Nick Baxter in saying, "What are you crabbing about? We never had it so good." Then off they'll go, drifting from one vague disappointment to the next, deep in the narcotic trance of advertised promise, never thinking of themselves but always of their diversions, entirely unaware that they are neither giving nor receiving anything of value. Feeling no part of the city where they work and uninterested in the monotonous bedroom area where they sleep, moored to nothing, they make no decisions. They say neither yes nor no when their Martinis are replenished, and it is a short step from this kind of acceptance to acceptance of crime in the cities, thievery in government, knavery in labor unions, unconscionable business practices, mindlessness in the public schools, and the disappearance of anything that could remotely be called the national will. Such are the penalties of drift; such are the results of moral failure around the house.

At the moment, suburbia has a long way to go if it wishes to head in the direction of reality, for as one suburbanite said, "If the networks were smart, *they'd* take the payola from the record companies instead of letting the disc jockeys get it."

When you hear remarks like this, you sometimes think that maybe fire should be fought with fire. For instance, could suburbia's immoral groupiness be turned to advantage? It is interesting to speculate that suburbia's salvation may depend on Sarah Howard's ability to make a fad out of not getting drunk at cocktail parties.

## Study suggestions

Through satire and extravaganza, Keats gives his impressions of mass production of a "wasteland of look-alike boxes stuffed with look-alike neighbors" of a "real-estate nightmare." Although the point of view is third person, as we watch Nick and Fran we are aware of the author's attitude, magnified as it is: "Here is a place that lacks the advantage of both city and country but retains the disadvantages of each."

1.    Analyze the satirical phrases that describe (1) the life of father, (2) of mother, (3) of the children. What are the implications concerning the family in the second and third paragraphs?

2.    Explain the "stratification" of social life.

3.    Reflect on the instability Nick piles up by the "not-paid-for" articles. How are Nick and Fran "trifling with their children's future?" Why does the author call Nick "immoral"? Note the effect of his repetitions of homogeneous, same, and boredom.

4.    What is his point of view concerning conformity? Explain "heresy," "ostracism," and "adjustment to the group."

5.    Is there any seriousness in this satire? Has the author over-

loaded his attack, or has he given facts? Are there dangers in such mass living?

6.    Write a 500-word theme on your point of view in regard to Suburbia or a criticism of the author's attack and style.

7.    Write a 500-word theme on conformity.

# TODAY'S WORLD

*Information is the key to understanding.*

ERWIN CANHAM

# THE FIRST CITIZENS OF THE ATOMIC AGE

*Norman Cousins*

Hiroshima wasn't what I expected.

I expected resignation; I found rehabilitation. I expected desolation; I found rejuvenation.

In Hiroshima I found people who, having survived atomic catastrophe, restored their lives, and, even more important, restored their faith in the human race and their faith in themselves. The citizens planned to make their city one of the most beautiful in the world.

From the back yard of the small inn where I stayed, I had a fairly good vantage point for viewing the city, with its many rivers and levees. In front of me, across the river, I could see perhaps six square miles of the city, stretching along the banks of the river and sprawling out beyond. The city itself is fairly flat, built at sea level. Hiroshima is a seaport, though from this vantage point it seemed completely surrounded by a ring of mountains.

The hurry-up, improvised quality of the wooden buildings on the other side of the river gave the city something of the appearance of an American mining town in the West a century ago. The resemblance was even stronger because of the mountains in the background.

From where I stood, I could see the general area hit hardest by the atomic bomb; I could see what is now the most famous landmark of the atomic explosion—the dome, or what used to be a dome, of the old Industrial Exhibition Hall. Just enough of the curved steelwork was left so that you could tell it was a dome. Another four- or five-story structure, off to the left a few hundred yards away, showed evidence of considerable damage.

Apart from these two buildings, Hiroshima was completely rebuilt—rebuilt, that is, on a sort of overnight basis. The homes, the stores, the industrial buildings were thrown up very hastily. But the greatest difficulty hasn't been putting up the new buildings and shacks. The greatest difficulty has been clearing away the rubble.

The river in front of me was at low tide; you could walk across its full width of about five hundred feet without getting your ankles wet. I looked out across the river and could see the streets clearly marked—electric and telephone poles, very little open area, and no rubble or evidence of the bomb whatsoever, except for the old dome skeleton.

Of course, when I actually walked through the streets I could see many wounds still open. There were the gutted foundations of the concrete buildings, even though four years of weeds and grass do a great deal to smooth over and conceal the old ruins.

Right next to the small inn where I stayed was the wreckage of what was once a fairly large two-story stone home. All that was left was part of a wall, the large concrete gateposts, and the iron gate itself—most of it twisted out of shape. I went poking around behind the wall and came across a family of five living under a piece of canvas propped up by boards, with the stone wall as the principal inside wall surface. Directly in front of their home, if you want to call it that, which measures about seven feet by seven feet, the family had cleared away the rubble and planted a vegetable garden.

On the fourth anniversary of the atomic bombing, I stood at the spot which is believed to mark the center of the atomic explosion. Directly in front of me were two fairly thick and round stucco columns or gateposts on a very small plot raised about one foot off the ground level as a marker and memorial.

These columns were all that was left of Dr. Shima's hospital, which was directly under the atomic burst. A new hospital had been built right in back of the old gateposts. It was a two-story affair, painted white. Patients waved from the windows.

As you stand at the spot marking the center of the atomic explosion, it's difficult to describe the things you feel. Here, four years ago, there was a flash of heat which at the split second of fission was many times the surface temperature of the sun. And suddenly, even before a stop watch could register it, the heart of a city was laid open with a hot knife. I talked to dozens of people who were in it—dozens who were crippled and burned and suffering from diseases of radioactivity—and their stories were very much the same.

The sudden flash of light brighter than the morning sun—much shorter, much more intense than lightning, much more intense than any light ever seen before on this earth. If you lived through that second, you found that your clothes were on fire, and your arms and legs and face were on fire, and you rushed out into the street and ran, for everyone else was running—no one knew where. And everything was now blazing, and you were inside the fire, trying to run somewhere. Then someone yelled, "Run for the river!" and you threw yourself into the river, and thousands of others did the same thing, and you wondered what happened to your family, to your children or your parents. No one knew where anyone was, but there were people all around you, and other people were jumping from the bridges into the river, and the dead bodies were all around you in the river; but you could hardly hear the people crying because the blaze was like rolling thunder sweeping over you. And all day and night the fire ate your city and burned your dead, and all night you stayed in the river to cool your burns; but the tide ran out and you buried yourself as deeply in the mud as you could and prayed for the tide to come back in again with the water from the sea to cool your fevered body, even though it was salt water and it cut into your burns, but at least it was cool. The hours passed slowly, and you searched the sky for the light of morning, but the city was a torch and it was difficult to see the sky. But then morning came, and you joined the thousands of others running through the black smoke, stumbling over the wreckage of the buildings, the sounds of the dying all around you. You were too much in a hurry to notice you had no clothes; it was hard to see that others had no clothes either, for their bodies were like charcoal.

This, then, was Hiroshima in the first hours of the Atomic Age. It was something new in the solar system—getting at the heart of matter and ripping it apart, and causing the smallest units of nature to smash each other and set off a flash as though a piece of the sun itself had broken away, and sending out strange rays that went through the bones and did things to the composition of human blood that had not been done before or dreamed of before. This was the triumph of mind over matter in the ultimate and most frightening sense.

As you stood in front of the large stone columns from the old hospital gateposts, and you reached over and felt the rough, raised surface of the stone, its composition altered because the surface had been melted by the explosion, you wondered why people would ever come back to the city again—not merely Hiroshima but any city—any city that man ever built, for by this bomb he had placed a curse on every city everywhere. You wondered what the lure could be that could bring people out from the hills and back to this place of compressed agony. You wondered, but you didn't have very far to look for the answer, for the answer was all around you. You could see it in the faces of the people who passed on the street. You could see it in the brisk life-loving walk of the young people. You could hear it in the full laughter of children. You could see it in the eagerness of young boys and young men playing ball with each other wherever there was a place to play ball. The answer you found was that there are deeper resources of courage and regeneration in human beings than any of the philosophers had dared to dream. The answer you found was that the greatest force on this earth—greater than any device yet conjured up in the laboratories—is the will to live and the will to hope.

As you looked around you in Hiroshima, you saw a young woman of about twenty-four or -five with a baby strapped to her back. She was wearing Western dress, though she had on Japanese wooden shoes. There was nothing defeatist about the girl. She was starting out to raise a family; she was going to do it in Hiroshima, and nowhere else; she believed in life, and nothing could change it. And as she passed you, and you looked at the back of her neck and down her left arm, you saw the seared and discolored flesh that is the badge of citizenship in Hiroshima today. The girl stepped to one side to allow a modern bus to pass—it was a bus filled with Japanese baseball players in uniform, for baseball has become the national pastime in Japan to an extent not approached even in America. The baseball players were singing, some of them, and you thought you saw, but couldn't be quite sure—you thought you saw the familiar atomic burns on one or two arms and faces.

Another thing you wondered about was what the people themselves thought about the bomb and America. You spoke to them about it, and it was hard to believe that what they said was the way people can or should feel after having lived through an atomic explosion.

There was no bitterness, except in one or two cases. They said, most of them, that if it hadn't been Hiroshima it would have been another city and that they had no right to ask exemption at the expense of their fellows.

They said, most of them, that they had taken part in something that would save the lives of millions, for they believed, most of them, that Hiroshima, in the words of the mayor, Shinzo Hamai, was an exhibit for peace, a laboratory that had demonstrated the nature of the new warfare so dramatically that it would destroy war itself.

They believed that two years of blinding, grinding warfare were squeezed into a single bomb and that the smashing of Hiroshima made it possible for many millions of Japanese to stay alive, for they then knew by this bomb that the war was forever lost to them.

Some of them, of course, said things they thought you wanted to hear, but their voices and their eyes would frequently give them away.

And then, as counter-balance perhaps, you would find a woman —a woman barber who took over the shop after her husband died in the explosion—who would turn her head and say that she never wanted to look at any American, for she was afraid he would see the hate she had in her heart for the people who could stain their honor as Americans did by dropping such a bomb. She lost her husband and two children, and when it pained her heart to think about it she would think of America and know that such evil could come only from evil people.

Then there were some who blamed it on the Japanese Government, who said that when Japan first bombed China they were certain that God would visit the crime on the Japanese a thousand-fold. Some blamed it on the Japanese Government because it had converted Hiroshima into a military base and shipping point, and they were certain that America would find this out and destroy the city.

This was the first I had heard about Hiroshima as a city of military importance. As I spoke to people and questioned them, the picture began to take shape. When a girl of nineteen told me about her experience in the bombing, she spoke of all the soldiers running past her house on the way from the barracks near the old castle. When the photographer who took films for me told about his experience in the bombing, he spoke of his sensation while riding a train two miles away from Hiroshima on his way to work. He said that when he heard the explosion he thought the large ammunition supply center near the old Parade Grounds had been blown up, for the explosion was too loud for even the largest bomb. Others on the outskirts of the city spoke of the same feeling. I spoke to one man who operated a bus to the ammunition dump; he gave me some idea of its size and said that many thousands worked there during the war.

It was freely admitted, once you referred to it, that Japan was divided into two military zones: the headquarters for the North in Tokyo, and the headquarters for the South in Hiroshima.

Later that evening I discussed with Mayor Hamai the military importance of Hiroshima during the war. He spoke freely and fully. Hiroshima had been Japan's chief port for sending soldiers overseas. It had housed large ammunition supply depots.

I asked the mayor whether it was true, as I had heard in some of my conversations, that as many as 60,000 soldiers had been stationed in Hiroshima at the time of the bombing. He was familiar with the reports but believed that the number may have been closer to 40,000. Then I learned for the first time something I had seen in no report about Hiroshima since the end of the war. I learned that 30,000 soldiers had died in the atomic bombing of Hiroshima and that this figure had been suppressed by the Japanese police, then under orders from the Japanese Government to conceal the military death toll and the military importance of Hiroshima as well as to minimize the general damage and civilian death toll. Japan had been taken completely by surprise, and didn't want the United States to know how effective the weapon had been, so that what little bargaining power she had at the peace table might not have been further reduced; and that, once having announced false figures, Japan was reluctant to embarrass herself by giving out the true ones.

I learned that the only figures since used by the American Government about Hiroshima have been supplied by Japanese sources and that the original figures supplied by the Japanese police had never been corrected. I further learned from Mayor Hamai, who was in charge of rationing in Hiroshima during the war and who was given the responsibility for issuing new certificates after the bombing, that the population of Hiroshima had decreased 110,-000 when a check was made three months after the bombing—and that this figure did not include 30,000 military personnel or the many thousands of volunteers from outside the city brought in to construct fire-retention barriers, or the thousands who have died since. The city's own estimate today, said Mayor Hamai, is 210,-000 to 240,000, which includes all those who have died since. The highest previous figure made public was 100,000.

The following day Mayor Hamai took me on a tour of Hiroshima's hospitals. It was an experience difficult to put out of your mind, and you tried hard to put it out of your mind because you saw things that whatever sanity you might have had cried out against. You saw beds held together with slabs of wood; nowhere did you see sheets or pillows; you saw dirty bandages and littered floors and rooms not much larger than closets with four or five patients huddled together. You thought back to what you saw in the D.P. camps in Germany, and you knew that nothing you had seen in Germany or anywhere else put human pride to such a strain.

You looked in on an operating room that seemed little better than a crude abattoir. You saw rooms where whole families had moved in with the patient. You saw all this with unbelieving eyes, and then you had some idea of what Mayor Hamai meant when he said that Hiroshima needed America's help to take care of the sick. For all the hospitals in Hiroshima were destroyed or gutted or severely damaged by the bomb, and hospital facilities in Japan are not easy to come by. People can throw up shacks to live in inside a week or two, but a hospital is nothing to be thrown together. Everything is needed that makes a hospital a hospital, Mayor Hamai said: surgical equipment and rubber gloves for operations and sterilizers and X-ray equipment and beds and pots and pans.

As he spoke, I thought of the millions of dollars being spent by the United States in Hiroshima in the work of the Atomic Bomb Casualty Commission—excellent work and important work, for it can tell what happens to people in atomic warfare. Nothing of those millions goes to treat the victims of the atomic bomb. The Casualty Commission only examines patients; it doesn't treat them. And you had the strange spectacle of a man suffering from radioactive sickness getting thousands of dollars' worth of analysis but not one cent of treatment from the Commission.

On the second floor of the Memorial Hospital in Hiroshima, near crowded rooms of children who are serious tuberculosis cases, a woman rushed out to me and fell at my feet, sobbing as I have heard few people sob. Dr. Akio Asano, the tall scholarly, youthful head of the hospital, told me that she had heard an American had come to Hiroshima and that she had just been praying to Kami for the American to come to the hospital so that he might be able to see how sick her little girl was and how badly she needed certain medicine they didn't have in Hiroshima. She had been praying when I walked in. The little girl was seven years old. Her father had been killed in the atomic explosion. Her name was Nobuko Takeuchi. She had been ill of tuberculosis for several months, complicated by a series of mastoid infections, for which there had been several operations. But now she had what Dr. Asano described as the worst case of tuberculosis he had ever seen in a child of her age, and she might not live for more than a few weeks unless she was able to get large doses of streptomycin. But nowhere in Hiroshima could you get streptomycin.

That night I became a black marketeer. We established contact with what are called sources in Japan, and a few grams of streptomycin were rushed over to the hospital. But little Nobuko needed forty to fifty grams, and we sent wires to Tokyo and even to the United States to get the medicine in time. The Church World Service in the United States heard about the appeal and rushed a fairly substantial package of streptomycin by air-mail. (The medicines kept Nobuko alive for almost a year; then her frail body succumbed to an attack of meningitis.)

After we left the hospital, Mayor Hamai told me of his dream for a modern hospital in Hiroshima that would become part of the Hiroshima Peace Center, for which the Reverend Kiyoshi Tanimoto, of the Nakaregawa Church of Christ in Hiroshima, had gone to the United States in search of support. I had been working with Mr. Tanimoto in the United States, getting groups together to advance the idea of a Hiroshima Peace Center, but not until now did I realize how important were the units that were to go into it. The Peace Center would have, in addition to the hospital, an orphanage, a home for the aged, a civic recreation center, a peace institute study center, and a medical research center.

The next tour was of the orphanages for children whose parents were killed in the atomic explosion. I should like to report on one of them in particular—the Yamashita Orphanage, located about eight miles outside the city on a hillside. It is operated by Mr. and Mrs. Yamashita as a public service with whatever help and support they can get from the city and its people, and from the outside world. It is the largest of the four orphanages for Hiroshima children, providing care for almost one hundred youngsters ranging in age from four years to seventeen years. The youngest was born just a few hours before the bombing.

Mr. and Mrs. Yamashita were able to survive the bombing despite severe burns. Mrs. Yamashita, who had been close to the center of the explosion, said that suddenly there was a bright light and her body was on fire. She was carrying her two-year-old baby at the time, and the first thing she did was to smother the flames that enveloped the child. Then she picked up the baby and ran until she reached the fields outside the city, where she lived for three days on the ground before word came that people were returning to the city.

On her return with the child she found Mr. Yamashita, already under treatment. Recovery was slow for both of them, but after six months they were able to resume their lives, and they decided to dedicate themselves to the care of orphans. They got land and homes outside Hiroshima and built their little colony.

Mr. and Mrs. Yamashita were now completely recovered, except that the old wounds burn and itch in extremely warm or cold weather. Mrs. Yamashita said that she had been unable to have a successful pregnancy since the bombing, having experienced four miscarriages. She spoke of other women in Hiroshima in like circumstances.

The Yamashita Orphanage was, I think, the high spot of my visit to Hiroshima. Living conditions were better and brighter than I had seen almost anywhere else in the city. The children there were more alert, more responsive, and seemed quicker and happier than I had seen almost anywhere in Japan. The food was adequate and well prepared; there was ample play space; and, what was more important, the children were not starved for want of affection. Dozens of the younger ones hung on to Mrs. Yamashita like kids hanging on to an American mother's skirts in a department store. The quality of the teaching in the orphanage was as high as you would find anywhere in Japan. There was only one thing wrong with the Yamashita Orphanage. There was not enough of it. It ought to be five times as large, and would be, if outside help were forthcoming.

Before coming to Japan, several people had told me that they would like to adopt Japanese children orphaned by the bombing. Under the Oriental Exclusion Act, however, these adoptions were not possible. It occurred to me that the next best thing might be *moral* adoptions. By moral adoptions I was thinking of Hiroshima children who would be adopted by American families and who would carry the names of the people adopting them. The children would continue to live in Japan—perhaps in some such place as Mrs. Yamashita's—but the American families would be responsible for their care and upbringing. Then, later, if Congress passed a law permitting Japanese children to come to America, these morally adopted children could become legally adopted as well.

The next morning Mayor Hamai took me to the site of the old castle that had been destroyed by the bomb. Here, on an artificial hillside, you could overlook the city with its seven rivers and its many bridges. You could see the many homes and stores going up. The sound of the city, with its old trolleys, and the sounds of the pile drivers and the hammers and saws blended into a drone, as it sometimes does high up in a skyscraper.

There on the hillside that morning, a small group of citizens broke ground for the Hiroshima Peace Center, and rededicated their city to the cause of peace by renaming it the Peace City. Mayor Hamai, in introducing me, spoke of his hope that within a few years there might rise on this site an institute for the study of world peace, as part of the Peace Center project.

I said I came to Hiroshima expecting to see the end of the world. Instead, I found the beginning of a better one. I expected to find that Hiroshima, like many of the cities I saw in Germany the previous year, would be flattened out, its only heights those of rubble. True, there were few stone or concrete buildings in Hiroshima by contrast with such cities as Cologne, Aachen, or Berlin, but the wounds here went as deep as, or deeper than, any city in any war had ever suffered. Yet what was most important about Hiroshima, I said, was not that the debris and the remains of the old city have been cleared away and that a new city is in the process of being rebuilt. What was most important was what has happened inside people. I was not referring to the lack of bitterness, for even if it were bitterness it is doubtful that history would completely withhold sanction. I referred to the proof of personal regeneration, the rediscovery and reinforcement of personal purpose, the capacity for personal rededication.

I tried to make the point that hope cannot exist, either in the individual or society, without the prospect of regeneration. And yet the power of regeneration is undervalued by modern man. The idea of regeneration in too many cases has been tied to the idea of immortality, identifying it as the principal means of achieving ends beyond life, rather than as an end in life itself, essential and attainable.

The sense of personal regeneration in Hiroshima was discernible and unmistakable. There was not only proof of the power of life over death, but of the individual discovery of fathomless physical, emotional, and spiritual resources. This regeneration soared far beyond personal rehabilitation to a restoration of vital faith in human destiny. There was in the making there, I said, a larger definition of the purposes of man than it seemed within our ken to imagine only a few years ago. In the days following the bombing many people in Hiroshima must have believed that they were witnesses to the death both of a city and of an age—and in a sense they were right. But that feeling had changed color and composition with the passing of the months. Today there was a new vision in Hiroshima. The city had a mission to explain itself to the world, to offer itself as a laboratory specimen in the making of world peace.

Such a vision was important and good, for personal recovery must be part of a larger pattern. However impressed we may be with man's capacity for regeneration, we must ask ourselves: regeneration for what? So that man may be afforded an even larger test of his capacity to survive atomic catastrophe? Hiroshima was an ideal classroom for history, but little will have been learned if the only lesson is that survival and regeneration are possible. Regeneration was possible in Hiroshima because it had the rest of the world to draw on. But what will the rest of the world draw upon?

Not survival but the condition of man is the problem. Not whether he can endure atomic fire but whether he can avert it. And in dedicating itself to this purpose the city of Hiroshima defined a mission as urgent as it was noble.

Even as we broke ground for a new Peace Center, we were aware that peace in the world was less a fact than it was a word and that while the will to peace was deep inside peoples everywhere there was as yet no adequate means by which this will could be translated into effective reality. There existed nowhere on a world level an agency responsible to mankind as a whole, an agency which could listen and act to the end that human life may be protected and developed. To say that such an agency is more easily imagined than achieved, and is therefore to be avoided, is to condemn the history of progress.

Certainly true peace will be difficult to achieve. Life itself is difficult. But an honest effort is required before we can be sure that what is difficult may not also be possible. And such an effort—a supreme, common effort in the name of the world's peoples—has yet to be called for, let alone attempted. The problem confronting us is neither interplanetary nor supernatural. It is a man-made problem, one well within our reach to examine and solve.

When I returned to the United States, I had in my pocket a message that Mayor Hamai asked me to convey to Americans. It was written in his own hand. It was appended to four large bound volumes containing the signatures of 106,000 citizens of Hiroshima sending their greetings to the American people. This was the Mayor's message:

"There is much I would like to say to America. First of all, I would like to thank those Americans who have helped us to bring a dead city back to life.

"It is not my place or purpose to try to tell Americans what ought to be done. But what I can do is to tell them about what will happen to the world's cities if something is not done to stop war. The people of Hiroshima ask nothing of the world except that we be allowed to offer ourselves as an exhibit for peace. We ask only that enough peoples know what happened here and how it happened and why it happened, and that they work hard to see that it never happens anywhere again.

"We the people of Hiroshima are sick at heart as we look out at the world and see that nations are already fighting the initial skirmishes that can grow into a full war. We know that stopping war is not a simple thing and that there are grave questions that have to be solved before the world can have true peace. We know, too, that peace is not to be had just for the asking; all nations must agree to it.

"But we also know that some nation must take leadership in building the type of peace that will last. And we are looking to America for that leadership. America can call for world law, and all the world will listen. Leaders of a few nations may not want to listen, but their people will hear. Let the call go out from America for a federation of the nations strong enough to prevent war, and a thrill will be known in the hearts of millions of people everywhere. This is the best hope for averting a war which would see thousands of Hiroshimas. And this is the message the people of Hiroshima ask that you take back to America."

## Study suggestions

1. Analyze the impact of the beginning sentences.
2. In the author's description of the bombing how does the author make one actually live through it?

3.    What answer does he give to his own question of why people returned to the city?

4.    What attitudes did he find toward the Americans? And what facts did he discover about the military and about the health conditions?

5.    Explain the belief of some of the people that Hiroshima was "an exhibit for peace." Also: "What was most important was what has happened inside the people."

6.    In the opinion of the author and the Mayor what is the hope for ending conflict? Discuss the Mayor's message to America.

7.    Discuss (or write) on your opinions concerning the hope for peace.

8.    Read *Hiroshima,* by John Hersey.

# SATELLITIS

*Richard Glenn Gettell*

When the Trustees of Mount Holyoke College presented me with the exciting opportunity of the presidency, I began to search for ways to fill the requirements of this new responsibility most effectively. One of the many "New Year's resolutions" that emerged from this process of soul-searching was a vow that I would spend at least my first year at Mount Holyoke concentrating on learning my job and trying to begin to understand the College. I swore to address myself solely to things of the College, to events and problems bounded by the campus. I assumed that I should forswear national concerns, minimize outside speech-making, and keep my mouth closed on public affairs so that I could keep my mind focused on educational affairs.

In recent months I have come to realize that this was a naive notion, suitable perhaps to the pre-war academic world in which I served my apprenticeship, but absurd and impossible today. The things of the College are inextricably interwoven with matters of national concern. No longer is there a lag of a generation before our students affect the world which they enter on graduation. No longer is it feasible, whether or not it is desirable, for our faculties to teach and conduct their research in aloofness from the world around them. No longer can colleges, even those with the distinctive qualities of the Seven, stand in cloistered isolation from the rest of the world of education. Our very survival as institutions is dependent, not only on what we do to adapt to an explosively changing world, but also on what that world may do to us.

Moreover, I quickly discovered that a vow of silence is not permitted to a college president. It is part of his job to make speeches —indeed, whether or not he has anything to say. And no one can have something worth saying as often as is demanded.

Today, however, there is something I do want to say. And while you probably look on this gathering as an opportunity to inspect the "new boy," I welcome it as a chance to emerge from my self-imposed cocoon and say a few words about matters which are of campus concern, but also are of tremendous national and international concern.

It will probably come as no surprise to you that, like almost everyone else in the country, I want to have my say about SPUTNIK.

Robert L. White, writing in the *New York Herald Tribune* earlier this month provided me with a text, and a point of departure. He phrased it nicely when he said:

Ever since the Soviet government announced last October [1957] that its experts had launched the world's first earth satellite this country has been in a state bordering on shock. First of all our own experts were set to work shooting off whatever they had handy, regardless of whether it could be expected to work, whilst our top echelon leaders were shooting off their mouths—and with just about the same amount of effect.

Mr. White goes on to develop the theme that, after the initial panic, there were soberer second thoughts. Some of them took the form of attacking our educational system for its failure to produce scientists, and as his third thought he presents the suggestion that industry should grant sabbaticals to some of the scientists it has enticed away from the campuses so that they can return to fill the shortage of teachers.

This is one possible sequence of second and third thoughts, triggered by the launching of SPUTNIK. And it is an engaging idea. But it is not the one I want to develop today. Instead I should like to go back to the initial shock of October 4, 1957, and then sketch a different sequence of second and third and fourth thoughts.

So let us start again from last fall when a new disease first swept the nation. More virulent than the Asian flu and much more widespread, it caused most of us to succumb to SPUTNIK fever, or, to make it sound more medical, should we call it "Satellitis"?

If this were a more nearly ideal world, the launching of a satellite could have been the object of worldwide, unqualified rejoicing. At last the dream of the science fiction writers had come true. Man was no longer chained to the earth. The greatest new frontiers were before us. The space age had dawned. If mankind were more perfect, this could have been the most exciting challenge in the history of civilization. It still can be, and probably must be, if there is to be any civilization left.

But instead of regarding SPUTNIK as a vehicle to the stars, our minds turned to the motive power of a military missile. Just so did nuclear energy lead first to the bomb, and only secondarily to a powerful new source of energy. It is not clear that the world will be granted the chance of a second such mistake.

So our first thoughts were panicky, not exultant. They set us on the track of a space race, of recriminations because we were not first, of military reorganizations, of criticism of our scientists, and of the system that produces them. In this feverish search for crash programs to "catch up" much has been made of the fact that the Soviet Union is training more scientists than we, and therefore we must rearrange our educational system lest we lag further behind in the future. A few lone voices raised a cry that "We must have the humanities, too," but the weight of attention, even today when we have had time to reconsider, is focused primarily on the means by which the United States can produce greater numbers of physical scientists.

I think this proposition needs further exploration and sounder third thoughts.

First, let's assume that the problem could be solved by these scientists, an assumption I will question in a minute, but let's accept it for now. Is the correct approach a quantitative one? Do we count noses, and compare our count of scientists with Russia's? And if our nose count is less, do we admit defeat? Obviously not, there are several major fallacies in this sort of reasoning.

To begin with, Russia has demonstrated its superiority in only one field: the field on which she chose to concentrate her talent. In no other field of technology does any sensible person claim that she can begin to match us. The material aspects of American civilization, its general scientific competence, its contributions to basic research, and particularly its ability to apply that research, to engineer, and to produce, is without rival.

As a matter of aesthetics and of world politics, one can and should question whether our scientific talents have been applied to the best advantages in all instances, but our inadequacies in this regard are the consequence of our social organization—of governmental and commercial policy—not of scientific inadequacy. Perhaps it also is a reflection of the willingness of our scientifically trained personnel to apply their talents in pursuits which will be most lucrative, but it is not, of itself, a reflection on their capacities. If it is socially desirable to have more basic research, or more teachers—or more rocketeers, we have the trained manpower to do so, far beyond that of any other country. But we have yet to determine how to apply the social pressures and provide the incentives that will induce these individuals to redirect their talents.

Then, too, our preoccupation with the comparative *numbers* of scientists misses another crucial point; scientific break-throughs are not mass-produced. The brilliant intuitions that advance fundamental research, the new ideas that make significant contributions to engineering applications, are not the result of cranking out extra thousands of individuals with B.S. degrees, nor of teaching elementary physics to extra tens of thousands of high school students. It is reported that Russia's SPUTNIK was the product of thirty-one good brains. It was the result of a gifted few. This is a fact of which more notice needs to be taken.

I venture to guess that if we wanted to maximize our chances of keeping a technical lead over the rest of the world, we would accomplish far more if we selected a few thousand—even a few hundred—of the most gifted youngsters in the country, the top brains with scientific aptitudes, and gave them the best possible training, with the most superior teachers, than if we tried to mass-produce, with indifferent teachers, hundreds of thousands or even millions of half-baked mediocrities.

The nature of the training we should give these gifted youngsters is, from past experience, pretty clear. Start them in the liberal arts colleges, where best they can gain some intellectual breadth, and where inquiring minds are most likely to be awakened. Graduate school seems early enough for full concentration on their ultimate field of specialization. It is no accident that a disproportionate share of our leading scientists and our most promising graduate students are products of a liberal arts training. There is something in the learning process that seems to make it so.

But let's go back to the earlier proposition: that we need greater numbers of scientists. I have suggested that numbers is not the answer, as much as quality. But do we need the scientists at this stage in our development as much as we need certain others?

It has often been said, but never sufficiently appreciated to the point of becoming the basis for our actions, that our social sciences lag behind our natural sciences. Man has yet to learn how to use the things he can create. He has yet to learn how to organize his society in forms that are not self-destructive.

There are two points worth mentioning here, as antidotes to SPUTNIK fever.

Our first answer at this moment is the classic one of military force. We cannot dare to be militarily weak. In the past, however, military strength was the means by which, when war came, it could be won. No one today pretends that anyone will win the next war. Everyone will lose, catastrophically. So the best we can hope for is the deterrent of massive retaliatory power—of creating an uneasy stalemate where none but a madman would launch a war. Our missile program is not conceived to win a war but only in hopes that it might prevent a war.

But we have long learned from history that the possession of force is not the cause of war; it merely offers a temptation to the aggressor. Neither is it the sure preventive of war for the non-aggressor; in a dynamic technology, a seesaw of offensive and defensive capabilities is almost inevitable. The causes of international friction, and, accordingly, the problems to study if war is to be prevented have to do with the motivations of individuals and groups, and with the form and activities of our social, political and economic organizations. More than anything else we need to know what causes tension and what can be done with men's minds, and men's institutions, to relieve the tensions that periodically lead to war.

These are problems of the social sciences. Beyond the negative, but currently necessary, policy of enlisting scientists to hold the fort in hopes of prolonging a military stalemate, what we need most is time for the social scientists to catch up, for our diplomats and politicians to find ways for nations to accommodate their differences, and for students of society to help them find their way.

For this reason it seems to me that the strongest possible case must be made that our need for scientists, while urgent and immediate, to buy time, is, at bottom, less urgent than our need to apply our most fertile minds to discover the means by which the scientists' instruments of destruction can be rendered unnecessary.

Political issues and political leadership seem to be more often a matter of emotion than of rationality. Perhaps we need to recognize that fact, and seek rational ends by emotional means. Certainly we need to study the strange phenomena by which individuals who, separately, have no urge to kill, are led, as members of a nation, to take pride in becoming organized mass murderers. If only the magnificent sense of unity that arises in wartime could be marshalled to meet the problems of peacetime, wonderful things could happen in the world, and with much less sacrifice.

If some of our best minds, with the same sense of urgency, addressed themselves to study the sources of friction among nations, and we all could be induced to accept the desirability of applying our national wealth and ingenuity to lubricate the points of friction, then the stalemate of power would be less uneasy. Then military power might become obsolete.

However, even if the natural scientists achieve a military stand-off, and our social scientists manage to seek out and solve the issues that tend to cause wars, so that mutual destruction is no longer the problem, we still have the problems of winning the peace. And this surely is a task for the social scientists.

Most will agree that in recent years the reputation and stature of the United States has declined from its wartime peak. We may not be losing the peace, but we certainly are not winning it. In the Middle East, in South East Asia, among our wartime allies, throughout the Western World, among the underdeveloped nations, the uncommitted, the neutralist ones—in all these areas we have suffered serious tactical defeats. And few victories.

We think our way of life is good. But it is not being adopted and copied by many other nations. Nor are we disposed to force it on them. Probably we couldn't without waging war ourselves. We are anxious, however, as a matter of self-protection, that an alien way is not forced on us, nor on our friends, and that a hostile one is not adopted in more and more other parts of the world. To prevent this from happening demands the arts of the politician, and the psychologist, and the development of far greater skills and far deeper understanding than economists and other social scientists have demonstrated to date.

What I am trying to say is this: As we conduct the national reassessment which seems to have been started by the circulation of a small man-made sphere around the earth, we recognize it is a triumph of science, and as a national threat. But in rearranging our thinking to adjust to the implications of a space age, and, particularly in rethinking the direction of education, we must recognize that for some time to come, man is not leaving the earth behind. He is still living on earth, and our primary educational problem is that of learning how men can live together.

So some of the best minds, and the best training must be devoted as much to the social as to the natural sciences, lest through science alone, man learns only how to perish.

A comparable plea can be made for the humanities, but perhaps I can establish this point with a single anecdote.

During a recent war, it is said that a soldier in uniform up-braided a civilian for not participating in the war. He said, with some belligerence:

"Why aren't you in uniform? Why aren't you fighting? What are you doing to justify yourself during this emergency?" The civilian replied:

"Who, me? I'm a poet. I'm the civilization you fellows are fighting to save."

There's lots more that needs to be said about the implications of SPUTNIK and the kinds of second and third thoughts that should follow our first panicky reactions.

There is one fourth thought which I'd like to present briefly: perhaps it is another way of making a case for the humanities.

We know, in the natural sciences, that the extension of man's knowledge has inherent dangers, that an automobile is at once a means of transportation and a source of traffic deaths, that nuclear energy can be harnessed for power or can make a bomb, and that rocket power can climb to space or conduct a lethal missile. We know that knowledge can be abused.

It is unfortunately true that the social sciences have the same inherent dangers. As we learn more about the make-up of men's minds, either singly or in groups, it will be easier to manipulate them. This would delight Madison Avenue and give new power to demagogues. It is possible to use economic power to destroy as well as to create. The art of politics can be practised by a Machia-velli as well as by a Jefferson or a Lincoln.

This raises a final question as to the real purpose of our education in America. It requires that along with the skills we impart, and along with the intellectual curiosity we excite, we have an even higher obligation: to teach ethics and morals. Somewhere in the educational process, as well as in the home, and the church, we need to inculcate a set of values which recognize individual freedom and human dignity but which count as paramount, while we are on this earth, man's responsibility to man. If we can do this, knowledge will not be abused, and the ultimate significance of SPUTNIK will be that mankind has at last deserved a trip to the stars.

**Study suggestions**

1. In this address delivered before the alumnae clubs of the seven associated colleges, Richard Glenn Gettell, the President of Mount Holyoke College, focuses on what problem in education?

2. What comparison does he make between the technology of Russia and of America?

3. Discuss his disbelief in mass-production of scientists—What is his concept of specialization? Note his statement that many of our leading scientists are products of training gained from the liberal arts.

4. What are his "antidotes to SPUTNIK fever? What does he call our primary educational problem?

5. Explain: "We know that knowledge can be abused."

6. What is "man's responsibility to man"?

7. Compare this speech with the ideas of Vannevar Bush for their beliefs in war, for their attitudes toward science, and for man's social needs.

# HOW TO TALK TO PEOPLE,
# IF ANY,
# ON OTHER PLANETS

*Ralph E. Lapp*

Is there somewhere in the depths of space an advanced society which can communicate with us? If so, how will we establish contact with these strangers and understand them?

Man has for so long considered himself centered in the glittering framework of the universe that he has imagined himself to be unique—the central intelligent actor upon a vast stage. Even after patient astronomers diligently catalogued a vast panoply of stars, few took seriously the notion that intelligent life might exist on planets circling these faraway suns. Thus before we inquire into the matter of communicating with distant relatives, we need to examine the question of life itself and the conditions under which it might arise and flourish.

Would intelligent beings—granting that they exist on other spinning planets—resemble Homo sapiens in any way? After all, man is a product of his environment. Such subtle factors as gravity, the nature of the atmosphere, and the strength of the sun's rays condition the form and substance of our earth-bodies. One is reminded of Voltaire's "very witty young man . . . Mr. Micromegas" who journeyed from Sirius to "our little anthill." Voltaire described Mr. Micromegas as measuring "from head to foot twenty-four thousand paces" but still possessed of human qualities, albeit in outlandish dimension.

It is often assumed that life on other planets would be so different as to defy comparison with anything on earth. Yet if we take inventory of our present knowledge about the universe we can postulate that all living things must have an elemental relationship. That is to say, life is an aggregate of chemical compounds which are in turn wondrously fashioned assemblies of atoms such as hydrogen, oxygen, carbon, nitrogen, and phosphorus—to name but a few. From microscopic bacterium to macroscopic mouse, there is a common substructure: atoms of chemical elements.

No planets beyond the rim of our solar system come within the view of even the most powerful telescopes. But studies of the stars prove that planets do exist around parent stars like our sun. According to astronomer Dr. Otto Struve, "billions of stars in our Milky Way possess families of planets. Evidence seems to be overwhelmingly in favor of the conclusion that all, or most, solar-type stars possess planetary systems resembling our own."

While we cannot see these far-off planets, we can observe their parent stars not only in our own galaxy, the Milky Way, but in galaxies so remote from us that the light emitted from the stars takes over a billion years to reach our planet. This starlight can of course be focused in a gigantic telescope and registered as a small blob of light on a photographic plate. Astronomers have an additional, very powerful tool for looking more closely at these blobs of light from the remote stars. They can pass the light through a spectroscope, an optical instrument whose principal part is a finely ground glass prism, and observe the patterns of light which are thus produced. The effect is to produce a spread of colors or *spectrum* just as raindrops cast a bright band of colors in a rainbow.

Each element emits a spectrum of light which distinguishes it from any of the other elements. This is true whether the light comes from a sample of the element made incandescent in a laboratory electric arc or in the fiery atmosphere of a blazing star. The faint stars in the recesses of space send us a wealth of information about themselves, and the combination of the telescope and spectroscope allows us to decode this message. As a result we know that the observable universe contains the same basic ingredients, the same chemical elements, with which we are familiar here on earth. This is not to say that scientists have a profound knowledge of the molecular basis of life or even that they understand fully the architecture of many complex molecules; but they do know enough to describe the approximate conditions under which a planet might qualify as "habitable."

Planets must be neither too hot nor too cold if they are to support life in even a rudimentary form. If the planetary environment is too frigid, then complex aggregates of atoms fail to form or form too slowly to survive and evolve. Too much heat destroys the union between atoms and curtails the molecular build-up so essential to the evolution of biological organisms. The range of temperatures hospitable to life may be translated into a zone of warmth around a sun. In the case of our sun, the zone runs from the orbit of Venus out to that of Mars. Temperatures on the sunny side of the closest planet, Mercury, are hot enough to melt lead, while on Pluto, the outrider, the thermometer dips to 375 degrees below zero.

In addition to the requirement that habitable planets reside in the temperate zone, we can also add a condition that their orbits be fairly circular so that extremes of temperature are avoided. We could also place conditions upon the nature of the planetary atmosphere and the spin rate of the planet. And since the evolution of complex organisms embraces a span of more than a billion years we must also require that the host sun be of even temperament. A single flare-up of the solar flame could snuff out a billion years of evolutionary progress.

These restrictions on habitable planets and even a few other stipulations do not appear unduly fierce when we consider the immense numbers of stars and probable solar systems that exist in the Milky Way alone. Even though only one in a thousand planetary families would be a candidate for the evolution of life, this yields many millions of potentially life-supporting planets within our local galaxy.

Life may be very common within the vastness of our universe but this does not mean that communication between planetary societies is going to be easy. For one thing—to focus upon our niche of the Milky Way—the space nearest us is dotted only here and there with a likely prospect. Alpha Centauri is our closest neighbor and it is 4.3 light-years or 26 million million miles away. It is, however, not a good candidate because it is a multiple star and stable planetary orbits are not probable. Tau Ceti, a star 10.8 light-years distant, might provide a habitable planet. But there are relatively few other stars within a distance of 20 light-years. It may well be that centers of life are a hundred light-years apart. Thus life could be both common and rare—common, from the viewpoint of the universe, and rare, from the viewpoint of any location within the firmament of stars.

Man is very limited in his ability to hurl objects into space. It has taxed his ingenuity to fashion chemically-powered rockets powerful enough to escape from the clutches of the planet's gravity. Even enormous chemical rockets will thrust quite limited payloads into planetary space and will inevitably require very long journeys —46 years for a one-way mission to Pluto at the "edge" of our solar system.

When man enters the strange, inky-darkness of space he must truck along the necessities and some of the creature comforts of his earth environment. Sheer necessities include about six pounds of food and drink per day, slightly more than two pounds of oxygen, and a rugged airtight capsule to shield against harmful radiation. On long voyages the astronaut might recycle liquid wastes and oxygen but even so the weight of his life-support system will be several tons. Trucking such payloads strains the weight-lifting capacity of chemical rocket fuels, and skyscraper-high rockets are required to thrust them into space. Furthermore, chemically-powered space vehicles are incapable of achieving high speeds with which to conquer light-years of space.

Nuclear energy might seem to be the ideal prime mover in the space transportation business. But nuclear fuel such as uranium cannot simply be "burned" in space and used to propel a massive rocket. One needs a massive machine to harness the release of nuclear energy. This device known as a nuclear reactor would have to contain the power of the Grand Coulee within its fiery core. All this power, which must be housed in a unit no bigger than a domestic freezer, would not lift the rocket off the ground unless it could be converted into propulsive thrust.

There are also attractive but even more remote prospects of using a nuclear-electric rocket or an ion rocket in which electrical power is used to impart propulsive thrust to tiny, electrically-charged bits of matter. But the electric rocket is still in the laboratory stage and it will probably take a decade to develop an ion engine capable of propelling small payloads. Because of the constant acceleration which this novel low-thrust motor makes possible it should be feasible to attain velocities of a hundred miles per second. Speedy as this may seem, it is a snail's pace in interstellar space. Alpha Centauri, our closest neighbor, is eight thousand years away for the 100-mile-per-second rocket.

Can man ever perfect a rocket which would race along through space and compete with a beam of light? In theory the problem would be solved by the development of a photon or quantum rocket. This is what I call an "Einstein flashlight." It is essentially a machine which converts mass into energy according to Einstein's $E=mc^2$ mass-energy equation and channels this energy into a stream of radiant quanta or photons as the equivalent of the rocket jet exhaust.

So far our earthly attempts to unleash nuclear energy tap only a thousandth part of the total mass-energy locked up inside the atom. Therefore even the development of a nuclear source of photons will not allow man to race to the stars. No one can of course predict the scientific break-throughs of a century or a millennium hence but there are physical limits to what technology can do. The sheer energy requirements for propelling a massive spaceship on interstellar flights are fantastic; they relegate such journeys to the realm of science fiction.

In practice we must conclude that the photon rocket is far beyond man's grasp. But it adds to the intellectual excitement of our space age to consider the consequences of bridging "the abysm of time," to use Shakespeare's words. Suppose that man, rather than being an eternal prisoner of time, could conquer its swift rush. According to the Einstein Theory a space traveler, let us say, one of a pair of twins, who rockets along at a speed close to that of light, could return to earth in the middle of the twenty-first century to find his twin brother long since dead. Yet the speedy space twin would have aged only twenty years! This "asymmetrical aging" is also known as the clock paradox. Or, as interpreted by Nobel Prize-winner Edwin M. McMillan, "The result, that travelers live longer than stay-at-homes, while sometimes called 'paradoxical,' is really in the 'strange but true' category."

If we accept the conclusion that our primitive technology restricts space travel to the vicinity of our solar system, we are then isolated in space and imprisoned by time. That is—so far as direct or instrumental contact with exo-societies is concerned. Here we use the new term exo-society to designate intelligent life beyond our solar system. This means that if we are to communicate with an exo-society we must resort to signaling through space.

What do we mean by the term space signal? The word space needs no definition since we have already specified our area of interest as that lying beyond our solar system. The word signal has a special meaning to a scientist or engineer. It is really a significant event which can be distinguished against a background of other events. For example, a seismologist recording the earth's tremors obtains a seismogram which is a long sequence of jagged wiggles. An experienced seismic expert can pick out specific wiggles which he distinguishes from the background or "noise." Anyone tuning in a radio hears static or noise in between stations, and tunes in to the signal of the radio station by moving the receiver dial back and forth. In the case of the seismologist the signal indicates a physical event such as an earthquake whereas in the case of the radio signal we have a signal fashioned by an intelligent society.

A person trying to tune in a very distant radio station is often troubled by the interference or static (technically called "noise") which drowns out the station's signal. In the same way, when we look into space we find that it is far from silent. The noisiness of space was first discovered by the late Dr. Karl Jansky of the Bell Telephone Company. The latter had inaugurated its radio-telephone transmission across the Atlantic only to find its service was subject to interference. The youthful Dr. Jansky set about searching for the causes of this static and in order to track these down he built a big radio antenna. The radio listening device consisted of an array of pipes mounted on a wooden scaffolding and insulated by means of glass cylinders. He attached four wooden-spoked automobile wheels to the apparatus so that he could rotate it in a circle. This wood and pipe skeleton was located on an abandoned farm near Holmdel, New Jersey, southeast of Perth Amboy.

Dr. Jansky put his apparatus into operation in the fall of 1931. He found three types of radio-frequency disturbances, two of which he attributed to local thunderstorms and to more remote atmospheric disturbances. The third type of annoying static puzzled him. Further experiments pointed to an extraterrestrial source for this high-frequency static. Dr. Jansky's data indicated that the radio noise came from space and he thought that the source was probably near the center of our Milky Way (26,000 light-years away). Karl Jansky had stumbled upon a discovery of great magnitude, yet for two decades it was largely ignored. Only after World War II did others, especially the British, develop the near-blighted science of radioastronomy.

Astronomers today have an important new instrument for exploring the heavens. It is the radiotelescope, the principal part of which is a huge rotatable metal grid or "dish." Just as a reflecting telescope focuses light rays with its accurately ground, superfinished mirror, the gigantic metal dishes catch radio waves and focus them. A number of radiotelescopes have been constructed in various countries, with the biggest at Jodrell Bank, England, where the University of Manchester has a 250-foot-diameter dish. Research to date has identified a variety of sources of what Dr. Jansky called "cosmic static." The sun, certain planets, points within our galaxy, and intergalactic objects send out space static. Some sources are faint while others possess incredible signal strength or radiating power.

Out of the hissing, spluttering noise of the universe a single radio frequency or unwavering note has been found. It is the 21-centimeter (1,420-megacycle-per-second) radio frequency discovered in 1951 by two Harvard physicists. This "song of the universe" has its origin in the chirping of the hydrogen atom—a steady drone that re-echoes through the vastness of space over distances as far as the Mt. Palomar telescope can peer. But the 200-inch telescope at Palomar can see only those fiery objects whose luminosity renders them visible. The cold hydrogen atom's faint note resounds from regions where even the most powerful telescopes see little detail. Radio-astronomers who tune their telescopes to the 21-centimeter radio wave are granted X-ray vision to scan the heavens. It turns out that space is remarkably transparent to this radio frequency—a valuable thing for us to know when we attempt to listen in for words from other worlds or to send signals of our own through space.

Because we can receive cosmic signals from remote space we know that there is a clear channel for communication with exosocieties relatively close to us. We need to broadcast and to listen on radio frequencies close to that of the 21-centimeter hydrogen note. But we cannot broadcast signals in all directions; this is wasteful dissipation of energy. We need to beam or concentrate our signal in the right direction.

Where do we point to locate the sought-after society in space? This is equivalent to asking: what stars close by are our best bets for harboring intelligent life? Dr. Su-Shu Huang, a University of California researcher, has taken inventory of the nearby stars, meaning those within 15 light-years of our sun. The Chinese-born astrophysicist analyzed the stellar census and selected two candidates—Epsilon Eridani and Tau Ceti—as the best prospects for exhibiting planetary life.

Tau Ceti is 10.8 years away if we measure the time for a light signal to cross the void and reach our earth. No signal can travel faster than the speed of light—this is an Einstein speed limit in space—so the irreducible sender-to-receiver time is 10.8 years for a signal from Tau Ceti. (Radio waves travel with the same speed as light waves.) And this time must be doubled if we are to measure the total time from transmission of a signal to acknowledgment of receipt of the message. A lull of 21.6 years in conversation is a distressing pause but there is no way for man to exceed the Einstein speed limit. As a matter of fact, a lull of 21.6 years is probably a lower limit for the time from query to reply on the space channel. We will probably have to look deeper into space to find an exo-society capable of communicating with us.

Initial findings at the U. S. National Radio Astronomy Observatory near Greenbank, West Virginia, are negative. About a year ago, scientists trained a huge, 85-foot electronic ear on Tau Ceti and Epsilon Eridani. The ear or "dish" is the business end of Project Ozma—named after the Queen of Oz, that mythical but well-known "place very far away, difficult to reach and populated by strange, exotic beings." Secluded in the mountains of West Virginia, strange structures are being assembled to probe the secrets of space. The first of these, the 85-foot radiotelescope, drew a blank when it looked for signals from our nearest neighbors in space. Some "bugs in the electronic circuit" gave the researchers a flurry of excitement but when the equipment was functioning properly it found nothing unusual—meaning "signs of technological life" on either Tau Ceti or Epsilon Eridani. This did not disturb Dr. Otto Struve, director of the radio observatory, whose advice was, in effect, "keep trying"—the same formula used when the party at the other end of the phone fails to answer.

Other radiotelescopes will probe deeper into space. The biggest of these is the U. S. Navy's "Big Dish" now under construction near the hamlet of Sugar Grove, West Virginia. Costing nearly $80 million, the Big Dish is an ear on the dimensions of Voltaire's Mr. Micromegas. The structure soars to the height of a sixty-six-story skyscraper and cradles a radio mirror with some seven acres of metallic surface. From edge to edge the mirror is twice the length of a football field. This stupendous contraption can be rotated and swung on its axis toward various points in space and stay "locked on" these points despite the earth's rotation.

The Navy's Big Dish has been delayed in completion owing to engineering difficulties but it is expected to go into operation by 1964. The receiving end of the radiotelescope consists of a small cylinder suspended above the mirror at its focal point; this is the observation cage where powerful amplifiers boost the electronic signals received and convert them into scientific data that will be continuously recorded by automatic instruments. The dancing swing of voltmeters and scribbling of recording instruments will represent the output of the telescope—quite a different view of the heavens from that photographed by the conventional astronomer with an optical telescope.

How will we "talk" with the exo-society we seek—with someone we have never met? Imagine that you were stranded at some inaccessible point and that your only contact with civilization was a telephone. Suppose further that you could only ring one number and the person at the other end of the line could not speak your language—in fact, neither of you could even *recognize* the other's language. How could you manage to communicate? *If* you both were quite intelligent and knew the Morse code, you might converse with verbal dots and dashes. In other words you would resort to a common code that you both understood. Communication in this hypothetical case would be greatly simplified by the nearly instantaneous telephone linkage. The situation is vastly different for space communication, where a simple acknowledgment may take decades.

Before we give up the problem as hopeless—as a layman might readily believe—we need to examine what we may have in common with intelligent beings on another planet. After all, if two strangers meet and wish to learn each other's language, the simplest procedure is to point to a visible object and identify it by name. The stranger repeats the name to indicate he understands and you approve with a nod. The process is repeated with the stranger's name for the object and translation is thus begun. At first glance, it would appear that "pointing" to common things across the void of space is impossible.

I believe that the problem can be solved. The basic reason for my optimism is that if we do establish contact with an exo-society it is probable that their technology is more advanced than ours. We may find that we are dealing with vastly brighter beings—so smart that they can even understand the incoherent space chatter of earthlings. A little reflection will make clear why this may in fact be the case.

Society X and our own human society do have something in common. In order to transmit and listen on a radio frequency there must be at both ends of the line a comparable, although perhaps not very similar, technology. The X transmitter may not look like ours but it must operate on the communicating frequency or wave length. This fact alone bespeaks a fairly sophisticated level of society. However, it would be a really weird circumstance if both the planet Earth and planet X arrived at the same level of technology at the same time. It is much more likely that society X is considerably more advanced than ours—it could not be less advanced and still be able to communicate.

Now, bearing this information in mind, we ask how we would respond to an intelligent signal from planet X. First, the simplest way to let planet X know that we have received its message is to beam back precisely the same signal—analogous to repeating a name for an object pointed out by a stranger. We could alter the pattern or sequence of the signals to make perfectly sure that society X would not think it was being tricked by some echo effect.

This playback of the received signal, whether it be a series of nonrandom blips or electrical pulses or a more complex electronic signal, is essentially equivalent to repeating "Hello!" as the opening word of a conversation. It does not solve the problem of more detailed communication. But here we have to remember that society X must have a considerable substructure of science in order to send a message across space and that numbers are the language and the metrics of science. Furthermore, we must concede that society X is more advanced than ours; it may even be a case of a genius talking with a moron. In any event, if we transmit a coded signal to society X we must assume that their cryptographers will decode it rather quickly. After all, we will not be trying to conceal our message, as in cryptography, but to reveal it.

Thus it seems clear that we will encode numbers into the scheme of our interstellar message. We can try many codes because we have a long time to wait before getting an answer. This is what we will have to do in sending messages prior to receiving any. Once we receive a clear signal, we will know better how to reply, assuming that we have the technical capacity to cram the information into a radio message. It would be wonderful if we could send television signals so that we could display graphically the content of our message, but the power requirements for television transmission across the vastness of space are far beyond our capability. We can hope to send back single picture frames from a moonship at a distance of one-quarter million miles, but the distance to planet X may be over 100 million times greater.

I believe that we can do more than transmit a numbered code. I believe it is possible to "point" to certain features of the physical universe and thus establish a space language. For example, we have mentioned the unique radio frequency of "cold hydrogen"— we could point to this (by shifting transmitter frequency to 1,420 megacycles) and then give this a characteristic number. In the same way we could identify all other elements—helium, lithium, and so forth—by using a simple multiplier for this number. We can also introduce a distance and time scale without too much difficulty. In addition, we can specify mass in terms of the hydrogen atom. We now have the rudiments of a physical system. Of course, we lack verbs, adjectives, and most of all pronouns; for we want desperately to know who "they" are. But we could communicate with society X even if "they" might look down their noses (or whatever part of their anatomy would be homologous) at our baby talk.

Of course, our listening may be rewarded with the monotony of steady static uninterrupted by any artificial signal. This silence can have numerous meanings. It may mean that we are truly alone or at least unique in our niche of the galaxy. It may mean that we are out of range of the nearest exo-society or that the latter is at too low a rung of the technological ladder. Some, who concede that other societies may have vaulted ahead of ours, place an ominous interpretation upon a noncommunicative planet; they believe that such an advanced society is self-destructive. Once a society masters space technology, it is presumably nimble enough to release the atom's energy and this spells its downfall. Nuclear technology thus becomes the final evolutionary step.

On the other hand, we may literally learn the secrets of the universe if we establish contact with society X. Suppose that this planet X boasts a technology which is more advanced than ours by a lead time of a million years—or even a thousand years. This after all is but a tick on the evolutionary clock. Imagine what kind of technology society X might possess! Perhaps the best way to do this is to project our earthly thoughts from the year 1900 to 2000 and compare the technological advances and then multiply these a thousand times. Society X may have already communicated with many other planets. We will in effect be plugging into a party line. Society X may even be a little blasé about contacting another planet such as ours, especially if we seem to *them* underdeveloped and sense-limited. But the excitement on our planet would be something! As Dr. Harold Urey expressed it: "Contact with *them* would be the most magnificent thing one can imagine."

Think of the knowledge we could gain if planet X is far advanced and is already familiar with the discoveries, inventions, and evolutionary steps which are still in our future. Think of the impact which such knowledge could have upon our lives, upon our philosophy and our religion. These matters are now being discussed quite seriously by reputable scientists. I suppose that it is only a matter of time before President Kennedy appoints a group of the nation's leading thinkers as members of the U. S. Committee for Space Communication.

## Study suggestions

1. Discuss the theories which indicate not only possible life on distant planets but even possible communication.

2. What are the problems to overcome for communication?

3. What attempts have been made to signal through space?

4. How will we talk and communicate with beings on another planet? What might we have in common?

5. What secrets of the universe might be learned?

6. Read more on this subject in Dr. Lapp's new book, *Man and Space: The Next Decade.*

# THE AMERICAN IMAGE OF SUCCESS

*Raphael Demos*

Americans have often been criticized, especially by the intelligentsia at home and abroad, for being too engrossed with success. I shall not join this chorus. Rather, I will claim that we should not be ashamed of ourselves for pursuing success, and that we should not pretend we are indifferent to it. Certainly, we want success both for ourselves and for our children. But, by the same token, we must be careful of what we mean by success, and know the areas to which the term success does *not* apply.

For instance, here we are—at the height of material prosperity —with a standard of living never before attained. Yet there are now more people more urgently seeking an easy access to "peace of mind" than ever before. Such a craving is clearly a symptom of a deep anxiety underlying the gleaming surface of our prosperity. This surely proves that success is not everything in life.

We are right in trying to eliminate poverty, and the cars, refrigerators, radios, and washing machines supplied by businessmen are surely useful things. But the good life—that is something different. While it depends to some extent, certainly, on material goods, it does not depend even largely on the possession of goods. Advertising subtly argues against this truism, giving the misleading impression that if you buy enough goods, you have secured the good life.

In a striking phrase, Edward C. Bursk wrote that "it is not easy to define . . . what the line is that separates the fraudulent from the dramatic." He went on to urge advertisers to go all out to think positively, not negatively, as they had recently tended to do since the payola scandals. Of course; as the old saying goes, if a thing is worth doing, it is worth doing well and forcefully.

Nevertheless, there are negatives and negatives—negatives which repress and negatives which reinforce. Eight of the Ten Commandments are couched in negatives, "Thou shalt not . . ." Any rule book is cluttered with negations. There is no tennis game without the white lines imposing a limit on where the ball should fall. The horse of advertising will run taste, integrity, and—dare I say it?—a certain philosophy of values.

Thus, perhaps some discussion of the goals of life will be especially thought-provoking to businessmen, who of necessity are concerned with material ventures, and who are not impervious to worries about what our country's drive toward material success implies. We can distinguish between kinds of success, and between the areas where it is a meaningful or meaningless concept.

Success refers to something subjective, and to something objective.

By subjective I mean what one gets for oneself—the element of reward, which takes a variety of forms, such as wealth or glory. It is precisely this factor of self-reference and selfishness which, according to our critics, throws a dark shadow over the image of success. In business such personal rewards are counted in terms of money, yet not of money only; we must not forget prestige and power. In addition, we all desire the success which consists in social appreciation. We like being appreciated by others; we have the need to be needed.

The meaning of objective success may be indicated by examples. A doctor is successful because he can cure diseases, a lawyer because he wins cases, a general because he wins battles, a scientist because he adds to our knowledge of nature. In these instances, success implies results, accomplishment, getting things done.

This is also true of business, of course. A successful businessman is not just a man who has made a lot of money; he is one whose name we associate with great accomplishments. He has built, let us say, new plants and factories; he has increased production; he has succeeded in extracting new mineral resources from the earth. (I use "business" in its widest sense, to include both production and its offshoots—for instance, industry, transportation, construction, management of money or of organizations.)

In this sense, business means nothing less than man's conquest of nature—what Bacon had in mind when he said that knowledge is power. Bacon's word "knowledge" has special relevance to the growth of business, for it is the application of science to production which has raised industry to its present heights. Our greatest success so far in this country has been in the area of business, that is to say, of technological achievement.

Can our nation not be proud of this accomplishment? Surely it can. What is involved is how man reacts to his material environment. Primitive people tend to be passive, even fatalistic; they take their environment as something given, to which they adapt themselves as best they can. Even nations with a highly advanced civilization, like India, have, in the past, refrained from fighting against the hostile environment. Rather, they have devoted themselves to cultivating the spirit alone, thus avoiding the battle with material nature.

The American ethos, on the contrary, has been neither to accept passively nor to ignore but to rebel against material circumstances, to modify the environment, and adapt it to the shape of human uses. That there has been a persistent pursuit of profits leading to ruthless and sometimes unscrupulous competition I do not deny. But these have been incidents of a magnificent effort: the struggle of spirit against matter in order to impress on it a human image. This is something to take pride in, not an occasion for shame or apology.

Will it surprise the reader to find that the ancient Greeks, whom we spontaneously associate with a respect for spiritual values, included a great deal of what I have been saying in their own image of man? For instance, this is what the tragic poet, Sophocles, says when he wants to praise man:

"Many are the wonders of the world but none so wonderful
as man;
Man makes his way through the perilous sea,
Steering his bark over the waters
While the waves break over his head.

He ploughs the earth and makes it yield food;
He snares the birds of the air, tames tribes of savage beasts,
And traps the creatures of the deep,
And devises remedies for sickness.
He is resourceful and has good counsel;
Language he has learned;
He has made cities and is sworn to keep law and justice.
Only death he cannot avoid."

What is especially noteworthy in these fine lines is that Sophocles seems to place man's material accomplishments on the same level with his spiritual achievements. He cites man's invention of language, his "good counsel," and his law-abidingness, but he also calls attention to man's successful battle with the elements, especially water, air, and earth. Aeschylus (who preceded Sophocles) includes man's conquest of the fourth element, fire, in the list. Here I have in mind the record of the things which Prometheus stole from the gods for the benefit of man:

"He brought radiant fire and skill;
Taught man how to build houses and boats to cross the sea;
Revealed to man hidden resources underneath the ground;
Copper, iron ore, silver and gold.
And he established blind hope in the hearts of men."

Fire stands for light, heat, and energy. Fire produces flame which shines; fire melts metal; fire yields energy for transportation. Fire, too, is something which goes on; it feeds on and perpetuates itself, until it may produce a holocaust. Fire stands both for creation and destruction. And fire symbolizes the radiance of a clear intelligence, also.

In these two famous odes, the Greek poets are exalting what today we call technology and industry, although naturally in the much simpler and cruder form of their day. They exalt technology just because they see in it the refusal of mind to submit to matter. Nevertheless, they dwell on some of the limitations of man's power over nature. Thus, Sophocles stresses that man can never conquer death, while Aeschylus warns that man's hope may be blind.

It is well to remember in this connection that Americans, as a whole, have been a hopeful people, confident that their efforts will be rewarded with success. In this country, faith has in fact moved mountains; and our confidence has been greatly justified.

Yet we find a deep and disturbing paradox. Business enterprise is an expression of man's determination to dominate matter. Nevertheless, the end result seems to be man's domination by matter. Production is tough and competitive; it requires and leads to hardening of the muscle and to tension. So far, very good. Yet production ultimately is for the sake of consumption; its purpose is to produce human satisfaction. But consumers' goods introduce a climate of wholly contrasted attitudes.

After a point, consumption induces a love of comfort and self-indulgence, a fondness for luxury rather than a provision for needs. Now that I have a car, I walk less than before, if at all. I drive even if I have to go only three blocks. Now that we have radios, the family no longer provides its own music. The more creative business is, the less creative, the less self-reliant is the consumer; in this sense, the enterprising quality of business is self-defeating.

Dynamic production, moreover, means dynamic selling, and selling cannot be continuous unless the consumer is persuaded that what was purchased yesterday is obsolete today. In a sense, Americans are the least materialistic of any nation, as the many car cemeteries scattered near the highways demonstrate. Yet even manufactured goods have the aura of personality because human thought and design have been incorporated into them. And the existence of various museums in which old makes of cars and the like are preserved is evidence of a counterfeeling of material nostalgia.

But, regardless of whether Americans are really or hopefully, materialistic, they certainly are conditioned to think in terms of success and failure—unfortunately even in realms where these terms do not apply. Success applies clearly to matters where measurement is possible. We can, for example, identify the number of bridges built by the engineer; the number of cases won by the lawyer, enemies conquered by the general, ailments cured by the doctor, profits made by the businessman; or the number of years a man and wife have lived in apparent harmony. Thus we can say, at this level, that each has been successful in accomplishing a particular thing.

But once we go beyond such easily quantifiable items, when we go beyond immediate accomplishments and enter realms of ultimate results, we find that terms like success or failure do not so easily apply. Especially when we try to measure the ultimate social consequences of our acts do we enter a realm of complexity where the variables are too many and too elusive to be measurable. Let me give an example:

We can predict that a given machine will produce a given amount of goods. But when we try to predict that our growing industrial machine will produce more and better goods for Americans and thus raise our standard of living, we enter a future realm where exact prediction is impossible.

And when we try to estimate the social consequences of technology on our civilization, we run into even great difficulty. Will it have effects that are good? Will it raise our standard of living at the expense of other less material goods of life?

As another example, our great cities are the unique products of our technology. In this sense they are good, a successful outcome of man's creative ingenuity. But when one considers how more and more people are now leaving the cities for the suburbs and the country, we can question their ultimate success as a social development. Are large cities really a successful social creation? It is difficult to know.

You can easily see how difficult it is to apply terms like success and failure to situations such as these.

Even in the restricted areas of the careers that we have already mentioned, the concept of success, sometimes, is hardly relevant. For instance, it is not easy to decide whether a teacher has been successful or not. Popularity alone is not a good test; Socrates, a great teacher by any sensible standards, made himself generally unpopular and had to pay the price with his life. Teachers who do not win applause from their students can often take satisfaction in the quality of the books they have written. Socrates did not write a single word.

The teacher's influence is something which operates in the long run. It has been said that education is like forestry in that it takes a generation or two before its effects become visible. Yet even this analogy fails; we can count the number of trees that have grown out of seeds and evaluate their quality. But as the young man grows up to be an adult, so many influences pour on him from all sides that it becomes impossible to trace this or that particular trait to the word of the teacher.

In medicine, sometimes a cure is clearly attained, but often the best that a physician can do is simply to tinker with the patient's organism and enable him to live with his sickness. Often, the most a political leader can hope for is merely to keep the ship of state from sinking. Even when he does not bring the ship to port, he manages to keep it afloat.

In the field of production, there are definite problems to be solved and definite techniques for solving them. But the good life is not a problem; here the very ends are unclear, and there are no specific formulas for achieving ends. The good life is not a production job; it is growth. It is a platitude that happiness will evade those who make of it a deliberate objective; nor are there scales by which to weigh character, yardsticks by which to measure love and hate, or thermometers by which to measure the temperature of happiness.

Go over the list of guests at the White House dinners, as published in the *New York Times*. You will find names of successful men, of diplomats, of high government officials, of big-businessmen, but not of ministers, artists, scholars, poets, or philosophers. (Of course, it is true that after the Sputniks appeared, the scientists were brought in.) It was not so in the time of Theodore Roosevelt. If you demur that it is the President's private affair whom he invites to dinner, then I beg to differ. The White House is the Pantheon of our values; the kind of people honored there set the tone for the country. Position, bigness, success—these are not our only values.

Consider now the relations between people, beginning with the most intimate type. Parenthood is not exactly a specialized occupation: still, like some of the careers already discussed, its function is the care of human beings. Indeed, bringing up children is a more important task than any mentioned so far. Yet the degree of our knowledge of the skills which it involves is in inverse proportion to its transcendent importance. Certainly, the parent has an obligation to provide guidance to his child and not to let him grow like the lilies of the field. But whereas in technology we can speak of man dominating and molding his inert material, the more a parent tries to dominate his child the less well is he doing his job. We speak of the influence of heredity, yet often the child surprises the parent; he is a creature of God rather than of the parent, and even more a creature of his own free choice.

We do not call an undertaking successful if it has not been completed, if the wrinkles have not been ironed out. But a family is an undertaking which is never finished. A family consists of a network of the most intimate, delicate personal relations conceivable. Its bonds are those of affection—but, like electric wires, they are subject to tension. Such tension is inevitable when the members of the family are independent and determined personalities; and when tension is absent, there must be something wrong either with the members or with the kind of relationship. Thus, domination by one partner may eliminate tension but crush the personality of the other.

Parents are united with children not by choice but by nature; so, to some extent, they are strangers to one another. A family provides a rich and satisfying experience to its members just because they represent different points of view. We want harmony but not the kind we expect to find in a regiment. The harmony of a family is one which accepts contrasts and even discords. In short, the very things we value in a family make for trouble.

So if we take success to mean elimination of tension and suffering, then, since there is no guarantee of happiness, to expect success is to hope for something which is both impossible and undesirable. The intimate togetherness of a family calls, not for driving pressure, but for patience, forbearance, and forgiveness. We may therefore wonder whether the increasing number of breakdowns in the family may not be due to the fact that we expect, indeed, demand, success in an area where it does not belong.

Similar questions arise in the international sphere. In the past, as a nation, we have been isolated from the general world by the two oceans. Thus, we were provided with the opportunity to concentrate on raising a civilization on this continent. But now the very technological skills which we have cherished have been so employed as to raze the barriers separating us from the larger world. Now we have been thrust into the jungle of international relations. The rivalry of nations is slow to heal, if ever, and quick results are not to be expected. However, we must not be defeatist just because accomplishment is difficult; neither must we be Utopian. Once more we need to cultivate understanding, patience, and forbearance, not to demand a finished job.

There are an infinite variety of ways of life, and the transcendental producer is putting on many different plays simultaneously in the vast theatrical stage of this world. The plot of the play in this country consists of struggle, striving, challenge, competition, success, and failure. Our business world enacts just this play. But there is another drama also in which we all play a role.

In this dimension of life, winning and losing, competing and succeeding, have no meaning whatever. Our national ethos, probably deriving from our Calvinistic heritage, requires that every man, no matter how rich, should work. By working, a man not only earns a living; he acquires a human status and dignity. In working, man proves himself to his fellows and to himself. As Aristotle said, the prizes in the Olympic games are awarded not to the great runners but to those who prove their merit by actually participating.

But counterbalancing this testing of oneself, there is the sheer acceptance of oneself, also. Human beings show unequal abilities in the contest of life; some of us go ahead and others fall behind. Yet, independently of how we come out at the end, all of us have an equal value as human beings.

Often success in a career is incompatible with a rich and vivid life, for the career may demand concentration to the point of narrowness and spiritual impoverishment. A man may attain the heights of wealth, power, and reputation for which he has striven all his life; yet may find that the cup of success, as it reaches his lips, is empty.

Life has these two facets—the career, on the one hand, and the warmth and substance of personality, on the other. There is *doing* —the life of action—and there is *being*. What a man is, is as important as what he does. Deeds are for all to see and admire; deeds are celebrated in song and poetry. But the quality of life and the flavor of a personality, while not measurable and not accessible to observation, are no less worthy of esteem.

The reader remembers what comes at the end of an article better than what was said in the beginning. Let me therefore repeat that this article is not a tirade against the concept of success. The American people have been distinguished among all nations for their drive, their refusal to bow down before obstacles. This has been one of their greatest contributions to the world at large. The inspiration to such deeds has come from the bright image of success. But we must not project this image into areas where it is not relevant. We should view success in perspective, as part of the total image of the good life.

## Study suggestions

1. Explain the writer's concept of success and compare it with your idea or interpretation of the word.

2. Differentiate between negatives which repress and negatives which reenforce, between subjective success and objective.

3. Contrast reactions of primitive people with those of the American—also of the Greeks.

4. In what ways are technology and creative business self-defeating?

5. Explain the analogy of education to forestry. Discuss the many influences that surround the students.

6. Explain: "The White House is the Pantheon of our values. . . ."

7. Do you believe that domination may destroy personality?

8. What is meant by "the jungle of international relations"?

9. Discuss the two facets of life he describes.

10. With what thought does he end this discussion?

11. Write on your concept of success.

# THE DECLINE OF HEROES

*Arthur M. Schlesinger, Jr.*

Ours is an age without heroes—and, when we say this, we suddenly realize how spectacularly the world has changed in a generation. Most of us grew up in a time of towering personalities. For better or for worse, great men seemed to dominate our lives and shape our destiny. In the United States we had Theodore Roosevelt, Woodrow Wilson, Franklin Roosevelt. In Great Britain, there were Lloyd George and Winston Churchill. In other lands, there were Lenin, Stalin, Hitler, Mussolini, Clemenceau, Gandhi, Kemal, Sun Yat-sen. Outside of politics there were Einstein, Freud, Keynes. Some of these great men influenced the world for good, others for evil; but, whether for good or for evil, the fact that each had not died at birth made a difference, one believed, to everyone who lived after them.

Today no one bestrides our narrow world like a colossus; we have no giants who play roles which one can imagine no one else playing in their stead. There are a few figures on the margin of uniqueness, perhaps: Adenauer, Nehru, Tito, De Gaulle, Chiang Kai-shek, Mao Tse-tung. But there seem to be none in the epic style of those mightly figures of our recent past who seized history with both hands and gave it an imprint, even a direction, which it otherwise might not have had. As De Gaulle himself remarked on hearing of Stalin's death, "The age of giants is over." Whatever one thought, whether one admired or detested Roosevelt or Churchill, Stalin or Hitler, one nevertheless felt the sheer weight of such personalities on one's own existence. We feel no comparable pressures today. Our own President, with all his pleasant qualities, has more or less explicitly renounced any desire to impress his own views on history. The Macmillans, Khrushchevs and Gronchis have measurably less specific gravity than their predecessors. Other men could be in their places as leaders of America or Britain or Russia or Italy without any change in the course of history. Why ours should thus be an age without heroes, and whether this condition is good or bad for us and for civilization, are topics worthy of investigation.

Why have giants vanished from our midst? One must never neglect the role of accident in history; and accident no doubt plays a part here. But too many accidents of the same sort cease to be wholly accidental. One must inquire further. Why should our age not only be without great men but even seem actively hostile to them? Surely one reason we have so few heroes now is precisely that we had so many a generation ago. Greatness is hard for common humanity to bear. As Emerson said, "Heroism means difficulty, postponement of praise, postponement of ease, introduction of the world into the private apartment, introduction of eternity into the hours measured by the sitting-room clock." A world of heroes keeps people from living their own private lives.

Moreover, great men live dangerously. They introduce extremes into existence—extremes of good, extremes of evil—and ordinary men after a time flinch from the ultimates and yearn for undemanding security. The Second World War was the climax of an epoch of living dangerously. It is no surprise that it precipitated a universal revulsion against greatness. The war itself destroyed Hitler and Mussolini. And the architects of victory were hardly longer-lived. After the war, the British repudiated Churchill, and the Americans (with the adoption of the 22nd Amendment), Roosevelt. In due course, the French repudiated De Gaulle (they later repented, but it took threat of civil war to bring him back); the Chinese, Chiang Kai-shek; and the Russians, Stalin. Khrushchev, in toppling Stalin from his pedestal, pronounced the general verdict against the uncommon man: the modern world, he said, had no use for the "cult of the individual." And, indeed, carried to the excesses to which the worshipers of Hitler and Stalin carried it, even to the much milder degree to which admirers of Roosevelt and Churchill sometimes carried it, the cult of the individual was dangerous. No man is infallible, and every man needs to be reminded of this on occasion. Still, our age has gone further than this—it objects not just to hero worship but to heroes. The century of the common man has come into its own.

This term, "common man," suggests the deeper problem. There is more involved than simply a dismissal of those colossi whom the world identified with a season of blood and agony. The common man has always regarded the great man with mixed feelings —resentment as well as admiration, hatred as well as love. The Athenian who refused to vote for Aristides because he was so tired of hearing him called "the Just" expressed a natural reaction. Great men make small men aware of their smallness. Rancor is one of the unavowed but potent emotions of politics; and one must never forget that the envy of the have-nots can be quite as consuming when the haves have character or intelligence as it is when they have merely material possessions.

Modern democracy inadvertently gave envy new scope. While the purpose of democracy was to give everyone a fair chance to rise, its method enabled rancorous men to invoke "equality" as an excuse for keeping all down to their own level. "I attribute the small number of distinguished men in political life," wrote Alexis de Tocqueville after visiting the United States in the 1830's, "to the ever-increasing despotism of the majority. . . . The power of the majority is so absolute and irresistible that one must give up one's rights as a citizen and almost abjure one's qualities as a human being, if one intends to stray from the track which it prescribes." James Bryce even titled a chapter in his *American Commonwealth,* "Why Great Men Are Not Chosen President."

History has shown these prophets unduly pessimistic. Distinguished men do enter American politics; great men have been chosen President. Democracy demonstrates a capability for heroic leadership quite as much as it does a tendency toward mediocrity. Yet Tocqueville and the others were correct enough in detecting the dislike of great men as a permanent potentiality in a democracy. And the evolution of industrial society appears to have given this sentiment new force. More and more of us live and work within great organizations; an influential book has already singled out

the organization man as the American of the future. The bureau-
cratization of American life, the decline of the working class, the
growth of the white-collar class, the rise of suburbia—all this has
meant the increasing homogeneity of American society. Though
we continue to speak of ourselves as rugged individualists, our actual life has grown more and more collective and anonymous. As
a Monsanto Chemical film put it, showing a group of technicians
at work in a laboratory: 'No geniuses here; just a bunch of
average Americans working together." Our ideal is increasingly
smooth absorption into the group rather than self-realization in the
old-fashioned, strong-minded, don't-give-a-damn sense. Where does
the great man fit into our homogenized society?

"The greatness of England is now all collective," John Stuart
Mill wrote a century ago: "individually small, we only appear capable of anything great by our habit of combining." He might have
been writing about contemporary America; but where we Americans are inclined to rejoice over the superiority of the "team," Mill
added somberly, "It was men of another stamp than this that
made England what it has been; and men of another stamp will be
needed to prevent its decline."

But was Mill right? Do individuals really have impact on history? A powerful school of philosophers has denied any importance at all to great men. Such thinkers reject heroes as a childish
hangover from the days when men ascribed everything to the action of gods. History, they assert, is not made by men, but by inexorable forces of irrevocable laws: if these forces or laws do not
manifest themselves through one individual, they will do so
through another. What has happened already has comprehensively
and absolutely decided what will happen in the future. "If there
is a single human action due to free will," wrote Tolstoi, "no historical law exists, and no conception of historical events can be
formed." If all this is so, obviously the presence or absence
of any particular "hero" at any particular time cannot make the
slightest difference.

This view of history is a form of fatalistic determinism; and Tolstoi's *War and Peace* offers one of its most eloquent statements.
Why, Tolstoi asked, did millions of men in the time of Napoleon,
repudiating their common sense and their human feelings, move

from west to east, slaughtering their fellows? The answers provided by historians seemed to him hopelessly superficial. His own answer was: "The war was bound to happen simply because it was bound to happen"; all previous history predetermined it. Where did this leave the great men? In Tolstoi's view, they were the most deluded figures of all. Great men, he said, "are but the labels that serve to give a name to an event and, like labels, they have the least possible connection with the event itself." The greater the man, "the more conspicuous is the inevitability and predestination of every act he commits." The hero, said Tolstoi, "is the slave of history."

There are many forms of historical fatalism. Toynbee and Spengler, with their theory of the inexorable growth and decay of civilizations, represent one form. The Marxists, with their theory that changes in the modes of production control the course of history, represent another. When Khrushchev denounced the practice of making "a hero" out of "a particular leader" and condemned the cult of the individual as "alien to the spirit of Marxism-Leninism," he was speaking the true spirit of his faith. And Marxism is not the only form of economic determinism; there are also, for example, economic determinists of the laissez-faire school who believe that all civilization is dependent on rigid adherence to a certain theory of the sacredness of private property.

Fatalists differ greatly among themselves. But, however much they differ, they unite in the conclusion that the individual plays no role of his own in history. If they are right, then nothing could matter less whether or not this is an age without heroes.

But they are not right. The philosophy of historical fatalism rests on serious fallacies. For one thing, it supposes that, because a thing happens, it had to happen. But causation is one matter; predestination another. The construction of a causal explanation after an event merely renders that event in some sense intelligible. It does not in the least show that this particular event, and no other, had to take place; that nothing else could possibly have occurred in its stead. The serious test of the fatalist case must be applied before the event. The only conclusive proof of fatalism would lie in the accurate prediction of events that have not yet happened. And to say, with Tolstoi, that all prior history predetermines everything that follows is to say nothing at all. It is to produce an explanation which applies equally to everything—and thus becomes so vague and limitless as to explain nothing.

Fatalism raises other difficulties. Thus it imputes reality to mystical historical "forces"—class, race, nation, the will of the people, the spirit of the times, history itself. But there are no such forces. They are merely abstractions or metaphors with no existence except in the mind of the beholder. The only evidence for them is deduction from the behavior of individuals. It is therefore the individual who constitutes the basic unit of history. And, while no individual can be wholly free—and, indeed, recent discoveries of the manifold ways in which we are unconsciously conditioned should constitute a salutary check on human vanity—one must assume the reality of an area of free choice until that assumption is challenged, not by metaphysical affirmation, but by verifiable proof—that is, consistently accurate prediction of the future.

Fatalism, moreover, is incompatible with human psychology and human morality. Anyone who rigorously accepted a deterministic view of life, for example, would have to abandon all notions of human responsibility, since it is manifestly unfair to praise or punish people for acts which are by definition beyond their control. But such fatalism is belied by the assumption of free choice which underlies every move we make, every word we utter, every thought we think. As Sir Isaiah Berlin observes of determinism, "If we begin to take it seriously, then, indeed, the changes in our language, our moral notions, our attitudes toward one another, our views of history, of society and of everything else will be too profound to be even adumbrated." We can no more imagine what the universe of the consistent determinist would be like than we can imagine what it would be like to live in a world without time or one with seventeen-dimensional space.

For the historian concerned with concrete interpretation of actual events, he can easily demonstrate the futility of fatalism by trying to apply it to specific historical episodes. According to the extreme determinist view, no particular individual can make the slightest difference. As slaves of history, all individuals are, so to speak, interchangeable parts. If Napoleon had not led his armies across Europe, Tolstoi implies, someone else would have. William

James, combating this philosophic fatalism, once asked the determinists whether they really believed "the convergence of sociological pressures to have so impinged on Stratford on Avon about April 23, 1564, that a W. Shakespeare, with all his mental peculiarities, had to be born there." And did they further believe, James continued, that "if the aforesaid W. Shakespeare had died of cholera infantum, another mother at Stratford on Avon would needs have engendered a duplicate copy of him to restore the sociologic equilibrium?" Who could believe such stuff? Yet, if the determinists do not mean exactly this, how can they read the individual out of history?

In December, 1931, a British politician, crossing Fifth Avenue in New York between 76th and 77th streets around ten-thirty at night, was knocked down and gravely injured by an automobile. Fourteen months later an American politician, sitting in an open car in Miami, Florida, was fired on by an assassin; a man standing beside him was killed. Would the next two decades of history have been the same had Contasini's car killed Winston Churchill in 1931 and Zangara's bullets killed Franklin Roosevelt in 1933? Suppose, in addition, that Adolf Hitler had been killed in the street fighting during the Munich *Putsch* of 1923, and that Lenin and Mussolini had died at birth. Where would our century be now?

Individuals, of course, must operate within limits. They cannot do everything. They cannot, for example, propel history into directions for which the environment and the human material are not prepared: no genius, however heroic, could have brought television to ancient Troy. Yet, as Sidney Hook has convincingly argued in his thoughtful book, *The Hero in History,* great men can count decisively "where the historical situation permits of major alternative paths of development."

This argument between fatalism and heroism is not one on which there is a lot to be said on both sides. The issue is far too sharp to be straddled. Either history is rigidly determined and foreordained, in which case individual striving does not matter; or it is not, in which case there is an essential role for the hero. Analysis of concrete episodes suggests that history is, within limits, open and unfinished; that men have lived who did what no substitute could ever have done; that their intervention set history on one path rather than another. If this is so, the old maxim, "There are no indispensable men," would seem another amiable fallacy. There is, then a case for heroes.

To say that there is a case for heroes is not to say that there is a case for hero worship. The surrender of decision, the unquestioning submission to leadership, the prostration of the average man before the Great Man—these are the diseases of heroism, and they are fatal to human dignity. But, if carried too far, hero worship generates its own antidote. "Every hero," said Emerson, "becomes a bore at last." And we need not go too far. History amply shows that it is possible to have heroes without turning them into gods.

And history shows, too, that, when a society, in flight from hero worship, decides to do without great men at all, it gets into troubles of its own. Our contemporary American society, for example, has little use for the individualist. Individualism implies dissent from the group; dissent implies conflict; and conflict suddenly seems divisive, un-American and generally unbearable. Our greatest new industry is evidently the production of techniques to eliminate conflict, from positive thoughts through public relations to psychoanalysis, applied everywhere from the couch to the pulpit. Our national aspiration has become peace of mind, peace of soul. The symptomatic drug of our age is the tranquilizer. "Togetherness" is the banner under which we march into the brave new world.

Obviously society had had to evolve collective institutions to cope with problems that have grown increasingly complex and concentrated. But the collective approach can be overdone. If Khrushchev worried because his collectivist society developed a cult of the individual, maybe we Americans should start worrying as our so-called individualist society develops a cult of the group. We instinctively suppose that the tough questions will be solved by an interfaith conference or an interdisciplinary research team of an interdepartmental committee or an assembly of wise men meeting at Arden House. But are not these group tactics essentially means by which individuals hedge their bets and distribute their responsibilities? And do they not nearly always result in the dilution of insight and the triumph of mish-mash? If we are to survive, we must have ideas, vision, courage. These things are rarely produced by committees. Everything that matters in our intellectual and moral life begins with an individual confronting his own mind and conscience in a room by himself.

A bland society will never be creative. "The amount of eccentricity in a society," said John Stuart Mill, "has generally been proportional to the amount of genius, mental vigor and moral courage it contained. That so few now dare to be eccentric marks the chief danger of the time." If this condition frightened Mill in Victorian England, it should frighten us much more. For our national apotheosis of the group means that we systematically lop off the eccentrics, the originals, the proud, imaginative, lonely people from whom new ideas come. What began as a recoil from hero worship ends as a conspiracy against creativity. If worship of great men brings us to perdition by one path, flight from great men brings us there just as surely by another. When we do not admire great men, then our instinct for admiration is likely to end by settling on ourselves. The one thing worse for democracy than hero worship is self-worship.

A free society cannot get along without heroes, because they are the most vivid means of exhibiting the power of free men. The hero exposes to all mankind unsuspected possibilities of conception, unimagined resources of strength. "The appearance of a great man," wrote Emerson, "draws a new circle outside of our largest orbit and surprises and commands us." Carlyle likened ordinary, lethargic times, with their unbelief and perplexity, to dry, dead fuel, waiting for the lightning out of heaven to kindle it. "The great man, with his free force direct out of God's own hand, is the lightning. . . . The rest of men waited for him like fuel, and then they too would flame."

Great men enable us to rise to our own highest potentialities. They nerve lesser men to disregard the world and trust to their own deepest instinct. "In picking out from history our heroes," said William James, "each one of us may best fortify and inspire what creative energy may lie in his own soul. This is the last justification of hero worship." Which one of us has not gained fortitude and faith from the incarnation of ideals in men, from the wisdom of Socrates, from the wondrous creativity of Shakespeare, from the strength of Washington, from the compassion of Lincoln, and above all, perhaps, from the life and the death of Jesus? "We feed on genius," said Emerson. "Great men exist that there may be greater men."

Yet this may be only the smaller part of their service. Great men have another and larger role—to affirm human freedom against the supposed inevitabilities of history. The first hero was Prometheus, who defied the gods and thus asserted the independence and autonomy of man against all determinism. Zeus punished Prometheus, chaining him to a rock and encouraging a vulture to pluck at his vitals.

Ever since, man, like Prometheus, has warred against history. It has always been a bitter and remorseless fight; for the heavy weight of human inertia lies with fatalism. It takes a man of exceptional vision and strength and will—it takes, in short, a hero—to try to wrench history from what lesser men consider its preconceived path. And often history tortures the hero in the process, chains him to a rock and exposes him to the vulture. Yet, in the model of Prometheus, man can still hold his own against the gods. Brave men earn the right to shape their own destiny.

An age without great men is one which acquiesces in the drift of history. Such acquiescence is easy and seductive; the great appeal of fatalism, indeed, is as a refuge from the terror of responsibility. Where a belief in great men insistently reminds us that individuals can make a difference, fatalism reassures us that they can't. It thereby blesses our weakness and extenuates our failure. Fatalism, in Berlin's phrase, is "one of the great alibis" of history.

Let us not be complacent about our supposed capacity to get along without great men. If our society has lost its wish for heroes and its ability to produce them, it may well turn out to have lost everything else as well.

## Study suggestions

1.    Would you *now* dispute the first statement, which was written in 1959?

2.    What reasons does the writer give for this lack?

3.    Explain: "Great men make small men aware of their smallness"; also, "Our actual life has grown more and more collec-

tive and anonymous"—"The increasing homogeneity of American society."

4. What, according to the writer, are the fallacies of "fatalistic determinism"?

5. How does he define "diseases" of heroism?

6. Discuss: "Individualism implies dissent from the group; dissent implies conflict; and conflict suddenly seems divisive, un-American and generally unbearable."

7. Explain John Stuart Mill's remark: "The greatness of England is now all collective. . . ."

8. Why does Isaiah Berlin call fatalism "one of the great alibis of history?"

Using one of the sentences from this article as a beginning write a paragraph or a theme:

"If we are to survive, we must have ideas, vision, courage."

"A bland society will never be creative."

"The one thing worse for democracy than hero worship is self-worship."

"Great men exist that there may be greater men."

# JOHN GLENN AND
# HIS DAY OF MIRACLES

Time *Magazine*

This was the moment. He had worked toward it for three years. Now he was alone, flat on his back on a form-fit couch inside the instrument-packed capsule *Friendship 7*. In an incredibly matter-of-fact voice, Lt. Col. John Herschel Glenn, Jr., began to count: "Ten, nine, eight, seven, six . . ."

A great yellow-white gush of flame spewed out from the Atlas-D missile. For nearly four seconds, it seemed rooted to its pad. Then, almost deliberately, it headed into the brilliant blue sky. "We're under way," said Glenn.

In the next four hours and 56 minutes, John Glenn lived through and shared with millions a day of miracles. There was beauty. "I don't know what you can say about a day in which you have seen four beautiful sunsets," Glenn said later, "—three in orbit, and one after I was back." There was the wonder of weightlessness. "This," said Glenn, "is something you could get addicted to." And there was danger: "This could have been a bad day all the way around."

After lift-off, the next crucial stage of the flight was the separation of rocket and capsule at the proper angle to put Glenn into the programmed orbit. When his orbit was confirmed at Cape Canaveral, Glenn jubilantly radioed back: "Capsule is turning around. Oh, that view is tremendous! I can see the booster doing turnarounds just a couple of hundred yards behind. Cape is go and I am go."

As he began to cross Africa, Glenn set out to test his reactions to the eerie world of weightlessness. He shook his head violently to see if the motion would induce space sickness. Nothing happened. "I have had no ill effects at all from zero G," he reported. "It's very pleasant, as a matter of fact. Visual acuity is still excellent. No nausea or discomfort whatsoever."

Glenn had with him a small hand camera to take pictures through his window. "It seemed perfectly natural: rather than put the camera away, I just put it out in mid-air and let go of it." With the camera suspended as though on an invisible shelf, he went on with other work, then reached back and plucked the camera out of the air.

Soaring over the Indian Ocean, Glenn began his first night in space. The stars were bright diamonds on black velvet. "If you've been out in the desert on a very clear, brilliant night when there's no moon and the stars seem to jump out at you, that's just about the way they look."

As he approached Australia, Glenn radioed Astronaut Gordon Cooper in the tracking station at Muchea: "That was about the shortest day I've ever run into. Just to my right, I can see a big pattern of light, apparently right on the coast." The glow was the city of Perth, which had prepared a welcome for Glenn that was also a test of his night vision. Streetlights were ablaze. Householders turned on their porch lights, spread sheets in their yards as reflectors. When the lights were explained to him, Glenn radioed Cooper: "Thank everybody for turning them on, will you?"

Then, in the first moments of dawn, Glenn saw a fantastic sight. At first he thought "that the capsule had gone up while I wasn't looking and that I was looking into nothing but a new star field. There were thousands of little particles outside the cabin. They were a bright yellowish-green, about the size and intensity of a firefly on a real dark night. As far as I could look off to each side, I could see them."

Glenn speculated that the particles might be the cloud of needles the U. S. Air Force had tried to orbit last October, or that they might be snowflakes formed by the cooling of water vapor from his jet nozzles. But he quickly rejected both theories. Best explanation of the phenomenon: the capsule was giving off electrically charged particles of water or gas vapor that were attracted to each other, built up the specks that Glenn saw.

Throughout his thrilling day, John Glenn recorded the emotions and impressions of being the United States' first tourist in orbital space. He had little sensation of speed. It was, he said, "about the same as flying in an airliner at, say, 30,000 feet, and looking down at clouds at 10,000 feet." Over California, he spotted part of the Imperial Valley to his left, and the Salton Sea; he could even pick out the irrigated acres around El Centro, where he once lived. Looking down on the Atlantic, he saw the Gulf Stream as a river of blue.

But Astronaut Glenn's adventure involved far more than mere sight-seeing. He encountered difficulties that turned his journey into a nightmare of suspense. Over Guaymas, Mexico, on his first orbit, the capsule's attitude-control system began to act up. A small jet, designed to release hydrogen-peroxide steam to keep the capsule in a stable position, was not working properly. The capsule, reported Glenn, "drifts off in yaw to the right at about one degree per second."

To return the capsule to its normal position, Glenn took over the controls himself and activated other jets. For most of the rest of the flight, he had to "fly" the capsule either by hand or by using a semi-automatic "fly-by-wire" system roughly akin to power steering on an automobile.

As he crossed the Pacific a second time, the erratic jets made the capsule "roll" (turn on its horizontal axis). A similar roll in last November's flight of the chimpanzee named Enos made it necessary to bring the capsule down after two orbits. Again John Glenn was able to overcome the trouble manually.

Worrisome as it was, this problem was nothing compared with another threat. Just as Glenn was beginning his second orbit, an instrument panel in the Project Mercury Control Center at Canaveral picked up a warning that the fiber-glass heat shield on *Friendship 7* had come ajar. If the shield were to separate before or during Glenn's reentry into the earth's atmosphere, he would perish in a flash of flame.

One by one, other tracking stations picked up the ominous signal. Project Mercury officials huddled tensely, trying to decide what to do. The final decision was made by Operations Director Walter Williams: an attempt would be made to hold the heat shield in place by changing the re-entry procedure. The retro-rocket packet was supposed to be jettisoned after the rockets themselves had been fired. But the packet itself was bound to the capsule by three thin metal bands. Williams figured that the bands might be strong enough to hold the shield to the capsule during the descent. He knew that the heat would eventually burn away the straps, but he hoped that by that time the air resistance would be dense enough to hold the shield in place.

Glenn took the news of the deadly threat with characteristic calmness. He made the adjustments necessary to keep the retro-rocket packet in place, hand-flew his capsule into proper attitude for descent—and braced himself. Timed by a pre-set mechanism in the capsule, the braking rockets fired in sequence. *Friendship 7* shuddered. "It feels like I'm going clear back to Hawaii," Glenn radioed. He could feel his body beginning to be squeezed by the buildup of G forces.

Outside the window he could see a fiery glow. "It became apparent that something was tearing up the heat-shield end of the capsule," Glenn said later. "There were large pieces anywhere from as big as the end of your finger to seven or eight inches in diameter coming past the window. You could see the fire and the glow from them—big flaming chunks."

On the ground, Astronaut Alan Shepard, the capsule communicator at Cape Canaveral, lost radio contact with Glenn. At the same time, other instruments tracking the capsule stopped registering. The blackout was predictable, caused by ionization from the heat of re-entry. It lasted for seven minutes and 15 seconds. Then came John Glenn's exultant voice. "Boy!" he cried. "That was a real fireball!"

Glenn had made it; he had successfully re-entered the earth's atmosphere. As it turned out, the heat shield had been in place all along; a monitor in the capsule had been flashing a misleading signal to the ground. But John Glenn could not be certain that he was safe until he saw the parachute which would lower his capsule gently into the Atlantic open. Said he the next day, "That's probably the prettiest ol' sight you ever saw in your life."

At 2:43 P.M. *Friendship 7* splashed into the Atlantic with a sizzle as the red-hot shield turned the sea water to steam. Surging ahead at flank speed, the destroyer *Noa* began to race helicopters from the carrier *Randolph* to the scene. The *Noa* won, plucked the capsule out of the ocean at 3:01. Across the United States, the millions of television watchers sagged weakly with relief.

John Glenn seemed almost destined for this day of triumph. As a test pilot and a combat flier with 149 missions in World War II and Korea (he holds five Distinguished Flying Crosses and an Air Medal with 18 clusters), he had lived with supersonic speed and the constant possibility of sudden death. To the millions who have now seen and heard him, it is obvious that he was a perfect choice to become the first American to orbit the earth.

He was raised in New Concord (population: 2000), a quiet, shirt-sleeves-and-overalls town in central Ohio, where his father, by turns, was a railroad conductor, proprietor of a plumbing business and owner of the local Chevrolet agency. As a boy, John swam in Crooked Creek, hunted rabbits, played football and basketball, read Buck Rogers, was a great admirer of Glenn Miller, and blew a trumpet in the town band.

In 1939 he entered Muskingum College, a small Presbyterian school in New Concord. He was a substitute center on the football team, got solid B grades, and schemed to get into the war as a pilot. He learned to fly in a Navy program for civilians at New Philadelphia, 35 miles away, then quit college as a junior to join the Navy's preflight program. In 1943 he took the Navy's option to join the Marine Corps, and won his gold wings and gold second lieutenant's bars. Then, resplendent in his dress-blue uniform, he came back home to New Concord to marry Annie Castor, daughter of the town dentist, and his sweetheart ever since he could remember.

There was never any question about John Glenn's flying skill. After his war duty, he developed a cocksure method of occasionally demonstrating it. Says Marine Lt. Col. John Mason, "Johnny would fly up alongside you and slip his wing right under yours, then tap it gently against your wing-tip. I've never seen such a smooth pilot."

As a test pilot for the Navy's Chance Vought F8U Crusader fighter after the Korean War, Glenn showed the determination that later landed him in the cockpit of *Friendship 7*. He had the F8U up to Mach 1.2 one day when something snapped and the plane veered sharply. Most test pilots would have gingerly guided the plane back to base. Glenn, scribbling notes all the while, stubbornly pushed the fighter up to Mach 1.2 two more times to see if it would happen again. It did. When he finally landed, he discovered that 24 feet of the trailing edge of a wing had been broken off.

Early in his career, Glenn developed the art of "sniveling." Explains Marine Lt. Col. Richard Rainforth, who flew ground-support missions beside Glenn in both World War II and Korea: "Sniveling, among pilots, means to work yourself into a program, whether it happens to be your job or not. Sniveling is perfectly legitimate, and Johnny is a great hand at it." In 1957 Glenn sniveled the Marines into letting him try to beat the speed of sound from coast to coast. Flying an F8U-1, he failed by nine minutes, but he did knock 23½ minutes off the coast-to-coast speed record by covering the distance in 3 hours 23 minutes at an average speed of 726 m.p.h.

Then, in 1959, Glenn resolutely set out to snivel his way into the toughest program of all: Project Mercury. He started with two handicaps: he lacked a college degree, and, at 37, he was considered an old man. But he managed to get permission to go along as an "observer" with one prime candidate of the Navy's Bureau of Aeronautics. When the candidate failed an early test, "Johnny stepped up, chest high," Rainforth recalls, "and offered himself. They took him."

Candidate Glenn and 510 others were run through a wringer of mental and physical tests. Doctors charted their brain waves, skewered their hands with electrodes to pick up the electrical impulses that would tell how quickly their muscles responded to nerve stimulation. Glenn held up tenaciously under tests of heat and vibration, did especially well with problems of logical reasoning.

To the surprise of no one who has ever known him, Glenn was one of the seven who were picked to become the nation's first astronauts. But even among the astronauts John Glenn stood out in his determination. By his own decision, he spent only weekends with his wife, son and daughter in Arlington, Va., lived Monday through Friday at Virginia's Langley Air Force Base so that he could better concentrate on the program. He ran two miles before breakfast every morning, sweated himself from 195 pounds down to a trim, flat-bellied 168.

To train himself to handle a capsule tumbling out of control, he spent hours spinning giddily in the fiendishly contrived "Mastif" (multiple axis space test inertia facility), which simultaneously rotates in three directions, like a carnival ride gone amok. Time and again he rode the giant centrifuge, which multiplies gravitational pull to simulate the strains of take-off and return. Despite his years, Glenn showed the least heart fluctuation of any astronaut. (At lift-off of *Friendship 7* Glenn's pulse rate was a relatively placid 110 beats per minute. Shepard's rate was 139, Grissom's 170 during their lift-offs. All three men normally register between 60 and 70 beats a minute.)

Not since Charles A. Lindbergh, in 1927, has the United States had such a hero. From the moment he stepped out of his capsule onto the deck of the *Noa*, Glenn has accepted his apotheosis as coolly as he handled *Friendship 7* on its flight through space. In the flood of press conferences, parades, appearances before Congress and Congressional committees, he has been articulate and at ease. There is honest pride in his great achievement, but he has gone out of his way to acknowledge the roles of hundreds of others who stood behind it. In greetings to his backstage co-workers at Canaveral, he put his feelings in this fashion: "There is much acclaim for this flight, but it is only one step in a long program. I'd like all of you who worked on it feel that I am your representative. I'm getting the attention for all the thousands of you who worked on it."

In terms of national prestige, Glenn's flight put the United States back into the space race with a vengeance, and gave the morale of the entire free world a huge and badly needed boost. Contrasted with earlier Russian shots, it was a great victory for the open society that produced Glenn—and proved the wisdom, in terms that Woodrow Wilson might have used, of "open shots openly viewed."

Technically, it justified and redeemed the long labors, careful planning and exacting standards of the U.S. space program, into which the nation has hopefully poured several billion dollars.

For man himself, it produced some valuable lessons. Because the Russians released little data about astronauts Gagarin and Titov, the world now knew with certainty for the first time that, at least for the period Glenn spent in space, a healthy and well-conditioned man can face the forces of gravity and weightlessness with no ill effects. By taking over the controls himself and proving that man can "fly" a capsule through space, Glenn also struck a blow for man's genius and versatility, answering the critics who claim that instruments can do anything better in space than man. Said Glenn, "Now we can get rid of some of that automatic equipment and let man take over."

At his first press conference, John Glenn emphasized the point that the exploration of space is still in its primitive stages. If the diameter of the earth were scaled down to about 80 inches, he said, his flight had brought us only 1 1/3 inches above it. "If you think of the enormity of space, it makes our efforts seem puny. But these are all step-by-step functions we go through. The manned flights we've had to date have added information. This flight, I hope, added a bit more."

## Study suggestions

1. Discuss the impact of the first sentence and of the entire paragraph. What is the significance of "incredibly"?
2. Comment on the use of Glenn's own words in this article over a third person narration of his reactions.
3. What qualities of character and training made him qualified for this "day of miracles"?
4. As a hero how did he show consideration and humility?
5. List the valuable lessons learned from this orbit.
6. What are future plans?
7. Write a comparison of this flight with that of Charles Lindbergh.
8. Write a theme as if you were astronaut Alan Shepard watching and communicating with Glenn.

# CAN MEN LIVE WITHOUT WAR?

*Vannevar Bush*

Nearly fifty years ago William James wrote an essay which he called "The Moral Equivalent of War." Since then many things have happened: there have been two world wars, a crippling depression, and now a phenomenal burst of fairly solid prosperity. The whole art of war has been profoundly altered by the application of science. A new kind of empire has arisen, rigidly controlled and avowedly bent on world conquest. The old colonial empires have disintegrated, and a new spirit of nationalism pervades lands that were once inarticulate. Most important of all, there is a growing understanding of what war may mean, and a deep yearning among all peoples for peace. It is proper, therefore, to review the arguments which James advanced and to do so in the light of the new circumstances.

James foresaw, with a clarity which was remarkable, that war would sometime end. At a time when warfare and the applications of science were poles apart, he said, "And when whole nations are the armies, and the science of destruction vies in intellectual refinement with the sciences of production, I see that war becomes absurd and impossible from its own monstrosity."

And so he turned to what might follow, with evident apprehension that men would become soft—that the virility which had brought the race thus far would give place to flat insipidity.

He first stated the case of the apologists for war, better than they themselves had stated it, repeating the only alternatives they offered: "a world of clerks and teachers, of co-education and zoophily, of 'consumers' leagues' and 'associated charities,' of industrialism unlimited, and feminism unabashed. No scorn, no hardness, no valor any more! Fie upon such a cattleyard of a planet."

With this extreme point of view he evidently had a genuine sympathy, for he added: "So far as the central essence of this feeling goes, no healthy minded person, it seems to me, can help to some degree partaking of it. Militarism is the great preserver of our ideals of hardihood, and human life with no use for hardihood would be contemptible. Without risks or prizes for the darer, history would be insipid indeed; and there is a type of military character which every one feels that the race should never cease to breed."

But when he then sought a moral equivalent for war he was far from convincing. His alternative was the struggle with nature as a substitute for the struggle between men and nations. Rugged though the struggle with nature sometimes is, we can hardly believe that it would fully serve to keep the red blood flowing hot in our veins, and to release the adrenalin which is the messenger between a virile mind and a fighting body. For the conquest of nature today involves only relatively few of us, and it is becoming an intellectual effort rather than a matter of brute strength. So James left me, at least, disappointed with his alternative and bewildered. Let us review his line of argument, in the present setting, and see whether there may be a way out of the dilemma.

His first point may indeed now be underlined. We strive for peace today with conviction and intensity, for great wars must cease if we are to pursue further the path of progress. And our striving is by no means hopeless. If great wars are outlawed—not by treaty, perhaps, but by a general realization of their absurdity—secondary wars will go on for a time by conventional means, and nations will maintain their postures of readiness to fight. But the end of all war is now definitely in sight for the first time in human history. No nation can today attack its prepared neighbor with the expectation of profiting immensely and securing a place in the sun, as has been attempted twice within our memory. The result today would be devastation for all, cities utterly destroyed, populations killed and maimed, starvation and disease rampant. That this is the brute fact is now obvious to the most obtuse. Nor can a tyrant or ruling clique, by bringing on a war, hope to advance their private interests or provide a diversion from popular discontent; no modern all-out war will leave in power anywhere those who perpetrated it.

War might, to be sure, come by accident, and this we must guard against assiduously. Little wars with the foolhardy use of weapons of mass destruction could lead to a great war; and if tempers rise, we shall need to curb the trigger-happy fools among us. Were we so gullible as to let down our guard too soon and invite a surprise mass attack which would prevent our retaliation and end the conflict at a single stroke, the invitation might be seized upon by those who still think of conquering the world by force of arms. It is not impossible that a group of desperate men could pull the temple down on all of us. But the conditions and concepts which brought on most of the great wars of history have now disappeared. We are all on notice, if we can read or listen, that indulgence in all-out war would be suicide. Self-preservation is a very powerful primary urge, and an understanding of the present monstrosity of war is increasing among the masses of people in spite of both iron and bamboo curtains. There is certainly more chance than ever before that we may now look forward to peace. In fact, we may conclude that we can have peace if we are not utterly gullible or careless.

The second point made by James also deserves emphasis. The main argument of the apologists for war has vanished as science has stepped into the picture. Whatever else may happen, the glamour of war is gone.

Where do the virtues of war lie today? Is courage needed to watch a radar screen or adjust a guided missile? Where is the daring of the soldier when the folks at home encounter equal risks? When one man guides a plane that can destroy a city, what becomes of the infectious influence of comradeship, the sense of being engaged with many others in a common hazardous campaign, the identification of self with a group which could inspire, or was supposed to inspire, even the common soldier with ideals and courage? Great war has become complex and must now be fought at a distance, if at all. It has lost forever those qualities that once had a real appeal for the red-blooded man.

Do we then look forward to some sort of Utopia? James had little use for Utopias, for he wrote in "The Dilemma of Determinism":—

> Why does the painting of any paradise or utopia, in heaven or on earth, awaken such yawnings for nirvana and escape? The white-robed harp-playing heaven of our sabbath-schools, and the ladylike tea-table elysium represented in Mr. Spencer's Data of Ethics, as the final consummation of progress, are exactly on a par in this respect,—lubberlands, pure and simple, one and all. . . . If *this* be the whole fruit of the victory, we say; if the generations of mankind suffered and laid down their lives; if prophets confessed and martyrs sang in the fire, and all the sacred tears were shed for no other end than that a race of creatures of such unexampled insipidity should succeed, and protract . . . their contented and inoffensive lives,—why, at such a rate, better lose than win the battle, or at all events better ring down the cur-

tain before the last act of the play, so that a business that began so importantly may be saved from so singularly flat a
winding-up.

We need have little fear of any such dismal outcome. Struggles
will not cease even if armed conflict ends. Between nations there
will continue to be political jockeying for position and very intense
economic competition. We shall still need to cope with penetration
and subversion and face the difficult task of guiding our friends
among the younger nations to positions of true independence and
stability.

Nor will struggle and conflict end in our internal affairs. We shall
have much to quarrel about.

Our racial antagonisms have by no means vanished. We hope
we have learned to avoid great depressions, but on this score we
should by no means be sanguine. Whether we can maintain full
employment without forcing inflation remains to be seen. The
division of our product between capital, labor, and management
can still lead to paralyzing strikes. We have narcotics, juvenile
delinquency, defiance of law. The preservation of our liberties
demands eternal vigilance. If we are easygoing, a swollen bureauc-
racy will certainly regiment us. Our political contests can still be
embittered and sordid.

If war ceases, it will be a different sort of world; and the apologists for war usually overlook one of its primary attributes, the
ending of which might greatly influence our lives in subtle ways.
During the past two decades this country has forged ahead at an
unprecedented rate until it stands as the unquestioned leader of
the free world, powerful, disciplined, even wise as it attempts to
press further by lifting its neighbors with it. War and the fear of
war produced this result—produced also our present great prosperity. And this did not occur because of war profits; for there are
no such things as war profits for a country as a whole; war merely
wastes man's goods and man's labor. In many nations the waste
has overbalanced all else, but we were fortunate. Our advance has
come about because the nation became internally united and went
to work, because secondary quarrels were submerged or tempered
in the common cause, because public opinion forced the chan-

neling of all effort in a single direction, because men's spirits rose and their blood ran hot as they faced together an enemy that all could recognize. Where would we now be had there been no such cement to hold us together during the past twenty years—if we had worked at cross-purposes, occupied ourselves with petty quarrels, or succumbed to the vices of intrigue and treachery?

Does this mean that, if peace comes and the fear of war is lifted, we shall again return to all the old quarrels and become a nation divided, split into factions with animosity and petty intrigues paramount? Does it mean that we shall lose the vision of a happy and prosperous nation, brought about by our own unity and determination, in which we can approach our disagreements objectively and in a spirit of relative good will? Does it mean that we shall forget how to battle with one another vigorously and with full conviction and determination, but standing up, and shall again thrash about in the mire of mutual suspicion? Do biting and kicking have to take the place of honest blows given and received?

The citizens of this country have shown that they take most of the guarantees of the Bill of Rights for granted, that they see no real danger to our primary liberties or any need to be keenly on the alert to preserve them; and in this complacency lies danger. But there is one element of the free life that is not taken for granted at all, that is highly valued, and that men are willing to fight for, if necessary, without question. This element is the opportunity for an individual to rise as far as his talents, health, and determination will take him, without artificial barriers of any kind.

We have by no means reached perfection in this regard. There are still artificial barriers of race, birth, and resources. Nor would we banish the paternal instinct, forbid the father to aid his son to make a good start in life, or frown on any effort of a man to help one of his fellows. There is a fundamental difference between this mutual aid—even the banding together of groups with mutual interests for mutual advancement—and the throwing of artificial obstacles in the path of a young man struggling to rise by his own efforts. We shall always have with us those who will drift, who will refuse to pull their weight in the boat, to whom opportunity means nothing; but the problem of their place in society is not one that concerns us here. It is the artificial obstacle in the path of the ambitious and able that we would banish, and this has not yet been fully accomplished.

But we have proceeded much farther toward the ideal than ever before in any country at any time. The workman at the bench recognizes the artificial limitations that surround him; and his own ambitions may be ended. But he knows, too, that for his son, his neighbor's son, or the bright attractive boy down the street there are genuine opportunities to rise to positions of influence and satisfaction. Luck, the caprice of men in high places, loyalty to dependents, an insidious bacterium or virus—any one of these may stop him in his tracks. Only a few will have the ambition to rise and the skill and personality that must go with it. But the opportunity is there, and it is real. The son of a tailor on the east side may become the honored surgeon, respected by men of power, loved by patients who owe their lives to him. The peddler of bananas may come to rule an industrial empire he has built. The painter's helper may become a labor leader and treat on equal terms with the captains of industry. The haberdasher may become president. It has happened. The bans and taboos are less than they ever were before. This is the land of opportunity, and we had better keep it so and enhance this central aspect of our liberty.

It is this which may yet bind us together in the ideal of brotherhood among men, not as a vague generality to which we pay lip service but as a living reality, exemplified by the opportunity for all to develop their talents to the utmost for their own benefit and the benefit of their fellow men.

We look forward to living in a new sort of world. The flowering of science, which has rendered war absurd, is also giving us wealth, comfort, and freedom from disease of the body or the mind. Our contests for position in the intricate fabric of society need no longer require that the unsuccessful shall suffer want and distress.

When individual progress is artificially barred, when men are divided into classes with impenetrable barriers, when men are serfs or slaves, or fettered by false restraint so that they cannot move, struggles on any subject are bound to be bitter. When a man knows that if he loses out, in competition with his fellows, those he loves will be ill-nourished and neglected, he must fight too desperately to care for the conventions of fairness and decency.

But when artificial barriers are gone, and men may rise if they have what it takes—when there is a floor beneath which no man need fall, a floor that will ensure a decent life—then the contests of men with one another may well be on a different plane. The key is the preservation and enhancement of individual opportunity in all its forms. Few will rise, for few are the places to fill at the top. But all will have dignity and satisfaction; and those who prefer for any reason to remain in humble and peasant status will do so by choice.

We can have peace. And with it we can have prosperity, greater than the world has ever seen, with a distribution of its blessings that preserves the necessary order of an industrial society while avoiding both arrogant opulence and cringing poverty. As we attain these things, whenever we do, shall we return to petty bickering and strife, sordid intrigue, and bitter recriminations? Or shall we tackle our problems as men, vigorously, with courage and convictions, pulling no punches, but with decency and fairness? We may, indeed, be able to rise to the latter if we keep our senses and our objectivity—and, above all, if we open the door of opportunity wide so that we battle as free men, in the pride and dignity to which only free men may aspire.

Here, indeed, may be an acceptable equivalent for war, preserving and enhancing in our people those virile attributes which conquered the old frontiers and built an industrial civilization beyond compare. When the foolhardy nature of international combat is fully recognized and great wars are banished, we may still struggle with nature and with one another and thus keep the vitality of the race from being sapped by insipid ease. If we do so as free men, independent, proud, seizing our opportunity in an open field from which artificial barriers have been removed, we may find that struggle, so necessary for the health of our race, can be entered upon in decency and dignity, and the vulgarity of war may give place to strife for worthy causes conducted with fairness and good will.

Yet, having said this, we have not come to the end of the matter. Man needs to exercise his virile attributes—in sport, in coping with the hazards of the wilderness, in honest and decent conflict with his fellows for just and worthy causes. No man has fully lived who has not experienced the fear, the exultation, of meeting great odds and struggling to prevail. But no man has fully lived who has not also experienced the joy of close association with worthy fellows or who has not known the thrill of individual creation. He who can say honestly to himself that he has discovered a set of facts or a relation between phenomena not known to any man before him in all history, and that by his insight and skill he has made them comprehensible to the human intellect—such a man experiences the same uplift of spirit as the one who first climbs a high mountain or first runs a mile in four minutes. And when the accomplishment results not from the lonely acts of individual genius but from the efforts of a team or group having mutual trust and confidence, supplementing one another's skills, compensating for one another's weaknesses, carrying the unfortunate over the rough places, heartening the leader by steadfast support—then all members of the group enjoy a satisfaction transcending that of accomplished creation, a satisfaction of success in their margin of effort to attain something that was beyond the capacity of any individual.

If war ends, we must still have outlets for our inherited energies; we need only attempt to render them dignified and worthy. But we shall also have increased opportunities for other satisfactions, not so intense but far more lasting and substantial. The unifying bond of war will be gone, but it can give place to a nobler bond, less universal, far more genuine and strong. This can appear in the midst of diverse careers. To me, naturally, the field of science stands out uniquely in its opportunities.

The country will be full of struggle and conflict as diverse causes are fought over. As individuals and citizens we enter if our consciences and inclinations so dictate. And by entering we may help to raise the level of the contests and render them worthy. But research centers such as the Carnegie Institution stand aside from all this.

Within the institutions dedicated to scientific research lies opportunity for the individual. They do not care about a man's origins—his country, race, or religion. They seek men who have an ambition to rise to the heights in their scientific professions, and insist, moreover, that among their talents should be a large measure of ability to rise by effective collaboration with others. They want men of generous instinct, and men who are devoted to science because they believe that the life of a scientist yields more satisfaction than any other career on earth and contributes more genuinely to the public weal. When they find a young man of this sort they welcome him with open arms. After that no artificial barrier stands in his path. He can rise as rapidly and as high in his profession as his own effort, judgment, and skill will carry him. He will be judged only according to the estimation in which he is held by fellow scientists—his peers. The requirements are rigorous, but the opportunity these institutions offer is real and complete. We must always keep it so.

No more war? Peace is indeed in sight if we are wise. But not an end of contest or struggle. And certainly not an end of opportunity, which may render the lives of those who follow us not insipid but virile, not belligerent but creative.

## Study suggestions

1.    From the opening paragraph discuss each of the items which have occurred in the last fifty years.

2.    Explain the opinion William James had concerning militarism as a preserver of hardihood.

3.    Compare this idea with that of the author. How does he challenge each point made by James? How effective is his use of the question?

4.    Discuss his belief in man's right to develop, and, too, man's need for outlets for his energies.

5.    What practical substitutes for war does he offer as a solution? How does he answer the question in the title?

6.    Write a theme on the values of competition in sports of various types, in politics, in science.

# THE FUTURE OF MAN

*C. P. Snow*

AUSCHWITZ AND HIROSHIMA. We have seen all that; in some of it we have acquiesced or helped. No wonder we are morally guilty. Men like ourselves have done such things—and at the same time men like ourselves, sometimes the same men who have taken a hand in the horrors, have been showing more concern for the unlucky round them than has ever been shown by a large society in human history. That is the moral paradox in which we have to live.

It is wrong to try to domesticate the horrors. The mass slaughter of the concentration camps was both the most awful and the most degrading set of actions that men have done so far. This set of actions was ordered and controlled by abnormally wicked men, if you like, but down the line the orders were carried out by thousands of people like the rest of us, civil servants, soldiers, engineers, all brought up in an advanced Western and Christian society. While it was people not like the rest of us but a great deal better, people who for imagination and morality, not to speak of intellect, stand among the finest of our race, people like Einstein, Niels Bohr and Franck, who got caught up in the tangle of events which led to Hiroshima and Nagasaki. The dropping of those bombs was on a lesser order of wickedness from what was done at Auschwitz. But Western man ought not to forget that he did it; Eastern man certainly won't.

At the same time we ought not to forget what there is to our

credit. Some kinds of optimism about man's nature are dangerous
—but so are some kinds of pessimism. Think of the care the
Swedes and Danes are taking of their old and poor, or of prisoners,
or of social misfits. Nothing like that has been done at any period
or in any place until our lifetime. We can congratulate ourselves in
Britain, too. The Scandinavians have not made anything like a
perfect society. In some ways we have not got as near to it as they
have. But we have both made a better shot at it than anyone before us.

Britain is a much fairer and a much kinder society than the one
I was born into in 1905. It may seem sentimental to have consciences troubled about capital punishment, about removing one
life when Western man has recently eliminated twenty million:
yet it is a sign of moral sensitivity. So is the attempt, however
grudging, to treat women as though they were equal human beings. So is the feeling behind the Wolfenden Report. So is the conviction—so urgent in the United States—that children have a special right to happiness.

Some of these feelings may lead to practical follies (I believe
that the American one is making a mess of their education), but
that is not the point. They are signs of a development of something
very rare in the world up to now, which one might call moral kindness. I have no doubt that in Scandinavia, England, some, though
not all, of the United States, and perhaps three or four other countries in the West, the amount of fairness, tolerance and effective
kindness within the society would seem astonishing to any
nineteenth-century man.

It would also seem astonishing to any nineteenth-century man
how much we know. There is probably no one now alive as clever
as Clerk Maxwell or Gauss; but thousands of people know more
than Clerk Maxwell or Gauss, and understand more of those parts
of the world that they spent their lives trying to understand. Put
those two down, or even greater men, such as Newton and Archi-
medes, in front of what is now understood—and they would think
it wonderful. So it is, and we can take pride and joy in it. It will
go on; the search to understand is one of the most human things
about us. Compared with our ancestors, there are some trivial

physical differences. We are a good deal taller and heavier, we live much longer. But above all, we know more.

All this it would be reasonable to call progress, so long as we don't expect of progress more than it can give. In each of our individual lives there is, of course, something beyond human help. Each of us has to live part of his life alone; and he has to die alone. That part of our experience is right outside of time and history, and progress has no meaning there. In this sense, the individual condition is tragic. But that is no excuse for not doing our best with the social condition.

To think otherwise, to take refuge in facile despair, has been the characteristic intellectual treachery of our day It is shoddy. We have to face the individual condition: for good or evil, for pettiness and the occasional dash of grandeur, we have to know what men are capable of: and then we can't contract out. For we are part, not only of the privileged North European-British American *enclave* of progress, but of another progress which is altering the whole world.

I mean something brutally simple. Most people in Asia still haven't enough to eat: but they have a bit more than before. Most people in Asia are still dying before their time (on the average, Indians live less than half as long as Englishmen): but they are living longer than before. Is *that* progress? This is not a subject to be superior or refined or ingenious about, and the answer is: *of course it is.*

It is because Western man has grown too far away from that elemental progress that we can't get on terms with most of the human race. Through luck we got in first with the scientific-industrial revolution; as a result, our lives became, on the average, healthier, longer, more comfortable to an extent that had never been imagined; it doesn't become us to tell our Chinese and Indian friends that that kind of progress is not worth having.

We know what it is like to live among the shops, the cars, the radios, of Leicester and Orebro and Des Moines. We know what it is like to ask the point of it all, and to feel the Swedish sadness or the American disappointment or the English Welfare State discontent. But the Chinese and Indians would like the chance of being well-fed enough to ask what is the point of it all. They are in search of what Leicester, Orebro and Des Moines take for granted, food, extra years of life, modest comforts. When they have got these things, they are willing to put up with a dash of the Swedish sadness or American disappointment. And their determination to get them is likely in the next thirty years to prove the strongest social force on earth.

Will they get them? Will the social conditions everywhere reach within foreseeable time something like the standard of the privileged Western enclave? There is no technical reason why not. If it does, the level of moral kindness will go up in parallel. These ought to be realistic hopes. One sees only one fatality that might destroy them. That is, it goes without saying, an H-bomb war.

No one can pretend that it is not possible. For myself, I think that it won't happen—then though we have seen how good and conscientious men have become responsible for horrors, even though two atomic bombs have been dropped already, and by Western man. But I still think, partly as a guess, partly as a calculation, that we shall escape the H-bomb war—just as I think we shall escape the longer-term danger of Malthusian overpopulation.

It may be that I am letting hope run away with me about the H-bomb war. Some of the wisest disagree with me. Let us imagine that they are right and that the H-bombs go off. Is that going to be the end? I find it difficult to believe. In England a lot of us would be dead, our children with us. A lot of Americans and Russians would also be killed outright. No one knows how many would die afterwards through effects of radiation. But I don't believe that men have at present the resources to destroy the race.

If that is so, and if after an H-bomb war a viable fraction of the world population were left untouched (my guess is that it would be a large fraction, at least two-thirds), then we should all be amazed how soon hope of progress took possession again. The human species is biologically a very tough one, and tough in a sense no animal species can be, through its intelligence, its organization of knowledge, the capacity of its members not to be totally bound within the rapacious self. After the most hideous H-bomb war, the inhabitants of Africa and India and South America would have the strength of those qualities to build on. The material and scientific gap, left through the devastation of the West and Russia, would be filled up at a speed not flattering to Western or Russian self-esteem. What would the moral scar be?

I think we can already answer that question, for we too have, as I said at the beginning, witnessed horrors and assisted at them. Most of us don't live constantly in the presence of Hiroshima and Auschwitz: the memory doesn't prevent us getting morally concerned about the fate of one murderer or cross because a lonely and impoverished old man doesn't have enough calls from the District Visitor.

It would be just the same if the Northern Hemisphere became more or less destroyed. Men elsewhere would not live under that shadow; they would be busy with their own societies. If those societies were less fair and morally sensitive than ours is now, they would soon catch up. Within a bizarrely short interval, after hundreds of millions of people had been incinerated by H-bombs, men in countries unaffected would be passionately debating capital punishment. It sounds mad, but it is the kind of madness which makes human beings as tough as they are, and as capable of behaving better than they have so far behaved.

So there remains a sort of difficult hope. As long as men continue to be men, individual man will perceive the same darkness about his solitary condition as any of us does now. But he will also feel occasional intimations that his own life is not the only one. In the midst of his egotisms, pettiness, power-seekings, and perhaps the horrors these may cause, he will intermittently stretch a little beyond himself. That little, added to the intelligence and growing knowledge of the species, will be enough to make his societies more decent, to sue the social forces for what, in the long sight of history, are good ends.

None of it will be easy. As individuals, each of us is almost untouched by this progress. It is no comfort to remember how short human history is. As individuals, that seems just an irony. But as a race, we have scarcely begun to live.

**Study suggestions**

1. Discuss the meaning of "moral paradox," as used here in the opening paragraphs.

2. Why does Snow feel that America is making a "mess of their education"? Give your opinions.

3. Write paragraphs using the following as topic sentences, but explaining your own thinking:

"The search to understand is one of the most human things about us."

"Each of us has to live part of his life alone."

4. How does the writer regard progress? With what does he seem to be most concerned? Why does he call the human species tough?

5. Explain the last paragraph.

6. What is Snow's purpose in this discussion? Is he pessimistic or optimistic? Defend your opinion.

# ALPHABETICAL LIST OF AUTHORS